THE TRUE FACE
OF JACK THE RIPPER

THE
TRUE FACE
OF JACK
THE RIPPER

Melvin Harris

MICHAEL O'MARA BOOKS LIMITED

For magnificent Maureen; tireless in times of
need; joyous in the realms of art and music;
and a bloody good cook to boot!

And for Andy Aliffe, dedicated organizer of
the 'Upper Baker Street Irregulars', who has
beavered away while all others slept.

First published in Great Britain in 1994 by
Michael O'Mara Books Limited
9 Lion Yard, Tremadoc Road, London SW4 7NQ

A CIP catalogue record for this book is available from the British Library

ISBN 1-85479-193-1

Designed and typeset from author's disks by Martin Bristow

Printed and bound in England by Clays Limited, St Ives plc

Contents

APPENDICES

Acknowledgments

My thanks to Philipp Reis and Alexander Graham Bell for inventing the telephone, and to all those who have patiently accepted my telephonic enthusiasms. They include: Francis X. King, Don Rumbelow, Martin Fido, Richard Whittington-Egan, Stewart Evans, Nick Warren, Sue Iremonger, Nicholas Easthaugh, Kenneth Rendell, Nick Warren and Leslie Shepard. And to Simon Welfare and my colleagues at Granite Productions who have cowered under the shadow of the Ripper for aeons.

The journalists who helped unmask the 'Ripper Diary' hoax deserve to be remembered; so many thanks to Phillip Knightley, first to reproduce the crucial fake diary handwriting, and to Maurice Chittenden for his extensive investigation. Special thanks to Joel Norris, Robert Ressler and Patricia Cornwell for their illuminating confirmations.

The article by Maurice Chittenden which is reproduced on pages 188-9 was published by the *Sunday Times* on 19 September 1993, and is reproduced by kind permission of Times Newspapers.

The English translation of the French poem at the end of Appendix One is copyright ©1994 by Marie Toft.

The illustrations of Druitt and Chapman in the plates section are by R. G. Trow.

The Thoughts That Chill and Kill

I've always wanted to kill legally…I have that feeling to take people out. I've always wondered what were going through, like, Yorkshire Ripper… Black Panther's mind. These had no compassion. They had no feeling. I want this feeling…it's like higher than any drug can get you…

Those chilling words were spoken in 1993 by a smiling British mercenary with the Croat Army. Over a century earlier another young man took up a foreign cause and fought in southern Italy. Sword in hand he too, killed legitimately. It was a brutalizing experience. A time of unleashed animal and brutal passions. At the impressionable age of 18, he became hardened to the sight of blood, death and mutilation. He went on to become the most notorious of all the Rippers – the one known as Jack…

Introduction

JACK THE RIPPER: why does that name still fascinate? He was not the first serial sexual murderer, as many imagine, and his crimes were quite overshadowed by earlier killers. The Texas Ripper alone killed nine women between Christmas 1884 and Christmas 1885, and all *his* killings were many times more brutal. So what was it about Jack's murders that made them so special? The short answer is: the time, the place and the publicity.

He struck at a time when London's police were the subject of intense debate; he struck in the capital city that claimed to be the very centre of the civilized world; and his butchery attracted press coverage that was unprecedented.

Those earlier murders in Austin, Texas, were hardly known, even in America; but the London murders became notorious throughout the world. And in the telling, the crimes became more horrifying. They were imagined to have spanned many years; the number of victims was increased from the actual five Ripper murders to fifteen or more.

The terror evoked by the Ripper was so great that lone women throughout Britain double-barred their doors long after he had retired. For years after, he was pictured as roaming throughout the Midlands, the North and beyond. There was a reported sighting in Belfast, another in Cork; and even one old lady in the far-off Orkneys testified that she lay petrified with fear each night, dreading a visit from the fiend.

The time came, eventually, when everyone accepted that the killings had finished, but even that failed to put the case to rest. Far from it; since no one had faced trial, a perplexing mystery was spawned. What manner of man could have mutilated with such taunting, callous indifference? How did he evade capture? Was there a cover-up?

The police were never able to answer these questions. They were crippled by unsophisticated notions of criminal mentality. In their minds there was no room for a cold, calculating killer who planned his stalks. He had to be a homicidal maniac, subject to outbursts of uncontrollable passion.

The Whitechapel murders came at a time when popular discontent with the Metropolitan Police was at a peak. A recently appointed Chief Commissioner, Sir Charles Warren, headed the force. Sir Charles was an army man, first and foremost. He filled five new senior police posts with army officers and introduced military discipline into a civilian force.

Warren quickly made enemies. He clashed with the Home Secretary Charles Matthews over the everyday running of the force, and he antagonized the trades unionists, radicals and labour bodies of of the day, by closing Trafalgar Square to all meetings and demonstrations. On 13 November 1887 this resulted in a head-on clash between demonstrators and 4,300 police aided by armed cavalry and foot-soldiers. One demonstrator died; 300 others were injured and Warren became a hated figure to thousands of ordinary people. He was never allowed to forget 'Bloody Sunday', so he entered 1888 handicapped by press hostility and public anger.

When the Ripper murders erupted and the killer remained free, hostile newspapers sniped away at Warren unmercifully. They branded him as inept, inflexible, and damaging to police morale. Even the man he chose to head the CID, Robert Anderson, was damned by association, and ridiculed for going on a 'rest cure' in Switzerland on the very eve of the first murder. Incredibly enough he remained abroad until well after the fourth murder, leaving Chief Inspector Donald Swanson to stand in for him. But the public heard and saw little of Swanson. The most visible of all the Ripper-hunters was the well-liked Inspector Frederick George Abberline. Abberline knew the East End and its denizens intimately, for fourteen years he had even served in Whitechapel itself.

In the 1900s all three policemen would air their views on the identity of the Ripper, each would clash with the others; but in 1888 not one of them had the slightest idea that the man they were looking for had moved around in police circles for almost twenty years.

For the first time, in this book, this man is investigated in full. He is unique. He is not a madman, or a fantasy candidate but an authentic suspect of the time. His indictment is based on solid evidence, without recourse to faked documents or journalists' inventions. The evidence is here in these pages. Consider his background, his cold-blooded personality, his strange actions, sayings and writings. Look without prejudice or preconceptions at the facts and you will see the true face of – Jack the Ripper, Master of the Killing Fields.

CHAPTER ONE

The Killing Fields

GHASTLY MURDER! REVOLTING AND MYSTERIOUS MURDER! EAST END HORRORS! DREADFUL MUTILATION OF A WOMAN! These were some of the garish newspaper headlines that petrified all England in 1888. Headlines that shrieked out the harrowing tidings of a faceless ghoul. A chilling creature who froze London with his unholy, merciless terror.

This bloody drama was played out to the full in one small area of the East End. Of the East End itself James Mackay wrote: '…it is the hell of poverty. Like an enormous black, motionless, giant Kraken, the poverty of London lies there in lurking silence and encircles with its mighty tentacles the life and wealth of the City and of the West End.' And of this area of grime and decay and hopelessness, the most wretched spot of all was Whitechapel. Jack London called it 'The Abyss'.

To starve on its streets was commonplace. To starve and die on its streets was unremarkable. And these filth-caked streets led to suffocating lanes and courtyards; and to even more sickening slimy-wastelands. There, in damp, mouldering houses were jam-packed the wretched of the earth; wretches who had lost every last shred of dignity and hope; wretches too drained, demoralized and apathetic to dream of raising the banner of revolt. They were doomed. Their heritage – a sunless day.

Into this setting came one man with a mission. He had no dream of uplift; he was no philanthropist; he had no message for the world. His mission was sordid beyond belief. He would take from the whores on those streets everything he craved. He would take their lives as an exercise in power. He would treat them like those specimens he had once carved up on mortuary slabs. It would be a brief reign of terror, but his memory would never die.

The women he chose to prey on were tragic, lost creatures. Not one of them had a fragment of allure. They justified the pity of anyone with a heart, but this heartless, fastidious man found their squalor an extra spur to his contempt. The women he came to terrorize were well pictured by a reporter from the *New York Herald*, who wrote:

> You can see them any evening, a dozen at least, on the pavement in front of the big old Spitalfields church. They are all over the adjacent district, but this is a sure place to find a group. They are old, actually or prematurely as the case may be. Their dress holds together but would not stand daylight. Their shoes are full of holes. Their bonnets would be rejected with nausea by a respectable rag-bag. They wear little, if any underclothing for several reasons, one of which is that it costs money. They are all bent, and walk slowly, the tottering gait of a wreck. And in all the scale of zoology there is nothing that can compare with the faces that look out at you in the flickering lights of the street.
>
> They are seamed and seared and wrinkled and bloated. Their eyes are dull like those of dead fish... They are not vicious... Depravity is a feeble word, degradation a familiar and inadequate expression to describe their condition...

From the ranks of these tragic discards the victims would be drawn. The stalker had studied them for years. He knew just where to find his prey. Every street, alley and lane was known to him of old. He could even choose the very spots to leave them on display. He could straddle them across the giant map of Whitechapel that lay seared in his memory. *His* would be the kingdom, the power and the glory.

CHAPTER TWO

The Terror Begins

In 1888 two prostitutes were murdered in the back streets of Whitechapel, well before the Ripper struck, but no one thought of linking these killings together. They were just two more of the brutalities that Whitechapel was long used to. Then, prostitute Polly Nichols was found mutilated and disembowelled in Buck's Row, just opposite the London Hospital, and the picture changed dramatically. Overnight the three killings were placed together. Now a pattern became observable; or so it seemed. But the observations were misguided; the Nichols murder was unconnected with the two earlier deaths. At the time only the killer knew that this murder was number one in a series that would dismay the civilized world. But in September 1888 belief that a single killer was responsible for all three deaths, dominated newspaper columns. The *Star* editorial for 1 September shows this well:

Have we a murderous maniac loose in East London? It looks as if we have. Nothing so appalling, so devilish, so inhuman – or, rather non-human – as the three Whitechapel crimes had ever happened outside the pages of Poe or De Quincey. The unravelled mystery of the 'Whitechapel Murders' would make a page of detective romance as ghastly as 'The Murders of the Rue Morgue'. The hellish violence and malignity of the crime which we described yesterday resemble in almost every particular the two other deeds of darkness which preceded it. Rational motive there appears to be none. The murderer must be a Man Monster...

And the account in the body of the paper spelled out the grim facts of the crime:

THE THIRD CRIME OF A MAN WHO MUST BE A MANIAC

The victim of the latest Whitechapel horror – the woman who was found yesterday in Buck's Row completely disembowelled and with her head nearly gashed from her body – was identified as Mary Ann Nicholls, also called 'Polly Nicholls'...

There is a terribly SIGNIFICANT SIMILARITY between this ghastly crime and the two mysterious murders of women which have occurred in the same district within the last three months. In each case the victim has been a woman of abandoned character, each crime has been committed in the dark hours of the morning, and more important still as pointing to one man, and that man a madman, being the culprit, each murder has been accompanied by hideous mutilation. In the second case, that of the woman Martha Turner, it will be remembered that no fewer than 30 stabs was inflicted. The scene of this murder was George-yard, a place appropriately known locally as 'the slaughter-house'. As in both other cases there was in this not the slightest clue to the murderer – no one was known to have any motive for causing the woman's death... The first murder, which, strangely enough, did not rouse much interest, was committed in Osborne-street. The woman in that case was alive when discovered, but unconscious, and she died in the hospital without recovering her senses, consequently she was unable to whisper a word to put the police on the track of her fiendish assailant, amd her murder has remained a mystery. All three crimes have been committed WITHIN A VERY SMALL RADIUS. Each of the ill-lighted thoroughfares to which the women were decoyed to be foully butchered are off turnings from Whitechapel-road, and all are within half a mile. The fact that these three tragedies have been committed within such a limited area, and are so strangely alike in their details, is forcing on all minds the conviction that they are the work of some cool, cunning man with a mania for murder.

How right they were! In the safety of his retreat the real killer would have revelled in these words. But the police and the public would have no truck with the idea of a cool cunning man. The killer had to have hate written all over his face; his manner had to be menacing and evil. In that frame of mind they began to hunt for the man known as Leather Apron. If the gossip was true, then everyone seemed to know him. He was unmistakable, so they said. But who was he? And, more to the point, where was he? The *Star* on 5 September tried to provide answers.

'Leather Apron' by himself is quite an unpleasant character. If, as many of the people suspect, he is the real author of the three murders which, in everybody's judgment, were done by the same person, he is a more ghoulish and devilish brute than can be found in all the pages of shocking fiction. He has ranged Whitechapel for a long time. He exercises over the unfortunates who ply their trade after twelve o'clock at night, a sway that is BASED ON UNIVERSAL TERROR. He has kicked, injured, bruised, and terrified a hundred of them who are ready to testify to the outrages. He has made a certain threat, his favourite threat, to any number of them, and each of the three dead bodies represents that threat carried out. He carries a razor-like knife, and two weeks ago drew it on a woman called 'Widow Annie' as she was crossing the square near London Hospital, theatening at the same time, with his ugly grin and his malignant eyes, to 'rip her up'.

...From all accounts he is five feet four or five inches in height and wears a dark, close-fitting cap. He is thickset, and has an unusually thick neck. His hair is black, and closely clipped, his age being about 38 or 40. He has a small, black moustache. The distinguishing feature of his costume is a leather apron, which he always wears, and from which he GETS HIS NICKNAME. His expression is sinister, and seems to be full of terror for the women who describe it. His eyes are small and glittering. His lips are usually parted in a grin which is not only not reassuring, but excessively repellant... His name nobody knows, but all are united in the belief that he is a Jew or of Jewish parentage, his face being of a marked Hebrew type...

Note the date of this report. Here is a woman stating that a man had threatened to 'rip her up'; at that time the killer had no name except Leather Apron. Did a hoaxing-journalist pick up the ripping reference and use it to forge a new name for the stalker?

CHAPTER THREE

Maniac at Large?

While all the talk raged about Leather Apron, came the second Ripper killing. In the backyard of No. 29 Hanbury Street, John Davis found the body of Annie Chapman with her throat cut and her body mutilated. Her neck was slashed so deeply that the head was almost severed. She had been disembowelled. And there, near the butchered body of this second victim was thrown a leather apron. Was it a taunt? Or had the killer left it behind in his haste? It was neither: the apron lay there after being cleaned outside under the yard tap. It belonged to John Richardson, whose mother lived at the place; so it had no significance whatsoever. Despite this, its discovery whipped up the fury against the strange, anonymous Jewish apron-wearer. This killing of 8 September convinced the *Star* that the time had come for popular action. Its leader on that day struck the keynote for its new campaign:

> London lies today under the spell of a great terror. A nameless reprobate – half beast, half man – is at large, who is daily gratifying his murderous instincts on the most miserable and defenceless classes of the community. There can be no shadow of a doubt now that our original theory was correct, and that the Whitechapel murderer, who has now four, if not five, victims to his knife, is one man, and that man a murderous maniac... London must rouse itself. No woman is safe while this ghoul is abroad. Up, citizens, then, and do your own police work!

Two days after this appeal for vigilantes, the news broke that, at last, Leather Apron had been cornered and hauled into a police cell. His name was now known: he was John Pizer, a Jewish boot-finisher, of Mulberry Street, Whitechapel. Crude broadsheets soon reached the streets proclaiming the arrest of the prime suspect. The killer-Jew had been ensnared. The rope would soon stretch his loathsome neck. But it was otherwise. On 12 September the *Pall Mall Gazette* announced that Emannuel Violenia had witnessed a quarrel between a man and a woman in Hanbury Street. The man had threatened to knife the woman and that man was believed to have been Pizer. An identification parade was held in the yard at Leman Street police station, with the result that:

> ...Violenia... Having keenly scrutinised all the faces before him, went up to Pizer and identified him as the man whom he heard threaten a woman on the night of the murder. Subsequently, cross-examination so discredited Violenia's evidence that it was wholly distrusted by the police, and Pizer was set at liberty.

Freedom for Pizer failed to satisfy the prejudiced, who were chained to the idea that the murders had to be the work of a 'low, dirty, foreign Jew'. No Britisher could sink to such depths. And while they seethed in their impotence the real killer, every inch a scholarly Englishman, struck again; not once but twice; his third and fourth killings delivered in one night.

The first knifing came in Berner Street, but it was interrupted; no time for the ritual mutilations. The interrupted ritual was hateful to the killer's plans; he needed a second victim fast. With his nerves stretched to screaming point, strident police whistles adrenalized him. With killing time running out, he sped swiftly through the back streets to a new place of anguish – a place he knew – this time on the territory of the City of London Police, Mitre Square. A square patrolled every fifteen minutes by a City policeman. He had this short time only to entrap, kill and mutilate.

The *Star* for Monday 1 October paints part of the picture for us, but concentrates on the Berner Street murder, where witnesses seemed to have proliferated:

> The first to find the body was Mr. Diemshitz, steward of the club. Interviewed by a *Star* reporter, Mr. Diemshitz said:- 'I was coming home from market at one o'clock on Sunday morning... After I had passed through the gate...on driving into the yard my donkey shied a little in consequence of my cart coming in contact with something on the ground. On looking down I saw the ground was not level, so I took the butt end of my whip and touched what appeared to me in the dark to be a heap of dirt lately placed there, a thing I was not accustomed to see. Not being able to move it, I struck a match end and FOUND IT WAS A WOMAN. First of all I thought of my wife, but I found her inside the club enjoying herself with the others. I said to some of the members there is a woman lying in the yard, and I think she is drunk. Young Isaacs, a tailor machinist, went to the door and struck a match,

and to our horror we saw blood trickling down the gutter almost from the gate to the club...'

In the case of this murder, there was an eye-witness who claimed to have been in Berner Street and seen a struggle between the murder victim, Elizabeth Stride, and a man. This eye-witness was a Hungarian called Israel Schwartz. Through an interpreter he made a statement, first to the police, and then to a *Star* reporter, who ran him to earth in Backchurch Lane. According to his story, he had witnessed a quarrel between a half-tipsy man and a woman. This took place in the entrance to the alleyway where the body was later found. Schwartz made no attempt to intervene since a second man came out of the doorway of a public-house, yelled to the tipsy man and rushed towards Schwartz. On seeing a knife Schwartz fled from the scene.

A great deal has been made of this statement by Schwartz. It has been construed by some to be evidence that Schwartz was later able to identify the Ripper beyond doubt. At the time his statement was made, however, the *Star* maintained that 'the truth of the man's statement is not wholly acceptable.' This clashes directly with Chief Inspector Swanson's verdict that there were no doubts about the honesty of Schwartz's statement.

There were similar claims to a sighting near to the spot where the second murder of that night took place. This was made by Joseph Lawende, who was walking past Mitre Square together with his friends Joseph Levy and Harry Harris. All three men saw a man and a woman talking there, but only Lawende was able to describe the man in any detail. These two 'sightings' have become part of a persistent myth that the Ripper himself was *definitely spotted* that night and later identified. Yet another myth grew out of that double event: the myth that the mutilations to victim Catherine Eddowes had been predicted in a letter to the Central News Agency.

Catherine Eddowes' murder in Mitre Square was the most sickening of all the killings up until then. Her intestines had been ripped from her body and thrown over one shoulder, the left kidney and uterus had been knifed out of her and her face had been systematically disfigured. Her killer was still an anonymous fiend, but not for much longer. Within days the the old cry of 'Leather Apron' was being replaced by a new one. An enterprising journalist had decided that the killer needed a memorable name, so he hit on 'Jack the Ripper' and used it first in a letter then on a postcard.

He sent off his hoaxing letter on 27 September, promising in it: 'The next job I do I shall clip the lady's ears off...' This was followed by a postcard posted on 1 October regretting that: 'Couldn't finish straight off. Had no time to get ears for police...'

These hoaxes were published in facsimile in the *Daily Telegraph* and this action led the *Star* (4 October) to lodge a protest:

> By the way, why does our friend, the *D.T.*, print facsimiles of the ghastly but very silly letters from 'Jack the Ripper'? We were offered them by the 'Central News', and declined to print them. They were clearly written in red pencil, not in blood, the obvious reason being that the writer was one of those foolish but bad people who delight in an unholy notoriety. Now, the murderer is not a man of this kind. His own love of publicity is tempered by a very peculiar and remarkable desire for privacy and by a singular ability to secure what he wants. Nor is there any proof of any pre-knowledge of the Mitre-square crimes, beyond the prediction that they were going to happen, which anybody might have made. The reference to ear-clipping may be a curious coincidence, but there is nothing in the posting of the letter on Sunday. Thousands of Londoners had details of the crimes supplied in the Sunday papers.

Foolish or not, from then on everyone, including the *Star*, accepted that the name would inevitably be 'Jack the Ripper'. And the killer himself, must have revelled in its gruesomeness. Then,while everyone was waiting for yet another knifing, the theorists began to refine their ideas. One such gentleman, a surgeon ill-received by the police, sought out the *Star* for help in promoting his views. Since these views were in line with those held by Archibald Forbes, the editor joined the two contributions together in a column on 6 October.

> 'Clearly,' said Mr. Forbes, 'the murderer is a man familiar with the geography of the Whitechapel purlieus. Clearly he is a man not unaccustomed in the manner of accosting these poor women as they are wont to be accosted. Clearly he is a man to whom the methods of the policemen are not unknown – the measured pace, the regular methodic round, the tendency to woodenness and unalertness of perception which are the characteristics of that well-meaning individual.
>
> 'Probably a dissolute man, he fell victim to a specific contagion, and so seriously that in the sequel he lost his career. What shape the deterioration may have taken, yet left him with a strong, steady hand, a brain of devilish coolness, and an active step, is not to be defined.
>
> 'The man's physical health ruined,' continued Mr. Forbes, 'and his career broken, he has possibly suffered specific brain damage as well. At this moment – I cannot use exact professional terms – there may be

mischief to one of the lobes of the brain. Or he may have become insane simply from anguish of body and distress of mind. Anyhow, he is mad, and his mania, rising from the particular to the general, takes the FELL FORM OF REVENGE against the class, a member of which has wrought him his blighting hurt, against too, the persons of that class plying in Whitechapel, since it was from a Whitechapel loose woman that he took his scathe.'

Now this exactly describes the man whom the doctor suspects. He is a man of about 35: He was not a fully qualified surgeon, but had a certain amount of anatomical knowledge, and had assisted at operations, including ovariotomy. He was the assistant to a doctor in Whitechapel, and KNOWS EVERY ALLEY AND COURT in the neighbourhood of the places where the murders were committed. He has been the victim of 'a specific contagion,' and since then has been animated by feelings of hate, not to say revenge, against the lower class of women who haunt the streets...

In later years this published theory would also furnish material for a lasting myth. A myth so persuasive and attractive that Leonard Matters, author of the first book on the Ripper published in English, *The Mystery of Jack the Ripper*, actually based his 'solution' wholeheartedly on it. Matters used the basic formula of a doctor bent on revenge and created a totally fictitious 'Dr Stanley', to fill the bill. His Dr Stanley was presented as an authentic man who lived, breathed, loved, killed and made a death-bed confession. There was one major difference, however: it was the doctor's *son* who caught the venereal disease, and the distraught father who sought the revenge.

So, were any of the contemporary theories ever more than inspired guesswork? In truth few of them had any kind of merit. But the most stubborn, underlying theme of many of these theories was one of anti-Semitism – an idea which gained strength from the very nature of the mutilations.

CHAPTER FOUR

Confusion Grows

Certain parts of some of the victims had been taken away, that much the public knew. It soon became known that the uterus had been removed from the scene in at least two cases. This was gruesome enough but then even more gruesome stories came in from the Continent suggesting a bizarre use for the missing organs. The *Star* ran one of these stories on 9 October 1888, which read in part:

> …certain facts…may throw a new light on the Whitechapel murders. In various German criminal codes…punishments are prescribed for the mutilation of female corpses, with the object of making from the uterus and other organs 'thieves' candles' or 'soporific candles'. According to an old superstition, still rife in various parts of Germany, the light from such candles will throw those upon whom it falls into the deepest slumbers, and they may, consequently, become a valuable instrument to the thieving profession…

When a similar account ran in *Police News* it was supplemented with a piece which said that such loathsome candles had also been introduced into the evidence at the trial of the Jew, Moses Ritter, a continental case of much bitterness.

Such words were honey to those who wished to fix the killings on the Jews. These people were sure to have been smugly satisfied by the news printed by the *Star* on 17 October:

WHITECHAPEL
A House to House Search Among the Jews

The police are making a house to house visit amongst the Jews at the East-end. They demand admission to every room, look underneath the beds, and peer into the smallest cupboards. They ask for the production of knives, and examine them. In some cases they have been refused admittance until proof was produced of authority...

Anti-Jewish feelings at the time ran high. As early as 15 September the *East London Observer* had reported a potential riot against the Jews:

On Saturday in several quarters of East London the crowds who assembled in the streets began to assume a very threatening attitude towards the Hebrew population of the District. It was repeatedly asserted that no Englishman could have perpetrated such a horrible crime as that of Hanbury Street, and that it must have been done by a *Jew* – and forthwith the crowds began to threaten and abuse such of the unfortunate Hebrews as they found in the streets. Happily the presence of a large number of police...prevented a riot actually taking place.

Adding to this anti-Semitism was the persistent chatter about a mysterious message left by the Ripper in Goulston Street just after the Mitre Square murder. It was something like 'the Jews not being blamed for nothing', or perhaps 'the Juwes not being blamed'; there was no certainty among the rumourmongers. Perhaps this was the fault of the police high-command. The writing had been rubbed out by order of Commissioner of Police Sir Charles Warren. Not even a photograph of the message had been allowed.

This growing hostility against the Jews was increased by a malicious story telegraphed to *The Times* from Vienna. The story alleged that the *Talmud* specifically sanctioned the mutilation by Jews of Gentile women. The Chief Rabbi, Dr Hermann Adler, wrote a bitter protest on reading this gross calumny:

...Many English and Irish workpeople in the East End are inflamed against the immigrant Jews by the competition for work and houses, by the stories of the sweaters and the sweated. If these illogical and ignorant minds should come to believe in the report heedlessly spread by a writer who is not quite just nor well informed himself, the results might be terrible.

Dr Adler's protest had little effect. The Jews were an easy target; they looked different; they ate differently; they spoke differently; and they were saddled with the collective responsibility for the death of Christ. Even the usually radical *Pall Mall Gazette* fell into the trap of using continental stories that reflected badly on the Jews. This led to a sorrowful letter from Samuel Montagu, the Jewish MP for Whitechapel:

Being a constant reader and in general accord with your policy of defending the weak against the strong, I felt much pain in reading in your yesterday's issue grave insinuations against the Jews who live in my constituency. In Jewish history there are frequent records that, when epidemics have occurred, or murders have taken place, false accusations have been made against the Jews, inciting the ignorant and the criminal classes to acts of violence. In this enlightened country, with an educated working class, no such fear need be entertained; but why recall the red spectre of bygone ages when religious persecution was a matter of course, whichever Christian creed was in power?

Few have greater experience than I of the Jew of this and of other countries, thus I am able to say with confidence that no similar class of human beings is as free from acts of violence as the Jews of Europe and America.

You may be right in blaming the authorities for not preserving a facsimile of the chalk inscription, which would have dispelled any chance of accusation against the Jews, although I cannot see how the atrocious acts of one man should affect a class. It has been generally admitted that the murderer had considerable practical knowledge of anatomy, and I do not believe that there exists such an individual among the Jews of East London. If the 'handwriting on the wall' was done by the monster himself, can there be any doubt of his intentions to throw the pursuers on a wrong track while showing hostility to the Jews in the vicinity.

Once again it is doubtful if these words of caution had any real effect. It is true that no one accused a specific Jewish doctor, but with 'Jewish wall-writings', and 'Jewish corpse-candles' in the public mind, it was inevitable that someone would hint that a Jewish ritual-slaughterman, or *shochet*, could be at work.

For a time the police actually took this seriously and checked on the men practised in *shechita* butchery. While all these futile diversions were taking up time and energy, the Ripper made his last foray, and made it the most spectacular of all.

CHAPTER FIVE

The Bloody Pinnacle

The Ripper chose the one day when all eyes would be centred on the City: the ninth day of November; Lord Mayor's Day. As the gilded coach stood waiting for the great procession, only a handful of people knew that the day would be completely dominated and overshadowed by the mocking killer.

Just a short distance away, in a shambles of a room, lay the most mutilated of all the victims. Mary Kelly had been unwise enough to usher the killer into her sordid bedroom. For the first time the Ripper had access to an improvised operating theatre. Every unexplored ritual could be carried out without haste or fear of interruption. *Police News* ran a report designed to sicken anyone who read it:

> The victim was another of the unfortunate class, who occupied a miserably furnished room in a court off Dorset-street, a narrow thoroughfare out of Commercial-street... Such a shocking state of things was there as has probably never been equalled in the annals of crime. The throat had been cut right across with a knife, nearly severing the head from the body. The abdomen had been ripped partially open, and both of the breasts had been cut from the body. The left arm, like the head, hung to the body by the skin only. The nose had been cut off, the forehead skinned, and the thighs, down to the feet, stripped of the flesh. The abdomen had been slashed with a knife across and downwards, and the liver and entrails wrenched away. The entrails and other portions of the frame were missing, but the liver, &c., it is said, were found placed between the feet of this poor victim. The flesh from the thighs and legs, together with the breasts and nose, had been placed by the murderer on the table, and one of the hands of the dead woman had been pushed into her stomach.

The first cries of horror from the newsboys cut through the cheering as Lord Mayor Whitehead drew near to St Paul's. All the gilt splendour failed to eclipse the black news from the East End.

Within days, the hysteria on the Whitechapel streets reached new heights. On 11 November, a crowd seized a Ripper suspect and cries of 'Lynch him!' were heard. Only swift action by the police prevented the man from being seriously injured. On 15 November, a City policeman in civilian clothes was surrounded by a small mob yelling that he was the Ripper. Within seconds the crowds had grown from dozens to hundreds, and escape was impossible. Once again, it was only the timely intervention by police constables that saved the man. And on the same day, one arrest caused more than usual excitement. As *The Times* reports:

> A man stared into the face of a woman in the Whitechapel Road and she at once screamed out that he was 'Jack the Ripper'. The man was immediately surrounded by an excited and threatening crowd, from which he was rescued with some difficulty by the police. He was then taken under a strong escort to the Commercial Street Police Station, followed by an enormous mob of men and women shouting and screaming at him in the most extraordinary manner. At the police station the man proved to be a German… He explained through an interpreter that he arrived in London from Germany on Tuesday and was to leave for America today.

At this turbulent time the Metropolitan police were shaken by the news that their Chief Commissioner, Sir Charles Warren, had resigned. His running battle with the Home Secretary, Charles Matthews, was over. An article by Warren in *Murray's Magazine* had contained too many indiscretions to be ignored and the two men met in a head-on clash. Resignation was Warren's only way of making one last protest, but few admired his stand; many in fact rejoiced in his downfall.

But was the hunt for the killer improved by this dramatic change at the top? If we judge by the results, then it made not the slightest difference, and as the year drew to its close nothing but false trails were explored. But did the police really have no clues to guide them? Well, they did have one incredibly detailed description of the man 'last seen with Kelly' on the night of her death.

This 'eye-witness' report counts as a classic in its own right. It is quite unbelievably detailed since the observation was conducted in the murk of a gas-lit street. Nevertheless this report was taken seriously, especially by the popular press. The *Star* ran the description on 14 November:

The story is told by George Hutchinson… He says: – '…about two o'clock on Friday morning…I came down Whitechapel-road into Commercial-street. As I passed Thrawl-street I saw a man standing at the corner of the street, and as I went towards Flower and Dean-street I met the woman Kelly, whom I knew very well, having been in her company a number of times. She said, "Mr. Hutchinson, can you lend me sixpence?" I said, "I cannot, as I am spent out going down to Romford." She then walked on towards Thrawl-street, saying, "I must go and look for some money." The man who was standing at the corner of Thrawl-street came towards her and PUT HIS HAND ON HER SHOULDER and said something to her, which I did not hear, and they both burst out laughing. He put his hand again on her shoulder, and they both walked slowly towards me. I walked on to the corner of Fashion-street, near the public-house. As they came by me his arm was still on her shoulder. He had a soft felt hat on, and this was drawn down somewhat over his eyes. I put down my head to look him in the face, and he turned and looked at me very sternly, and they walked across the road to Dorset-street. I followed them across, and stood at the corner of Dorset-street. They stood at the corner of Miller's-court for about three minutes. Kelly spoke to the man in a loud voice, say-ing, "I have lost my handkerchief." He pulled A RED HANDKERCHIEF out of his pocket, and gave it to Kelly, and they both went up the court together. I went to look up the court to see if I could see them, but could not. I stood there for three-quarters of an hour to see if they came down again, but they did not, and so I went away. My suspi-cions were aroused by seeing the man so well-dressed, but I had no suspicion that he was the murderer. The man was about 5ft. 6in. in height, and 34 or 35 years of age, with dark complexion and dark moustache, turned up at the ends. He was wearing a long dark coat, trimmed with astrachan, a white collar, with black necktie, in which was affixed a horseshoe pin. He wore a pair of dark 'spats' with light buttons over button boots, and displayed from his waistcoat a massive gold chain. His watch chain had a big seal, with a red stone, hanging from it. He had a heavy moustache curled up and dark eyes and bushy eyebrows. He had no side whiskers, and his chin was clean-shaven. He LOOKED LIKE A FOREIGNER…'

This pen-portrait soon became transformed into an 'artist's impression' that featured front-page in the 24 November *Police News* and influenced the public vision of the killer. Over the years the features depicted in this artist's wood-engraving have been positively identified as those of Walter Sickert; Frederick Deeming; George Chapman; Neill Cream; Pedachenko; Eddy, Duke of Clarence; Sir Randolph Churchill and James Maybrick! The choice is yours.

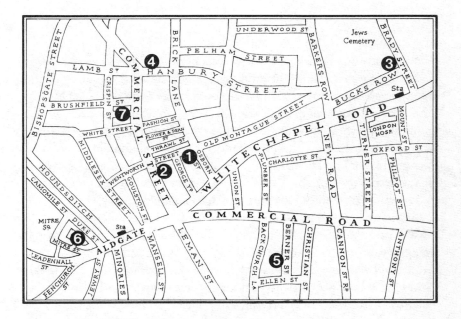

Map of the Whitechapel Murders

1. Emma Smith
2. Martha Turner
3. Mary Ann Nichols
4. Annie Chapman
5. Elizabeth Stride
6. Catherine Eddowes
7. Mary Kelly

After Kelly's murder *Police News* published this map and added to the confusion since only the last five were genuine Ripper murders

CHAPTER SIX

The Year Ends,
the Fears Remain

Given that good clues were elusive, one event on 19 December seemed to throw a new light on the killer's methods. It all began with the finding of a dead woman in Poplar; a woman later named as Rose Mylett.

Sensational reports at the time said that the dead woman's throat bore the unmistakable white mark of a strangler's cord. Despite this she was still a victim of Jack the Ripper! This strange conclusion resulted from some ideas put forward by Dr Matthew Brownfield, the police surgeon at Poplar. He was of the opinion that the Ripper victims were all first strangled by a cord because this rendered them unconscious and gave the killer the chance to cut their throats so much more cleanly and deliberately. By cutting the throat along the line of the cord he would obliterate all traces of partial strangulation, and add to the mystery. Evidence that the mark on her throat had been caused by too tight a collar was obviously dismissed with scorn by the inquest jury who decided it was murder. But in his autobiography Sir Robert Anderson (one-time Head of the CID) swept aside the jury's verdict of 'Murder by person or persons unknown' and wrote: 'The Poplar case of December, 1888, was death from natural causes, and but for the "Jack the Ripper" scare, no one would have thought of suggesting that it was homicide.'

Whether he was right or wrong is of little account. The murders had ended with the death of Kelly. No one but the Ripper knew that the killings had stopped (if only for the time being); but everyone was still waiting for the next outrage, so naturally, any type of attack on the 'unfortunates' in the East End was enough to raise the cry of 'The Ripper'. This is exactly what happened in 1889.

The first Ripper scare of 1889 erupted on 17 July, when the body of Alice McKenzie was found in Whitechapel's Castle Alley. Her throat was cut and her abdomen seemed to be gashed. But Dr Bagster Phillips soon ruled her out as one of the series. The abdominal wounds were superficial, not the extensive slashes favoured by Jack. And the throat had been cut with a short-bladed knife, very different from the long blades used by the Ripper. The press was not impressed; this had to be another Ripper job, and they were determined to stress the point. Their readers went on believing them and when a second body was discovered under a railway arch this simply showed that the press was right. But this second corpse, dumped just off Backchurch Lane, was headless and legless. The woman in this case had been dead for some days; all the cuts had been made cleanly and with decision; there was not the slightest hint of frenzy. It could well have been the work of some leisurely medical student. There was nothing to connect it with the killings of 1888.

Only one more pseudo-Ripper murder gained wide coverage. On 13 February 1891 a prostitute named Frances Coles was found slashed and ripped under a railway arch off Royal Mint Street. There was still a small spark of life left when she was found, so the killer must have darted off just seconds before the police arrived. Search parties were organized within minutes and the area was sealed off, but all the efforts were in vain.

A lead to the possible killer came from Coles' lodgings. A man with a bleeding hand had called looking for her. He had spun a yarn about being robbed and injured, then he went off to find a hospital. The tale sounded suspicious; could this be the Ripper at last? The man was swiftly traced and identified. He was James Saddler, a ship's fireman, who not only knew Frances but had even bought her a hat the day before.

For a while the case against him looked firm and he was arrested and charged with her murder. But the Stokers' Union came to his aid. Their solicitor, Harry Wilson, demolished, bit by bit, the case for the prosecution. Finally, in the interests of justice the Attorney-General decided that the case had to be dropped. With that Saddler slunk out of the limelight and the last great Ripper scare petered out. But theories about the Ripper went on multiplying.

He was now abroad, said some, and stories from both Nicaragua and Jamaica lent support to their claims. In both those places prostitutes had been slain and mutilated by an unknown killer; in Managua six women had been butchered in under ten days. Whether these horrors were inspired by reports about the London murders is an open question, but they were found to be unconnected with the man known as Jack.

Many of the other theories make strange reading. And there are famous names among the theorists; names like William Morris, Walter Crane, George Moore, Bernard Shaw, and other socially minded thinkers of the period. A whole book could be made up from these musings alone. Reading them one is struck with the thought that some of these men may well have known the Ripper and never once suspected him. For at one time he moved in the same circles as Bernard Shaw and even Conan Doyle, without being named by either of them. Did the creator of Sherlock Holmes ever have the faintest idea that the quarry was nigh? And were the police any brighter?

CHAPTER SEVEN

Fairy Tales?

Until 1910 the only published clues to the main police suspects were contained in the short account given by Major Arthur Griffiths in his *Mysteries of Police and Crime*. He confirmed that the police had suspected

> several persons, all of them known to be homicidal lunatics. Against three of these they held very plausible and reasonable grounds of suspicion… One was a Polish Jew, a known lunatic, who was at large in the district of Whitechapel at the time of the murders, and who, having developed homicidal tendencies, was afterwards confined in an asylum. The second possible criminal was a Russian doctor, also insane… The third person was of the same type, but the suspicion in his case was stronger… He also was a doctor in the prime of life, was believed to be insane or on the borderland of insanity… On the last day of that year (1888) his body was found floating in the Thames, and was said to have been in the water a month. The theory was that …his brain entirely gave way, and he became furiously insane and committed suicide.

No priority is given in this account to any one of the three candidates. This state of limbo changed when Sir Robert Anderson wrote his memoirs. The first version of the significant part of these memoirs appeared in the March 1910 issue of *Blackwood's Magazine*. This was followed soon afterwards by book publication under the title *The Lighter Side of My Official Life*. His comments on the identity of the killer led to a frosty rebuke from Sir Henry Smith, late of the City Police, and to two further objections: one from a City of London solicitor, George Kebbell; the other from the well-known 'expert in lunacy' Dr Forbes Winslow. These are Anderson's words that caused the furore:

> One did not need to be a Sherlock Holmes to discover that the criminal was a sexual maniac of a virulent type; that he was living in the

immediate vicinity of the scenes of the murders; and that, if he was not living absolutely alone, his people knew of his guilt, and refused to give him up to justice. During my absence abroad the Police had made a house-to-house search for him, investigating the case of every man in the district whose circumstances were such that he could go and come and get rid of his blood-stains in secret. And the conclusion we came to was that he and his people were certain low-class Polish Jews; for it is a remarkable fact that people of that class in the East End will not give up one of their number to justice.

And the result proved that our diagnosis was right on every point. For I may say at once that 'undiscovered murders' are rare in London and the 'Jack-the-Ripper' crimes are not within the category...I will only add here that the 'Jack-the-Ripper' letter which is preserved in the Police Museum at New Scotland Yard is the creation of an enterprising London journalist.

Having regard to the interest attaching to the case, I am almost tempted to disclose the identity of the murderer and the pressman who wrote the letter above referred to. But no public benefit would result from such a course, and the traditions of my old department would suffer. I will merely add that the only person who ever saw the murderer unhesitatingly identified the suspect the instant he was confronted with him; but he refused to give evidence against him.

In saying that he was a Polish Jew I am merely stating a definite ascertained fact. And my words are meant to specify race, not religion. For it would outrage all religious sentiment to talk of the religion of a loathsome creature whose utterly unmentionable vices reduced him to a lower level than that of a brute.

Major Smith's rebuke prompted no visible activity, but solicitor Kebbell's comments provoked an appeal to a Magistrate at the Bow Street Court. A report of these proceedings was carried by the *Umpire* on Sunday 31 July. In part, it ran:

WHO WAS JACK-THE-RIPPER?
ENGLISH SHERLOCK HOLMES ON THE MANIAC'S IDENTITY

Again the identity of the notorious murderer who called himself Jack-the-Ripper has cropped up. This time a lady living in Melbourne writes to Dr. Forbes Winslow, the Sherlock Holmes of these East End murders, and asserts that the fellow is a native of Melbourne, a college graduate, was called 'Jack', always carried an ugly sheath knife, and had told her that he was the perpetrator of the frightful series of crimes.

Quite recently the controversy was reopened by Sir Robert Anderson, formerly head of Scotland Yard, who contended that the miscreant was a Jew and that he was not arrested because the only man who could identify him was a co-religionist who refused to speak.

Mr. George Kebbell, a City of London solicitor, controverted this by declaring that Sir Robert was entirely in the wrong in that 'Jack-the-Ripper' was an Irishman who had been a medical student but had sinned, had been cast out by his family and had descended in the social scale until he became a casual fireman on board a cattle boat. Mr. Kebbell declared that this man, just after the Whitechapel murders, was caught in the very act of mutilating a woman, who, by a miracle, escaped death and gave evidence against him. The fellow was sentenced to ten years' penal servitude...

Dr. Forbes Winslow spent many days and nights hunting for the 'ripper', and, as a result, he asked Mr. Marsham, the Bow-street magistrate, to advise him as to what could be done in the case of the Irish medical student, who, in February, 1895, was sentenced to ten years' penal servitude for wounding a woman in Whitechapel.

Proceeding, Dr. Forbes Winslow said that while the student was serving that sentence statements were made, prompted probably by the nature of the offence, of which he said he was innocent, that he was none other than 'Jack-the-Ripper'.

In court Dr. Forbes Winslow said: 'I knew that there was no foundation for these statements, and I took up the man's case. A few days ago I received a letter from a lady in Australia. The object she had in writing this letter to me was to clear the Irish medical student I have referred to from the accusation that he committed these murders. This lady was acquainted with a man who left England in 1889, the last year in which these murders were committed.

'He went to Australia, and the lady became engaged to him there; but from certain facts which came to her knowledge, and from a confession made, she concluded that he was none other than "Jack-the-Ripper."...she is convinced in her own mind, that the real "Jack-the-Ripper" was the man who went to Australia, and who is at the present moment working in South Africa...'

Speaking of the various attempts to identify Jack-the-Ripper, Dr. Winslow remarked to a special representative of the *Umpire*: 'Of the many people who saw and spoke to the unknown murderer, there came never a suggestion that he was either a Jew or an Irishman.

Again, I should say that Mr. Kebbell is mistaken in his man for several reasons. To begin with, if he noticed that the man he defended before the magistrates was an Irishman, then some of my informants would have noticed it also. Now, I traced Jack-the-Ripper from one lodging to another, and all my first-hand descriptions fail to tally with Mr. Kebbell's in every way.

'I am convinced that the murderer of the eight unfortunates during 1888 and 1889 was an epileptic maniac, a man who at times was a homicidal maniac and at other times was quite sane.

'At the time of the crimes I threw my whole heart and soul into the subject, and I am still of the same mind – that Jack-the-Ripper was an Englishman, probably thirty-five years of age; that he was well educated, and had studied surgery in his earlier days. His conversation was often quite above the heads of his hearers, and he would talk by the hour on the morality of people.

'I have no doubt that when seized by homicidal mania he believed that he had a mission to perform, namely, to strike such a blow at open immorality that women would henceforth not dare to parade their vices... So well-known was my association with the hunt for Jack-the-Ripper that he actually wrote to me. These two epistles are, I firmly believe, genuine, because the writing corresponds with various inscriptions chalked under Whitechapel arches, while on one occasion he sent me the date on which he would commit his next outrage, and he kept his word, even though I had given notice to the police. This crime was carried out on Lord Mayor's day, and while the crowd was at its thickest to view the show newsboys were crying in the streets, "Another Whitechapel Murder!"...

'If the police will co-operate with me,' concluded Dr. Winslow, "Jack-the-Ripper" can be safe in prison in London in six months' time. I should be prepared to go out myself with a policeman and fetch him.'

Now Dr Lyttleton Forbes Winslow came from a family of asylum owners, and had given expert testimony in criminal cases, so his views seemed to have some weight behind them. In fact at the time of the murders he was regarded as an outstanding authority on the real personality of the Ripper. Of his own powers he had no doubt. He even wrote:

Day after day and night after night I spent in the Whitechapel slums. The detectives knew me, the lodging house keepers knew me, and at last the poor creatures of the street came to know me. In terror they rushed to me with every scrap of information which might to my mind be of value. To me the frightened women looked for hope. In my presence they felt reassured and welcomed me to their dens and obeyed my commands eagerly, and found bits of information I wanted.

Who could possibly dismiss such a worthy fellow as a humbug and a fantasist and a liar? But that is what he was. His claim to have warned the Yard *before* the Kelly murder is false. The letter he later produced to try to prove his claim can be shown to have had its date altered. It was originally dated 19 October 1889, and was one of a spate of such letters sent at that time. But the year has been crudely altered to read '1888'. And a thoughtful examination of the text confirms that it is based on events of 1889 beyond doubt. Thus at least two of Anderson's protagonists are not to be taken seriously. Major Smith, by contrast, had a valid point when he said: 'Surely Sir Robert cannot believe that while the Jews, as he asserts, were entering into this conspiracy to defeat the ends of justice, there was no one among them with sufficient knowledge of the criminal law to warn them of the risks they were running?'

But, despite Major Smith's objections, could Anderson possibly have truth on his side?

CHAPTER EIGHT

The Riddles of Zion

Anderson's Polish Jew remained anonymous until a few years ago when writer, Martin Fido, began to look at this neglected man. He reasoned that Anderson had been writing about Kosminski, one of the three listed by Macnaghten. This may seem an obvious linkage but Don Rumbelow, for one, had earlier concluded, '…it seems abundantly clear that Anderson was accusing John Pizer (Leather Apron) of being the Ripper'. But Martin Fido was certain that only one man fitted Anderson's description, and he began searching through the records of public asylums and workhouse infirmaries. His diligence paid off. In the records of admissions for Colney Hatch Asylum he found an entry for Aaron Kosminski. Was *this* the man he was hunting for? Unfortunately for his theory this Kosminski was not taken in until 6 February 1891. This simply failed to match. The man indicated by Anderson had to have been inside an asylum in March 1889. In addition lunatic Aaron was simply a poor wretch suffering from delusions; a sad figure impelled to search for bread in the gutters of the streets. Fido came to the reluctant conclusion that: '…with eighteen months of harmless scavenging from the gutters from 1888 to 1890, Kosminski could not have been the Ripper.'

A revised theory had to be quickly evolved. Perhaps there had been a confusion of names at some point? Maybe the killer had been penned up under a name quite like Kosminski? From that point Martin Fido made a fresh search and came up with Nathan Kaminsky, a Polish Jew who on 24 March 1888, began a six-week course of treatment for syphilis at the Whitechapel Workhouse Infirmary. After that the records were bare. No trace of the man anywhere. Fido met this challenge by theorizing that Kaminsky had been incarcerated under some other name and then concluded that a Colney Hatch patient logged as David Cohen was identical with the missing Kaminsky. Cohen had been brought in on 21 December 1888 and had died there on 20 October 1889. He was an extremely violent man more often found in a strait-jacket than without. He was also, in Fido's view, unmistakably Anderson's Polish Jew. In other words, Jack the Ripper.

It was a theory that was in dire trouble within weeks of its first appearance. On 19 October 1987 the *Daily Telegraph* published some notes made by Chief Inspector Donald Swanson in 1910. These had been jotted down on the pages of his copy of Anderson's autobiography, and at the point where Anderson states that the murderer had been identified by a man who refused to testify against him, Swanson wrote: 'because the suspect was also a Jew and also because his evidence would convict the suspect, and witness would be the means of the murderer being hanged which he did not wish to be left on his mind. And after this identification, which suspect knew, no other murder of this kind took place in London.'

On the endpaper of the book Swanson wrote a most remarkable observation. It is badly worded, but its meaning is clear:

> Continuing from page 138 after the suspect had been identified at the Seaside Home where he had been sent by us with difficulty in order to subject him to identification, and he knew he was identified. On suspect's return to his brother's house in Whitechapel he was watched by police (City CID) by day and night. In a very short time the suspect with his hands tied behind his back, was sent to Stepney Workhouse and then to Colney Hatch and died shortly afterwards – Kosminsky was the suspect.

Swanson puts no dates on record, but the Seaside Home he mentions was the Police Convalescent Home at Brighton, which only opened in March 1890. By that time David Cohen was dead and buried. Apart from that, Cohen had no next-of-kin, hence no 'brother's house' to return to. Martin Fido's Ripper Cohen is patently not the same as Swanson's Ripper Kosminski. Despite that, Fido has gone on record saying: 'I am quite convinced that he [Swanson] confirms my thesis that Aaron Kosminksi who lived at "his brother's house" in Whitechapel was somehow confused with David Cohen, who probably committed the Whitechapel Murders…'

I am not alone in failing to see how these two conflicting pieces of police testimony can be reconciled. So, was the original yarn about Kosminski simply an idea that Swanson came to nurse and passed on to Anderson? Did it get garbled in the same way that many of the police reminiscences became garbled? Major Smith, for a start, was wildly inaccurate at times. So was Macnaghten. And in the case of Inspector Reid we have his absurd statements that the Ripper only left '…a number of slashes all over the body of the victim, even after the murderer knew his victim was dead [and] at no time was any part of the body missing.' He also believed that the Ripper had nine victims!

Did the police, then, have any certain evidence that allowed them to make a solid, sober, definitive identification? Do the existing records persuade us to trust Anderson on this score?

CHAPTER NINE

Without a Clue

Anderson has been regarded as inaccurate and dogmatic by several historians. I personally mistrust anyone whose thinking has been governed by fundamentalism of any sort: religious, political, scientific, it doesn't matter which, rigid dogmatism always stands in the way of clear thinking. It promotes a feeling of certainty where caution should rule. For that reason I am convinced that Anderson was simply repeating the truth as he had come to see it.

But this is not objective, historical truth. His writings are not those of someone possessing real knowledge – that is why they are so sketchy. At no point does he say, 'I was there when the identification was made.' He is trading in second-hand information, and yet the solution to the great mystery would have dragged any sensible police chief from one end of the country to the other. So what did he really know?

Some have argued that a crucial sighting of the Ripper was made on the night of the double event. One group favours the sighting by Schwartz at Berner Street, another opts for Lawende's sighting near Mitre Square. One of these eye-witnesses, so the reasoning runs, was much later able to finger Kosminski.

Let us spell out what this implies: on 30 September the police knew for certain that the murderer had been seen, beyond doubt. They knew, as well, that they had testimony from a person who could pick out the killer without hesitation. In short they had an invaluable clue in their hands and it only needed a face-to-face confrontation between their witness and the killer to tie the whole case up. Is this at all possible? Not on your life! Anderson's own words prove this to be absurd. Consider first of all his report to the Home Secretary of 23 October 1888. The telling part reads:

> I wish to guard against its being supposed that the inquiry is now concluded. There is no reason for furnishing these reports at this moment except that they have been called for.

That a crime of this kind should have been committed without any clue being supplied by the criminal, is unusual, but that five successive murders should have been committed, without our having the slightest clue of any kind is extraordinary, if not unique, in the annals of crime. The result has been to necessitate our giving attention to innumerable suggestions, such as would in any ordinary case be dismissed unnoticed, and no hint of any kind, which was not obviously absurd, has been neglected.

Does it really have to be hammered home that this alone destroys the fallacy that a key witness was known? Perhaps it does need hammering, since the significance of these words seem to have been missed by too many people. Very well, the man is confessing without reservations that he does not have *'the slightest clue of any kind'*. No witnesses; no trails leading to a hideout; no bloody clothing that can be fitted to a suspect; nothing. And years later Anderson confirmed that they had been without clues and that their efforts had resulted in 'non-detection'. His admissions came in a front-page interview given by him to the *Daily Chronicle,* on 1 September 1908. It was an interview prompted by the Luard case and Anderson first compared the British police procedures with those of the French – to the detriment of the British. In France, he argued, a tight control would be exercised over access to crime-sites. Clues would be protected from destruction by this control. Not so in Britain. He then went on:

> Something of the same kind happened in the Ripper crimes. In two cases of that series there were distinct clues destroyed – wiped out absolutely – clues that might very easily have secured for us proof of the identity of the assassin. In one case it was a clay pipe. Before we could get to the scene of the murder the doctor had taken it up, thrown it into the fireplace and smashed it beyond recognition. In another case there was writing in chalk on the wall – a most valuable clue; handwriting that might have been recognised at once as belonging to a certain individual, but before we could secure a copy, or get it protected, it had been obliterated…I told Sir William Harcourt, who was then Home Secretary, that I could not accept responsibility for the non-detection of the author of the Ripper crimes, for the reasons, among others, that I have given you…

Since the police were so baffled, they inevitably had free scope to develop individual theories. In time, these theories became hardened into certainties. But, with hindsight, we can see that they were all based on a hopelessly inadequate store of knowledge. They had not the dimmest vision of the person they should have been looking for. Some of them actually knew the killer, but never suspected him. They would have recognized him as the killer, only if they had found him standing over a corpse, ritually carving away.

CHAPTER TEN

Cover-Up?

Since 1965 all serious research into the police suspects has been inspired by an odd document penned by Commissioner of Police Melville Macnaghten. This lengthy document is dated 23 February 1894 and in it he names three men as his prime suspects. But why bother to go to such lengths at that time? The murders had long since ceased and no spiky Home Secretary was pressing for quick answers. The truth is that his need to write was forced on him by outside pressure from the newspaper world.

It all began with a whisper conveyed to a reporter on the *Sun*. A patient held behind bars at Broadmoor Asylum was believed to be none other than the Ripper, but his connection with those murders had been hushed up. This was enough for the newspaper to mount an investigation and by 13 February 1894 the *Sun* presses were ready to roll off the first instalment of their great scoop. It took five days to tell the whole story and after the sensation had animated enough interest, the editor, Member of Parliament, T. P. O'Connor, decided that an editorial was called for. It appeared on 19 February:

> Slowly, but steadily, the public has come to the same conclusion as that to which we have been forced by months of investigation – that in the witless wretch who is at present in Broadmoor Lunatic Asylum we have traced the author of the Whitechapel murders. We are not surprised that our statement should at first have been received with a certain degree of incredulity...
>
> What reserve we had to make to defeat the arts of rivals, we were bound still further to increase by our sense of public welfare and our desire to spare feeling. Many correspondents have written to us to demand that we should give the name of 'Jack the Ripper' to the public. We may have to do so in the end, but we shall do so unwillingly, for it is hard to make the innocent suffer for the guilty, and to expose the

unhappy relatives – if such there still be – to the reprobation which will gather around his name. But we shall send to the police, when they ask for it, all the material at our disposal. The names which we had to veil under initials will be revealed to them. We have likewise the addresses, the occupations, all the particulars, with regard to all the persons who can either entirely reveal or throw considerable light on the mystery we claim to have solved. We understand that the attention of the highest police authorities has been called to our statements, and we confidently look forward to our story being subjected to the closest and most searching investigation. We believe that with others, as with us, facts will point irresistibly to the conclusion that the man we point out is undoubtedly the long-sought criminal.

Macnaghten was alerted and alarmed by the suggestion that the *Sun* would name the inmate. He already knew about the man held in Broadmoor and he sensed trouble if the name was made public, since it would not take long for people to discover that inmate Cutbush was the nephew of Executive Superintendent Charles Henry Cutbush, of Scotland Yard. A grave risk presented itself: the risk of an outcry fanned by a hostile press. The charge would inevitably be 'cover-up by the police, for the police'. It was an outcome that Macnaghten dreaded. Ever since the Turf Frauds Scandal of 1877 the police blanched at any hint of concealment or corruption in their ranks. The public outcry at that time; the imprisonment of Chief Inspector Palmer and the detectives Druscovitch and Meiklejohn; was still remembered in every agonizing detail. The last thing needed was a revival of the acid atmosphere of those days. So, as a precaution Macnaghten prepared a statement and filed it at the Yard. There it lay, potential ammunition for his underlings in the event of a disclosure. Though marked 'Confidential', it was never meant to be a secret document – only the names were meant to be kept under wraps. Indeed, this document was carefully leaked to friendly outsiders, like Major Arthur Griffiths. Its full text reads:

> The case referred to in the sensational story in 'The Sun' in its issue of 13th inst, & following dates, is that of Thomas Cutbush who was arraigned at the London County Sessions in April 1891, on a charge of maliciously wounding Florence Grace Johnson, and attempting to wound Isabelle Frazer Anderson in Kennington. He was found to be insane and sentenced to be detained during Her Majesty's pleasure.
>
> This Cutbush, who lived with his mother and aunt at 14 Albert St. Kennington, escaped from the Lambeth Infirmary, (after he had been detained there only a few hours, as a lunatic) at noon on 5th

March 1891. He was rearrested on 9th idem. A few weeks before this, several cases of stabbing, or jabbing from behind had occurred in the vicinity, and a man named Colicutt was arrested, but subsequently discharged owing to faulty identification. The cuts in the girls' dresses made by Colicutt were quite different to the cut made by Cutbush (when he wounded Miss Johnson) who was no doubt influenced by a wild desire of morbid imitation. Cutbush's antecedents were enquired into by Ch. Inspr.(now Supt.) [unreadable], by Inspr. Race, and by P. S. McCarthy C.I.D. (the last named officer had been specially employed in Whitechapel at the time of the murders there) and it was ascertained that he was born, and had lived in Kennington all his life. His father died when he was quite young, and he was always a 'spoilt' child. He had been employed as a clerk and traveller in the Tea trade at the Minories, & subsequently canvassed for a Directory in the East End, during which time he bore a good character. He apparently contracted syphilis about 1888, and, – since that time, – led an idle and useless life. His brain seems to have become affected, and he believed that people were trying to poison him. He wrote to Lord Grimthorpe, and others, and also to the Treasury, complaining of Dr Brooks, of Westminster Bridge Rd, whom he threatened to shoot for having supplied him with bad medicines. He is said to have studied medical books by day, and to have rambled about at night, returning frequently with his clothes covered with blood, but little reliance could be placed on the statements made by his mother or his aunt, who both appear to have been of a very excitable disposition. It was found impossible to ascertain his movements on the nights of the Whitechapel murders. The knife found on him was bought in Houndsditch about a week before he was detained in the Infirmary. Cutbush was a nephew of the late Supt. Executive.

Now the Whitechapel Murderer had 5 victims and 5 victims only, – his murders were

(i) 31st Aug '88. Mary Ann Nichols – at Buck's Row – who was found with her throat cut – & with (slight) stomach mutilation.

(ii) 8th Sept '88 Annie Chapman – Hanbury Street: throat cut – stomach & private parts badly mutilated & some of the entrails placed round the neck.

(iii) 30th Sept '88. Elizabeth Stride – Berner's Street: throat cut, but nothing in the shape of mutilation attempted, & *on same date*

Catherine Eddowes – Mitre Square, throat cut & very bad mutilation, both of face & stomach.

(iv) 9th November. Mary Jane Kelly – Miller's Court, throat cut, and the whole of the body mutilated in the most ghastly manner.

The last murder is the only one that took place in a *room,* and the murderer must have been at least 2 hours engaged. A photo was taken of the woman, as she was found lying on the bed, without seeing which it is impossible to imagine the awful mutilation.

With regard to the *double* murder which took place on 30th Sept. there is no doubt but that the man was disturbed by some Jews who drove up to a Club (close to which the body of Elizabeth Stride was found) and that he then, 'mordum satiatus', went in search of a further victim whom he found at Mitre Square.

It will be noticed that the fury of the mutilations *increased* in each case, and, seemingly, the appetite only became sharpened by indulgence. It seems, then, highly improbable that the murderer would have suddenly stopped in November '88, and been content to recommence operations by merely prodding a girl behind some 2 years and 4 months afterwards. A much more rational theory is that the murderer's brain gave way altogether after his awful glut in Miller's Court, and that he immediately committed suicide, or, as a possible alternative, was found to be so hopelessly mad by his relations, that he was by them confined to some asylum.

No one ever saw the Whitechapel Murderer, many homicidal maniacs were suspected, but no shadow of proof would be thrown on any one. I may mention the cases of 3 men, any one of whom would have been more likely than Cutbush to have committed this series of murders:-

(1) A Mr M. J. Druitt, said to be a doctor and of good family, who disappeared at the time of the Miller's Court murder, and whose body (which was said to have been upwards of a month in the water) was found in the Thames on 31st Dec. – or about 7 weeks after that murder. He was sexually insane and from private info I have little doubt but that his own family believed him to have been the murderer.

(2) Kosminski, a Polish Jew and resident in Whitechapel. This man became insane owing to many years indulgence in solitary vices. He had a great hatred of women, especially of the prostitute class, and had strong homicidal tendencies: he was removed to a lunatic asylum

about March 1889. There were many crimes connected with this man which made him a strong 'suspect'.

(3) Michael Ostrog, a Russian doctor, and a convict, who was subsequently detained in a lunatic asylum as a homicidal maniac. This man's antecedents were of the worst possible type, and his whereabouts at the time of the murders could never be ascertained.

And now with regard to a few of the inaccuracies and misleading statements made by the 'Sun'. In its issue of 14th Feb., it is stated that the writer had in his possession a facsimile of the knife with which the murders were committed. This knife (which for some unexplained reason has, for the last 3 years, been kept by Insp. Race, instead of being sent to Prisoners' Property Store) was traced and it was found to have been purchased in Houndsditch in Feb.'91 or two years and 3 months *after* the Whitechapel murders ceased!

The statement, too, that Cutbush 'spent a portion of the day in making rough drawings of the bodies of women, and of their mutilations' is based solely on the fact that 2 *scribble* drawings of women in indecent postures were found torn up in Cutbush's room. The head and body of one of these had been cut from some fashion plate, and legs were added to show a woman's naked thighs and pink stockings.

In the issue of 15th Inst. it is said that a *light* overcoat was among the things found in Cutbush's house, and that a man in a *light* overcoat was seen talking to a woman in Backchurch Lane whose body with arms attached was found in Pinchin St. This is hopelessly incorrect! On 10th Sept.'89 the naked body, with arms, of a woman was found in some sacking under a railway arch in Pinchin St: the head and legs were never found nor was the woman ever identified. She had been killed at least 24 hours before the remains (which had seemingly been brought from a distance) were discovered. The stomach was slit up by a cut, and the head and legs had been severed in a manner identical with that of the woman whose remains were discovered in the Thames, in Battersea Park, and on the Chelsea Embankment on 4th June of the same year; and these murders had no connection whatever with the Whitechapel horrors. The Rainham mystery in 1887, and the Whitehall mystery (when portions of a woman's body were found under what is now Scotland Yard) in 1888 were of a similar type to the Thames and Pinchin St. crimes.

It is perfectly untrue to say that Cutbush stabbed 6 girls behind – this is confounding his case with that of Colicutt.

The theory that the Whitechapel murderer was left-handed, or, at any rate, 'ambidextrous', had its origin in the remark made by a doctor who examined the corpse of one of the earliest victims; *other doctors did not agree with him.*

With regard to the 4 additional murders ascribed by the writer in the 'Sun' to the Whitechapel fiend:-

(1) The body of Martha Tabram, a prostitute was found on a common staircase in George Yard buildings on 7th August 1888; the body had been repeatedly *pierced,* probably with a *bayonet.* This woman had, with a fellow prostitute, been in company of 2 soldiers in the early part of the evening. These men were arrested, but the second prostitute failed, or refused, to identify, and the soldiers were accordingly discharged.

(2) Alice McKenzie was found with her throat cut (or rather *stabbed*) in Castle Alley on 17th July 1889; no evidence was forthcoming and no arrests were made in connection with this case. The *stab* in the throat was of the same nature as in the case of the murder.

(3) Frances Coles in Swallow Gardens, on 13th February 1891 – for which Thomas Sadler, a fireman, was arrested, and, after several remands, discharged. It was ascertained at the time that Sadler had sailed for the Baltic on 19th July '89 and was in Whitechapel on the night of 17th idem. He was a man of ungovernable temper and entirely addicted to drink and the company of the lowest prostitutes.

(4) The case of the unidentified woman whose trunk was found in Pinchin St on 10th Sept. 1889 – which had already been dealt with.

M. L. Macnaghten

Macnaghten is mistaken on a number of points; Druitt for example was never a doctor; Ostrog was a Polish Jew who was more of a confidence trickster than a killer; while Cutbush was much more violent. Yet these notes of his have served as the basis for most of the serious research undertaken by Ripperologists.

Now it is not my intention to be disparaging, but I contend that the efforts put into looking for Jack the Ripper among the main police suspects have been sadly misdirected. The police were never looking for a serial sexual murderer, they were hunting for their imaginary homicidal lunatic. Druitt alone, of the selected three had never been an asylum inmate;

but his suicide brought him into the insane category and this matched police expectations. And all other candidates had to measure up to these same archaic standards.

In Druitt's case, some thirty years of searching by numerous writers has failed to connect him in any way with the murders, or even with Whitechapel, but he went insane at the crucial time and that was enough to list his name as a *possible*. 'Many homicidal maniacs were suspected...' wrote Macnaghten, and this needs to be stressed over and over again. The police were so convinced that this was what they were looking for that their minds remained closed to the real nature of the killer.

Interestingly enough, only one of the top men at the time of the murders ever rejected Macnaghten's list of madmen. This was Inspector Abberline, the man on the streets in 1888, for in 1903 he named a man who had never even been considered before. His choice was the Polish wife-poisoner, George Chapman. Very odd! What governed that odd choice? Some writers have mistakenly echoed Abberline's own words and imagined that the Solicitor-General's opening statement at the Chapman trial linked Chapman with Whitechapel. But the trial record proves that Abberline was at fault. The opening speech does *not* place Chapman in Whitechapel at any time, neither does it even place him in the East End in 1888. Since this speech obviously offered no impetus for fresh thoughts, the answer to the Chapman conundrum must lie elsewhere.

CHAPTER ELEVEN

What Manner of Man?

In the 1880s few people understood anything about the varieties and lures of sexual aberrations. When the police were faced with a serial sexual murderer they could only draw on their inadequate experience and conclude that they were being challenged by a madman. Their conclusions would be inevitably coloured by the shallow thinking and prejudices of the day, so even their hypothetical madman was most likely a foreigner and probably not a Christian. It is no accident that the three men listed by Macnaghten are thought of as insane; that two of them are Polish Jews; and that the odd man out is most likely a homosexual. These were men beyond the pale and naturally given over to lust and despoilment.

Our present-day state of knowledge tells us that such a view was far too simplistic and even dangerously wrong. This does not mean that the police of the day were incompetent, they were simply without the experience that alone could give them guidance. Today we have the misfortune to have far too much experience of serial sexual murderers, but that unwanted experience does at least give us knowledge. The systematic study of such killers has shown us what we should look for. Forget the madmen and the obvious types, the killer will not be among them. He will be someone normal-looking, intelligent even, perhaps a pleasant person. Someone like an innocuous next-door neighbour, a man hard to suspect, if at all. These people give no outward signs of the rages within; their secret lives stay submerged; only their victims ever get to glimpse the hidden monster who craves power over them. Such killers are so very different from the old-fashioned stereotypes that once dominated popular – and even police – thinking. They plan, they stalk, they savour every stage of the hunt, they are not creatures of impulse. And when their victims are despatched, they then savour the hue and cry, and the fear they engender in the world around them. Looking back at everything that was written about the Whitechapel murders, I can only find one man (a reporter) who was able to come anywhere near to an accurate assessment of the killer's personality. His views, as published in the *New York Herald* (London ed.) on 21 July 1889, are remarkable for their foresight.

I have been trying for a year to form in my mind a harmonious conception of the murderer, and had been unable to do so. I have had some experience with various forms of mania in several lunatic asylums as an amateur specialist, but the combination of qualities which the Whitechapel murderer presents is so incongruous, that I could not reconcile them in one man. To me – and I have watched the case closely, been on the ground shortly after every murder, and seen every victim – the man is a sane man with a blood mania, who is well educated, excessively keen, excessively cool, and more determined and resolute than ninety-nine men in a hundred. He is also a humourist in his ghastly way. He combines with his horrible purpose a mockery of the police which savours of fun...

Second to our anonymous newsman comes Dr Thomas Bond. In his report on the five victims he says:

The murderer must have been a man of physical strength and of great coolness and daring. There is no evidence that he had an accomplice. He must in my opinion be a man subject to periodical attacks of Homicidal and erotic mania. The character of the mutilations indicate that the man may be in a condition sexually, that may be called satyriasis. It is of course possible that the Homicidal impulse may have developed from a revengeful or brooding condition of the mind, or that Religious Mania may have been the original disease, but I do not think either hypothesis is likely. The murderer in external appearance is quite likely to be a quiet inoffensive looking man probably middle-aged and neatly and respectably dressed. I think he must be in the habit of wearing a cloak or overcoat or he could hardly have escaped notice in the streets if the blood on his hands or clothes were visible.

Assuming the murderer to be such a person as I have just described he would probably be solitary and eccentric in his habits, also he is most likely to be a man without regular occupation, but with some small income or pension. He is possibly living among respectable persons who have some knowledge of his character and habits and who may have grounds for suspicion that he is not quite right in his mind at times. Such persons would probably be unwilling to communicate suspicions to the Police for fear of trouble or notoriety, whereas if there were a prospect of reward it might overcome their scruples.

The dominant view of the day, however, still directed the search towards the madmen. 'Enquiries were also made,' says a police report of 19 October 1888, 'to trace 3 insane medical students who had attended London Hospital. Result 2 traced, one gone abroad.' Earlier, on 11 September, Doctors Cowan and Crabb, informed the police that Joseph Issenschmidt, who had spent ten weeks in the Colney Hatch Asylum, was most likely the Ripper. Issenschmidt was once more taken to an asylum on 17 September 1888, and while locked up there the murders continued, so his innocence was established beyond doubt. And there were other mentally disturbed men around in the area who were taken in for questioning or harassed by ignorant mobs. The fallacies of the day continued to rule.

From his chosen bolt-hole the real killer could afford to gloat and smile. He was certain that no trace of wildness or madness would ever govern his features, his speech or his movements. All his actions were calculated, controlled, and designed to promote in others a feeling of trust and ease. His civilized veneer warded off all suspicions. His peaks only came at the time of killing. Even so, with time, this man proved to be vulnerable.

So who was he? In 1930 Fleet Street journalist Bernard O'Donnell began to ask that question. It did not come to him spontaneously, but was put in his mind by Hayter Preston, editor of the *Sunday Referee*. Preston was a friend of the poet Victor Neuburg, and Neuburg had once been one of Aleister Crowley's dupes. His health had been threatened by Crowley's demands until Crowley's business manager took pity on him and helped him break away. This business manager was an American lady called Vittoria Cremers.

She was the widow of Baron Louis Cremers, at one time attached to the diplomatic corps at the Russian Embassy in Washington. She also had a strange story to tell about the Whitechapel murders.

Neuburg had heard of some of the events from her own lips, but not enough to be able to give O'Donnell material for a story, so Preston urged O'Donnell to visit the lady at her retreat, somewhere in Caerleon-on-Usk, in Monmouthshire. O'Donnell was intrigued. He was certain that no one had ever claimed to have known the Ripper intimately. So this had to be very different from the usual Fleet Street assignment. O'Donnell was inspired enough to make the long trip to Caerleon. But his journey was wasted; the lady had returned to London, without leaving a forwarding address. O'Donnell was too good a journalist to despair. The capital was an enormous place but someone must know her whereabouts. And he was right. His searches paid off and he tracked the lady down to 34 Marius Road in Balham, south-west London.

On his first visit he found her a formidable person, but she soon came to appreciate his professional zeal, and so, in 1930 Vittoria Cremers began to unburden herself at length for the first time. She wrote small pieces for him over four years until at last O'Donnell was able to view her complete memoirs for the years 1888 to 1891. She gave him all her reminiscences without taking anything for them. She was completely without mercenary motives.

But the one thing about this lady that impressed O'Donnell more than anything else was her ability to talk to him about events that must have been alarming, in a quiet, matter-of-fact manner; and without any attempt to colour her accounts. This, he came to realize, resulted from her basic view of life; she was almost fatalistic in her beliefs. From his angle this was all to the good. The story he wanted would be sensational enough without any added colourings or exaggerations prompted by remembered fears or hates.

O'Donnell himself was never to publish her story. He spent some years trying to trace the main character in her pages, but was thwarted. The man she wrote and talked about did not exist in public records. There were articles of his, even a book; but no birth certificate, no marriage-lines, and no trace of his death.

There was a good reason for this. The name he was known by was assumed; and his true identity was not established during O'Donnell's lifetime. But, the Cremers memoirs in the end proved to be one of the most significant documents in the whole history of the hunt for Jack the Ripper.

For the first time, we have believable and verifiable testimony from someone who was close to the killer day after day for over eighteen months. When she wrote, she recorded facts that she could not have drawn from the literature of the day. Some of these facts were only checkable as late as the 1960s. All the documentation and testimony we can now draw on confirms her story as reliable, accurate and invaluable; and she was not alone in naming her colleague as the Ripper. Others who knew him well, thought the same.

Her story began in New York in 1886, when in a bookshop, she came across a copy of *Light on the Path* by Mabel Collins. It was one of the treasured books of the Theosophical movement and its opening words read: 'These rules are written for all disciples, attend you to them.' For some reason the words struck deep into Cremers and she felt impelled to buy the book, 'It was as though some unseen force was driving me to take it home with me to read,' she explained.

This one, slim book was to change her life. First, it made such a profound impression on her that she eagerly joined the American Theosophical Society. Then, in 1888 on arriving in Britain she went to the HQ of the British Society to enrol and there met Madame Helena Petrova Blavatsky, the greatest name in Theosophy. Blavatsky, on learning that Cremers had been involved in publishing, asked her to take over the business side of the society's monthly magazine *Lucifer,* and Cremers agreed.

Work at the Theosophists' headquarters in Holland Park (17 Lansdowne Road) was unexacting and Cremers often dreamed of meeting up with the woman who had inspired her. She now knew that Mabel Collins was a notable novelist and a one-time spiritualist medium. She also learned that Mabel lived near at hand, so a meeting was just a matter of time.

But the full story of that meeting and its fateful consequences must be left to Vittoria Cremers herself. What follows are her own words. The only changes made involve the supplying of full names where she used initials. This was an irritating Theosophical habit that we can well do without.

CHAPTER TWELVE

The Fateful Paths Converge

The events of 1888 were crystal clear in Vittoria Cremers' mind when she unfolded her story in the 1930s. In her detached, unemotional fashion she recalled her first meeting with the alluring Mabel Collins, and her first brief contact with the turmoil surrounding the Ripper murders.

It was inevitable that I should meet Mabel Collins at some time or other, because she was associate editress of *Lucifer* and our paths were bound to cross. I had settled down to my job at No. 17 and like the rest of those engaged in Theosophical work, lived there with Madame Blavatsky. Among others prominent in the Theosophical movement here, were Dr Archibald Keightley and his cousin Bertram.

But it was Mabel Collins in whom I was chiefly interested, and when one day, she strolled into the *Lucifer* office in company with the Keightleys and began to chat with me in a most friendly way I felt strongly drawn towards her. She was living at 34 Clarendon Road, the garden of which backed onto that of 17 Lansdowne Road. So that Helena Blavatsky and Mabel Collins were in the habit of signalling to each other across the gardens whenever they wanted to see one another. In addition to her theosophical work and the novels she wrote, Mabel Collins was also the fashion writer on Edmund Yates' periodical, *The World*; and I can recall her dashing about London in hansom cabs in pursuit of news on the latest fashions.

I told her that *Light on the Path* had been the direct cause of my joining the Theosophical movement, and as a result I was invited to her home, and from that time onwards we became close friends.

One day in the December of 1888, I went into the big room behind my office. It was the sanctum where the Blavatsky Lodge was held, and the moment I entered I sensed a state of suppressed excitement in the room. There stood the two Keightleys, one on either side of Helena Blavatsky who was seated at a card-table with a newspaper spread out before her. The two men were leaning over her shoulder plying her with questions the gist of which I gathered in snatches such as, 'Jack the Ripper – Yes – Is it true? – Yes – Did Crawford write it? – Yes – Black Magic –.'

I was young in years – about twenty-eight – and densely, pathetically ignorant of things occult. The words I heard meant absolutely nothing to me. I was still but a newcomer to the Theosophical movement, and so far as the Ripper murders were concerned knew little beyond the shrieking headlines. Such things did not interest me and I did not read the reports. As for Black Magic, I had never heard of such a thing any more than I knew that the Earl of Crawford and Balcarres was one of the leading occultists of that day.

I only know that when I went into the big room on that December afternoon, the occupants were in a state of tension. Later on when I chanced to mention it to Mabel Collins she explained that the article over which they were poring was one written by Lord Crawford for the *Pall Mall Gazette,* suggesting that Jack the Ripper was a Black Magician.

The incident of the article in the *Pall Mall Gazette* passed from my mind, and I devoted myself to my theosophical studies, seeking from Mabel Collins such enlightenment as I felt she could give on *Light on the Path.* Somehow I found her either incapable or unwilling to give me any help, but even so I managed to qualify for entry into the *Esoteric Section* (Secret Section) of the Society of which I was now a fully-fledged member.

In 1889 I had occasion to sail for America in connection with certain business, and it was February 1890 before I returned to England breaking my journey to spend a few weeks in Paris. While there I wrote to Mabel Collins inviting her over to stay with me, pointing out that she could combine business with pleasure as there were several big fashion shows in progress. I received no reply to my letter, and decided that I would look her up when I got to England.

Cremers finally landed in England in early March, after suffering a wretched, all-night Channel-crossing. She made straight for her usual lodging-place, run by Mrs Heilmann at 21 Montague Street, off London's Russell Square; there she tumbled straight into bed. Although worn out and tired, she was unable to asleep, her thoughts were in a turmoil over Mabel Collins. Was Mabel angry with her, or was she ill? Cremers was so preoccupied that she actually rose, dressed and went to Mabel's new address in elegant York Terrace, just behind Madame Tussaud's in Marylebone Road.

When she arrived, the maid told her that Mabel Collins was away in Southsea, writing a new novel; the maid gave her the address there, and the very next day Cremers took a train to visit Mabel.

On arriving at the address Cremers was appalled. The contrast between the splendour of York Terrace and this shabby, dingy street was overwhelming. Could it be that Mabel was seeking colour for her new novel? Or did this mean she had something to hide?

At the drab uninviting house, an unkempt, slatternly looking woman answered the door and led her along a narrow, dingy passage to a flight of stairs. The stairs led to a poorly furnished bedroom on the first floor. As Cremers relates:

> It was a comfortless-looking place containing an unmade single bed, a dressing-table with a few cheap china ornaments upon it; and, with the cinders of a previous fire still in the grate, it presented an utterly cheerless appearance.
>
> I began to pace up and down to keep myself warm. I wished I had not come. Then I heard the front door open, the murmur of voices, one unmistakably Mabel Collins', the other a man's. Then came the quiet shutting of the door followed by footsteps hurriedly coming up the stairs. A moment later Mabel Collins burst into the room in a flurry of embarrassment; or so it seemed to me.
>
> 'Well, Vittoria – so you've caught me at last... How are you?'
>
> That was her first greeting. We neither kissed nor shook hands for people in the occult movement dispense with all conventions of that kind. Personality is avoided as much as possible, although one must be natural and one's acts not enforced.
>
> Mabel Collins flung herself onto the unmade bed and settled herself Eastern fashion. It was over a year since I had seen her and there was much on both sides to talk about. But Mabel Collins rattled on about nothing in particular until suddenly she paused and regarded me closely.
>
> 'Do you remember an article in the *Pall Mall Gazette* about Rider Haggard's *She*?' she asked. It was signed "D'O", if you remember?'
>
> I said that I remembered her mentioning the article to me early in 1889, but I had never read it, and could not recall the signature of the writer.

'Do you remember that I told you I had written to the author care of the *Gazette*?' she then asked.

'No, I can't say that I do,' was my reply.

'Well – I did write to him, and after some weeks received a reply. It was only a few lines saying that the writer was ill in hospital, but as soon as he was better he would write and make an appointment. Again some weeks passed by before I heard anything and then a letter arrived from a Dr D'Onston making an appointment – a marvellous man, Vittoria, a great magician who had wonderful magical secrets.'

She paused to light another cigarette, for she was smoking furiously throughout our talk. Then she went on:

'He's here with me now – still very ill. I'm taking care of him – as soon as he is better we are coming back to London, and we will all go into business together. The three of us.'

I made no comment.

She rose from the bed, and smiling, said: 'But it's cold up here; let's go downstairs where it is warm, and we'll have tea. You will be able to meet D'Onston, for he will soon be back having just gone out for a short walk.'

It required no powers of deduction on my part to realize that D'Onston had been *sent* out while Mabel Collins told me of her association with him. Anyway the suggestion of tea was very welcome, and I gladly followed her down the stairs. A fire and tea went right home, but her mention of a 'marvellous man' and a 'great magician' meant nothing to me.

Having thawed out over tea, my tongue became loosened and I rattled on about my Paris trip, the nature of my business there, and my meeting with Sarah Bernhardt. I did full justice to the meal provided, and we were about halfway through tea when there was the sound of a key grating in the lock of the front door.

'Here he is…' exclaimed Mabel Collins.

I rose and pushed my chair nearer the wall to make room for the 'marvellous man' whom I assumed would be glad of a hot cup of tea.

'Oh – you needn't bother, Vittoria,' commented Mabel Collins in a casual voice, 'he never eats.'

This statement struck me as very peculiar, but I was to recall it later on when I knew more about Dr D'Onston. I had no time to make any reply however, for by this time he had entered the room so quietly that I was surprised to find him there. I noticed afterwards that there was an uncanny absence of sound in all his movements, and I can honestly say, that throughout the years of our association he was the *most soundless human creature I ever knew.*

I found myself looking up into the face of a tall fair-haired man of unassuming appearance. A man at whom one would not look twice. He held a cap in one hand while under his arm was tucked – in true military fashion – a short cane. I was not unduly impressed. To me there was nothing of the 'marvellous man' about him, and yet – there was an indefinable *something*.

'So this is Vittoria?' he remarked as he took my hand.

I nodded assent and Mabel broke in.

'I have told her all about you, 'she said, 'so there is no need for an introduction.'

Dr D'Onston moved noiselessly over to an armchair in which he seated himself. I had noticed that his voice was pleasant and cultured…

As for myself I was busily sizing up the man sitting opposite me…it was a habit of mine. The sum total of my estimate of D'Onston was nil – absolutely nil – gentle, silent – one who would remain calm in any crisis – maybe because he was ill. I wondered what was the matter with him…

That was the chaotic burden of my summing-up of him between snatches of conversation. I also indulged in a mental analysis of his physical qualities.

Tall – not an ounce of superfluous flesh upon him – military bearing unmistakable and a suggestion of strength and power. Pale; his face had a queer pallor – not a particle of colour anywhere; underlip, pink – upper lip hidden by a fair moustache. Fair hair, thinning at the sides – teeth slightly discoloured (from pipe-smoking I decided).

But it was his eyes which impressed me most. They were pale blue, and – *there was not a vestige of life or sparkle in them.* They were eyes which one might expect to find set in the face of a patient in the anaemic ward of any hospital.

One other thing impressed me about D'Onston. That was his appearance of super-cleanliness. He looked as though he had just emerged from the bathroom; he was well-groomed about the head, and his clothes, though obviously old and worn, appeared to have suffered from assiduous brushing rather than wear and tear.

Such was my first meeting with Dr Roslyn D'Onston as he called himself…

Cremers' short visit to Southsea convinced her that it was more than the sharing of occult interests that tied Mabel and D'Onston together. She saw that Mabel was deeply infatuated with this enigmatic man, and she was right. The man may have seemed to be a nobody, but perhaps there were hidden depths, and again she was right.

A fortnight later, when Mabel and D'Onston returned to London, Mabel had a problem: where was D'Onston going to stay? She was so prominent as a novelist, Theosophist and socialite, that she had to be discreet, and protect her reputation. Cremers, at once, came to her rescue and persuaded Mrs Heilmann to house D'Onston for a while. It turned out to be a short while indeed, as Cremers explains:

He only stayed for a few weeks because he appeared never to eat anything, and, like a good landlady, Mrs Heilmann became very worried.

As she put it to me: 'Those who don't eat *die,* and I don't want him to die on my hands'...I learned later that during one of his many wanderings over the earth, he had been wounded in the stomach, and that a Chinese slug was still lodged in his intestines, this being the cause of his illness and lack of appetite. Mrs Heilmann asked me to persuade him to find other accommodation, but fortunately the difficulty straightened itself out.

Mabel Collins had followed up the suggestion she mooted to me at Southsea about going into business together, and we all three engaged in discussing the project. D'Onston, said Mabel Collins, was possessed of certain little-known recipes for beauty creams and potions, which she thought could be turned to advantage. Beauty parlours as we know them today, were practically non-existent in the nineties, but feminine vanity was by no means lacking, and I felt that the idea might prove a good business proposition.

Mabel Collins and I put up the money, and D'Onston provided the recipes from which the various unguents and lotions were prepared. We formed a company named the Pompadour Cosmetique Company, and took premises in Baker Street on the site where Baker Street Tube Station now stands. It was then a street of houses and our office must have been just opposite the fictional residence of Sherlock Holmes.

We had an office on the first floor, consisting of one large room, where all the business was conducted and the 'treatments' made up, and a smaller room immediately behind it. The second floor was occupied by a private family while I had a flat on the third floor. The problem of D'Onston's accommodation was solved by letting him live in the small back room on the first floor. This was a suggestion of Mabel Collins' and it certainly was a way out of our difficulty. It was she who furnished it for him in a kind of monastic comfort. There was just a bed and table, a wash-stand (no toilet basins with H & C in those days), a chair and a *huge zinc bath*. I had my own maid; part of her duties was to prepare D'Onston's morning bath, and I can assure you that in the matter of his daily ablutions, he was fastidious to the point of fanaticism.

Cremers' new business interests did not interfere with her work for the magazine *Lucifer*. Since she knew D'Onston was always hard-up, she persuaded Blavatsky to commission an article from him. His piece of November 1890, was called *African Magic* and it contained some chilling revelations. But at the time, Cremers had no idea of its importance. In fact, as she testifies:

> I did not see the article and never bothered to read it till it was brought to my notice years later in 1931. Even if I had read it at the time, I doubt whether I should fully have understood it, and I certainly would not have associated the writer with the Ripper crimes which, by the end of 1890 had almost faded from public memory.

CHAPTER THIRTEEN

The Mask Begins to Slip

Initially then, Cremers summed up D'Onston, as inoffensive. She was so dismissive of the man that she blinded herself to the fact that he could be anything other than innocuous. The notion that he could be cold, hard, brutal and a killer; someone to dread and fear, never once crossed her mind. At first, in her open, trusting way she treated him as a friend, and provided him with a good listener one who didn't probe, moralize or judge. But her view of him began to change dramatically when she lived and worked along-side him at their place in Baker Street. It was then that her easy and compliant attitude led D'Onston to open up to her in an singular way and reveal, bit by bit, his true character. Cremers relates how her doubts about him began to grow:

> The first time I ever really got behind the mind of D'Onston occurred one evening when I returned to Baker Street and was mounting the first flight of stairs to enter the office. As I reached the landing I saw D'Onston standing outside the door of his room. What intrigued me however, was that he appeared to be drawing some sort of sign upon it with his thumb.
>
> There he stood, silent as the grave, an expression of the utmost solemnity on his face. As I passed him, I noticed that he was tracing with his thumb the outline of a *triangle* on the door. It seemed such a child-ish thing for a grown-up man to do, that I felt amused as well as amazed.
>
> I said nothing but simply passed on into the office. A few seconds elapsed and then the door was silently opened and D'Onston entered the room closing the door gently behind him. He fixed his eyes upon me as I busied myself at the desk, and then asked:
>
> 'Did you notice what I was doing, Vittoria?'
>
> 'Yes, D'Onston,' I replied, smiling at his serious expression. 'You were drawing something or other on the door, weren't you?'

'Did you notice what it was?'

'Looked to me like a triangle.'

'It *was* a triangle.'

'But you'd got it upside down.'

D'Onston smiled coldly. 'Yes, Vittoria,' he said. 'It *was* "upside down", as you describe it, and I'll tell you why.'

He seated himself upon one corner of the desk, and then went on:

'Years ago a friend of mine dropped in just before nightfall and suggested a walk. I told him I would run upstairs for my pipe and join him in the hall. I dashed up to my room and went across to the mantelpiece for my pipe.

'Then as I turned to go downstairs I suddenly sensed some horrible *Presence* outside the open door. I stood still, unable to move so petrified was I with terror. I felt that I dared not venture outside that door – that if I did I should drop down dead from sheer fright.

'At last I summoned up sufficient will-power to creep to the door and peer out. There was nothing to be seen, Vittoria. I scurried down the stairs to join my friend as though the whole of Hell was at my heels. Together we went out into the night, I was in a sweat of fear of *something*, I knew not what. Only once in my life since that day Vittoria, have I known the fear of that *Presence*. Later on I learned how to guard against its intrusion by making the sign of the triangle on the door of my room before entering. It is a thing I never fail to do.'

This was quite true, as I discovered during our residence in Baker Street, for on several other occasions I witnessed the same weird performance. More than once I chaffed him about it when I came upon him in the act.

'Keeping the spooks out?' I would remark, but he never replied and never ceased to complete his 'upside down' triangle. I had not the least idea at the time that there was any Magical significance either Black or White, about this sign of the triangle nor that its inversion indicated the Black Art. D'Onston said nothing about it, and beyond appearing a silly thing to do, his action made no impression upon me.

As for his story of the 'horrible *Presence*', it faintly recalled the awe-inspiring description of the *Presence* which figured in Bulwer Lytton's *Zanoni*. I had read this book on the recommendation of Helena Blavatsky soon after I joined her. To those who may not have read this very fine work I would explain that at one period of the story Zanoni endeavours to invoke the friendly spirit *Adon-ai*; instead he found at his side, 'the Evil Omen, the implacable Foe, with exultation and malice burning from its hell-lit eyes. . . As an iceberg, the breath of that Presence froze the air; as a cloud it filled the chamber and blackened the stars from heaven.'

And then comes the terrible threat from this hideous *Thing*.

'Thou art returned to the Threshold,' it tells Zanoni. 'Thou, whose steps have trodden the verges of the Infinite! And, as the goblin of its fancy seizes on a child in the dark, mighty one, who would conquer Death, I seize upon thee.'

Fiction! it may be said. Maybe, but those beliefs were a grim reality to Bulwer Lytton, through several of whose works runs the same strain of mysticism; just as was D'Onston's belief in the *Presence* which had scared him so thoroughly, a reality.

Of course I had no knowledge of D'Onston's association with Bulwer Lytton till forty years later when Bernard O'Donnell brought the *Borderland* article to my notice. At the time of which I am writing, it was only a casual recollection of Lytton's creature Zanoni which flashed through my mind when D'Onston related his story about *The Dweller on the Threshold*.

In drawing attention to Lytton's novel, Cremers was very much on the right track. This work was of enormous significance for many caught up in the thralls of magical thinking. Blavatsky borrowed from it in creating her *Isis Unveiled*. It was also drawn on by the creators of magical societies, like clergyman Charles Leadbeater, coroner Wynn Wescott and antiquarian Kenneth Mackenzie. In short it was taken seriously, as a veiled message to an elite. But its teachings about the *Presence*, were not elitist; they were, and are still, shared by hordes of people within the Christian churches and within other religions.

Whenever an exorcism takes place, the idea is invoked. Listen to the words of Roman Catholic exorcist, Malachi Martin:

From the moment the exorcist enters the room, a peculiar feeling seems to hang in the very air. From that moment in any genuine exorcism and onward through its duration, everyone in the room is aware of some alien *Presence*. This indubitable sign of possession is as unexplainable and unmistakable as it is inescapable. All the signs of possession, however blatant or grotesque, however subtle or debatable, seem both to pale before and to be marshalled in the face of this *Presence*.

There is no sure physical trace of this *Presence*, but everyone feels it. You have to experience it to know it; you cannot locate it spatially –

beside or above or within the possessed, or over in the corner or under the bed or hovering in mid-air.

In one sense, the *Presence* is nowhere, and this magnifies the terror…Invisible and intangible, the *Presence* claws at the humanness of those gathered in the room…

By openly acknowledging his fear of the *Presence*, D'Onston showed the extent of his dependence on magical ideas. But by employing his protective symbol, he revealed his belief that he had power enough to control even the forces of darkness. Such a delusion is enough to make a warped man contemptuous of humane values. Such a man lives for the exercise of power and the total annihilation of anyone bent on thwarting him. In D'Onston's case these drives were well concealed at first; with time he grew bolder, more openly contemptuous and more loose tongued.

CHAPTER FOURTEEN

A Glimpse of Brutality

It was in an off-hand way that D'Onston first revealed his indifference to the sanctity of human life. One afternoon he spoke to Cremers about an incident involving his favourite cousin. This cousin was in love with a girl who had rejected him as a suitor but had accepted him as a friend. One day the cousin came to D'Onston in great anguish. The girl he loved had been made pregnant by another man and this seducer had deserted her and left the country.

D'Onston asked for a handkerchief belonging to the girl and said:

'Tell her that neither of you will see nor hear from me until I can send or bring proof that she has been avenged.'

His hunt for the seducer took all of fifteen months and at last he caught up with him in California.

'I dipped the handkerchief in his blood,' said D'Onston, 'and on my return flung it into her lap without a word.'

After summarising this story Cremers continued:

I remember thinking what a braggart he was and yet his story was not told in any sense of vainglory but simply in matter-of-fact tones; tones such as one would use in recalling an ordinary incident of life. That is how it struck me at the time, and I attached no more importance to it than that.

D'Onston's recitals were always spontaneous, seeming to arise out of nothing particular in the way of conversation. It was not in response to any questioning by me that he told his stories, for from earliest days, I have been possessed of an almost abnormal faculty never to ask questions, never to interrupt a conversation, but allow a speaker to carry on with his or her talk to the bitter end. So it was with D'Onston. I never invited a confidence and never broke into anything he might be telling me. In fact, looking back, I think I must have been the most silent of any of his listeners. It had always been my belief that if I was destined to have certain knowledge, it would come to me without my seeking. Consequently when he related his varied and colourful experiences to me, I did not trouble to question his stories, but appeared to accept them. And in repeating them now, I am doing so, not in consecutive order as they may have been told to me over the months, but as they occur to me after a lapse of forty years.

For example, I do not precisely remember *when* he recounted the following experience during a Californian gold rush, he said:

'My mate and I had been weeks prospecting to set up a claim and eventually settled on one which eventually turned out of little account. Some time later it was rumoured that a Chink had found a nugget larger than any hitherto found in those parts. My mate and I put our heads together for we felt sure the Chink would sell his claim, and we decided that we could handle the matter with greater efficiency than a damned Chinaman. We watched and waited for him to make a move towards town to effect a sale. Sure enough things turned out exactly as we anticipated.

'Late one night he set off and we followed him. For a couple of days we were on his heels – unseen. We knew the trail he must travel, and on the second day we managed to get ahead of him and lay in wait behind a rock. Sure enough about three hours later Mr Chinaman came along, and unfortunately for him, as he passed nearby, my mate's pistol accidentally went off...'

No details you will observe; no mention of any sequel to that *accidental* death of the Chink; no information as to what happened to the claim; nothing but a plain unvarnished story of villainy, which, whether true or not throws an illuminating light on the working of D'Onston's mind and his attitude towards the taking of human life. Related as casually as when he referred to his slave-trading activities in the *Pall Mall Gazette* with a brief – 'That by the way.'

I got another glimpse of this callousness when he was relating an experience he had with the Garibaldean army in 1860. First of all he described the ghastly conditions under which he worked.

'I had got my MD,' he said, 'but was not yet in practice when I learned from a friend of the terrible plight the medical services of Garibaldi were in for want of doctors. I at once crossed to Italy and offered my services. The conditions were terrible, Vittoria. There were scarcely any medical supplies, no anaesthetics, very few bandages, while surgical equipment was almost non-existent. I had to perform many an amputation without anaesthetic, and the poor devils I operated on must have suffered agonies. There was nothing else for it, and it was no good being squeamish. More often than not they fainted and knew nothing about it till it was all over. Scores of those I dealt with never came through at all, but I gained a wonderful experience which it would have taken me twenty years to acquire if I had stayed at home.'

I remembered thinking at the time, 'Flint-hearted devil'. His callous reference to the sufferings of those upon whom he operated without anaesthetic; his casual mention that 'scores never came through but I gained a wonderful experience' irked me. That was all it meant to him and I was angry.

In the same callous, indifferent fashion he went on to mention yet another brutal act of his:

'I had gone to bed after days in action without rest or sleep, when I was suddenly awakened by a subaltern who said that a wounded prisoner had just been brought in. The youngster wanted to know what he should do with him. I was only half awake and thoroughly irritable. "Take him outside and shoot him, but leave me in peace!" I told the subaltern, and turned over and went to sleep. My order was carried out to the letter Vittoria, and I may say there was a devil of a row about it; but – what did it matter? The man was an enemy, and that's what enemies are for – to kill.'

After considering these tales Mrs Cremers concluded: 'So much for the outlook of D'Onston, so far as human life was concerned – a matter of small consequence.'

CHAPTER FIFTEEN

The Ghost from the Past

In all these reminiscences D'Onston seemed to be unmoved by tender-ness, compassion or human warmth, but gradually he began to reveal that he had once been emotionally vulnerable and wounded. An incident from his youth had crippled his capacity to love, as Vittoria Cremers reveals.

All this time I would mention, the association between Mabel Collins and D'Onston, was of the closest nature. I had no doubt in my mind that she was greatly infatuated with him, for in those early days, she could talk of little else, and D'Onston was a regular visitor to her flat behind Madame Tussaud's about two minutes walk from our office.

For myself, I neither liked nor disliked him. He was Mabel Collins' friend and simply part of the day's work so far as the business was concerned. I could not, however, help but notice D'Onston's reactions to the obvious affection shown him by Mabel Collins. She had taken him away to Southsea to recuperate after his illness; she had provided him with his creature needs and comforts; had furnished for him the room in Baker Street; had supplied him with money, and was ready to do anything for his happiness.

As regards D'Onston, I never saw the least sign of any emotional response to this kindness throughout the whole of their association. He was always courteous and polite; but never once did I notice his eyes light up, or his actions reveal any degree of pleasure when he and Mabel greeted one another.

It was to Mabel Collins that D'Onston confided the story of his shattered romance with a woman named Ada. In due course she unbur-dened herself of the story to me. And – there was something pathetic about Mabel as she did so. It became clear to me that she had been compelled to realize that whatever the bond existing between her and

D'Onston, it only occupied a secondary place in his mind. More than once she made this apparent when discussing her lover.

'D'Onston loved Ada,' she would say. 'Loved her in a way that sometimes frightens me, Vittoria.'

'I didn't think he ever loved anybody but himself,' I told her bluntly; but over and over again when we were talking, she would sadly remark, 'He loved Ada and will never get over her loss. No other woman will ever take her place.'

Now Mabel Collins was an extremely level-headed woman. She had already written a number of books and novels and was extremely popular with those who knew her. And, although I lived in the same house with D'Onston, and was in regular daily contact with him, there can be no doubt that Mabel Collins knew him better than any other living person.

She, more than anyone else, was able to get behind the mind of the quiet, reticent, soundless man who was Roslyn D'Onston. She was a psychologist who had gained a vast knowledge of the human mind, as any reader of *Light on the Path* will agree.

Consequently, I was more than usually interested when she began to unfold what she referred to as 'the love story' of D'Onston; and when she constantly reiterated, 'He loved Ada,' I quite understood that she did not mean he was sexually attracted to her. Love, not sexual attraction invariably means sacrifice, and Love is sacrifice. And that is what Mabel Collins wanted to convey – D'Onston's readiness to make a sacrifice for Ada.

According to D'Onston, he had at one time held a commission in the Army. Of yeoman family, his father was fairly well off. When the daughter of a wealthy neighbouring family fell in love with D'Onston, the match was looked upon with great favour.

But things were 'not to run well for D'Onston', as Mabel Collins put it. On one of his jaunts to town with some brother officers, he fell in with a woman of the streets to whom he became strongly attracted. On each subsequent visit he made a point of meeting this woman until he found himself wildly in love with her. This was the woman Ada.

I realize now – at this late hour – how my faculty for not asking questions, has resulted in obscurity on many points which, had I been more inquisitive, might have been cleared up. For example, we do not know Ada's surname, or anything else about her. And certainly it never occurred to me that Ada's surname would ever be of any importance, especially at this length of time when it would have been interesting to check up on her existence.

Mabel went on to tell me that D'Onston became so infatuated with Ada that he determined to marry her and take her away from her miserable life. He told his family of his intention and they were aghast. His brother officers were equally shocked, and tried to talk him out of his decision. They reasoned, expostulated, and pointed out the inevitable consequence which would follow any such alliance, but D'Onston was adamant.

Neither the efforts of his officer friends, nor the broken-hearted appeals of his parents had the least effect. He loved Ada and intended to save her from herself.

As for Ada, there appears to have existed – in spite of her mode of life – a certain decency of character. As Mabel told me, 'Ada loved D'Onston, just as he loved her. I am convinced of it, Vittoria.'

D'Onston set Ada up in rooms where he used to visit her. To bring him to heel, as it were, his father cut off his allowance with the result that the son's need for money became desperate. Always a gambler, D'Onston was found at the tables more often, plunging more wildly than ever. His misalliance with Ada had been kept a close secret in the family, as it was still hoped that D'Onston would get over his infatuation and break with his mistress.

Then, one night he lost a large sum of money. He realized that he could not pay his gambling debts. In desperation he sought out his father and explained his position. What took place at that interview Mabel Collins never learned. There was some sort of scene, and in the end, D'Onston told Mabel, he agreed to give up Ada and marry the heiress.

That same night he journeyed to London. He visited Ada and told her all that had happened; told her that he had come to see her for the last time, but – she would be provided for through his father's solicitor.

There were no tears, no recriminations, no protests. 'Ada loved me,' D'Onston told Mabel Collins. But, before they said goodbye they entered into a solemn pledge, that dead or alive they would meet at midnight on the anniversary of their parting, and their meeting place should be the middle of Westminster Bridge where they had first met.

So they parted, and within an hour of her lover's departure Ada threw a shawl over her head and walked to the spot where they had met but a few months before; determined that she would not stand in the way of her lover's career, Ada flung herself into the river below.

According to what D'Onston told Mabel Collins the story of his association with Ada came out at the inquest; but already he was beyond all care; for, as a result of the anguish which gripped him when he heard of her tragic death, he went down with brain fever, and subsequently had to go abroad to recuperate.

About a fortnight prior to the anniversary of Ada's death, D'Onston returned to England, still so broken in health that he could scarcely walk and had to be wheeled about in a bath-chair. He had resigned his commission in the Army; his prospective marriage to the heiress had also come to an end. This did not matter to D'Onston, whose one thought now was to keep the appointment which he had made with Ada on the night she took her life; that 'living or dead' they would meet on Westminster Bridge on the anniversary of their parting.

On that night, D'Onston ordered his man to wheel him to the bridge and on reaching the Westminster end, he bade him stop. D'Onston got out, and telling the man to remain where he was, he tottered along to the middle of the bridge. He leaned over the parapet from which Ada had hurled herself to death twelve months before; Big Ben chimed the midnight hour, and then (D'Onston told Mabel) he heard the click-clack of heels coming towards him. The sound came nearer and nearer and paused beside him. He strained his eyes but could see nothing. Minutes passed by. There was no further sound of any kind, and so, with lagging feet he returned to the end of the bridge where his man awaited him.

'Did you see anyone pass this way?' D'Onston asked.

'No, sir,' replied the servant. 'I saw nothing, but I distinctly heard the sound of footsteps, but although I looked saw nobody.'

D'Onston entered his chair and was wheeled home.

When Mabel Collins told me this story, I remarked, 'Fiction! He was imagining things.' At that time you must remember, I had no knowledge of the contents of the *Pall Mall Gazette* or *Lucifer* articles, and those in *Borderland* (which I also knew nothing about till years later) had not been written.

It was not until some time later that the story of Ada assumed any degree of significance in my mind, and then only after my suspicions had been aroused that D'Onston was in fact Jack the Ripper. That however, comes later in my story.

It is ironic that Cremers never knew that the tale of the lost love though true in substance, was drastically altered in parts. But even if she had realized this she would still have failed to discover just how this tale embodied one of the trigger-factors that led to the Whitechapel murders. Neither would she have known that the full story could lead to the truth about D'Onston's past and to the identity of his 'vanished' wife. And yet this full story had actually appeared in print not once, but three times over!

CHAPTER SIXTEEN

Sordid Symbols

Without the real keys to D'Onston's history, Cremers had to rely on the guarded references D'Onston made from time to time. As she recollects:

Apart from the self-revelations contained in the stories he told me, D'Onston displayed a strange reticence regarding himself. Except when describing his magical experiences or his adventures abroad, he seldom talked of his own being. Regarding his private life, his origin, or his family, never a word.

On several occasions Mabel Collins endeavoured to break through this reserve but without success.

'Who the devil are you?' she once asked him pointblank.

But D'Onston simply smiled his usual lifeless smile, 'Does it matter?' he replied and uttered not another word.

I remember too my curiosity when he brought to me the article for *Lucifer*. I just glanced at the title and then noticed that it was 'by Tautriadelta'.

'Why D'Onston...' I commented, 'what a funny way of signing yourself. Why don't you sign your name?'

He only smiled the slow inscrutable smile in which there was never a trace of mirth.

'That is my own name,' he answered.

'Tautriadelta?' I repeated. 'But what does it all mean? It seems so strange to me.'

'Yes Vittoria,' said D'Onston. 'A strange signature indeed, but one that means a devil of a lot if you only knew. A devil of a lot!' he repeated with sardonic emphasis.

'But what does it stand for?' I enquired, breaking through my usual rule never to ask questions.

'Before the Captivity,' D'Onston explained, 'the Hebrew Tau was always shown in the form of a Cross. It was the last letter of the sacred alphabet. Tria is the Greek for three, while Delta is the Greek letter D which is written in the form of a triangle. So the completed word signifies Cross-Three-Triangles...'

He paused for a moment or two as though reflecting.

'And Vittoria,' he went on, 'there are lots of people who would be interested to know why I use that signature. In fact, the knowledge would create quite a sensation.' And then, as though in defiance, 'But they never will find out, Vittoria, never.'

I did not press the matter because quite frankly it sounded like so much gibberish, and was far above my head. Mabel Collins had told me that he was a most learned man who had a vast knowledge of the Kabbalah, and I accepted her estimate. But – I still could not understand why he had adopted such a strange and involved nom de plume, or why he did not prefer the use of his own name.

That Tautriadelta embodied a taunting reference to murder and mutilation quite eluded Baroness Cremers. But then, it was meant to tantalize. Its hidden meanings were part of the dangerous game of unveiling cherished secrets; but only to those able to understand the rules of the game; only those could pierce the thick veils of deception.

This was in line with the age-old traditions of the occultists, who would sometimes bury three or more meanings in their writings and grow conceited about their abilities to create enigmas and puzzles, and to fool the rest of the world. Dr Edward Getsinger has given us valuable insight into this mentality:

Those among the ancients who were in possession of the ancient mysteries of life and certain secret astronomical cycles never trusted this knowledge to ordinary writing, but devised secret codes by which they conceal their wisdom from the unworthy... As ages progressed other systems were invented until human ingenuity was taxed to the utmost in an endeavour to conceal and yet perpetuate sacred knowledge...

In all my twenty years of experience as a reader of archaic writings I have never encountered such ingenious codes and methods of concealment as are found in the manuscript called *Le Très Sainte Trinosophie*. In only a few instances are complete phrases written in the same alphabet; usually two or three forms of writing are employed, with letters written upside down, reversed, or with the text written backwards...

Is it any wonder that Cremers never attempted to decipher D'Onston's strange name? Much more puzzling at the time was Cremers' discovery of some unwholesome, foul pieces of candle found burning on D'Onston's mantelpiece.

'Good God, D'Onston,' I exclaimed. 'Where on earth did you get those filthy-looking candles?'

'I made them,' he answered quietly.

'Made them?' I queried in surprise, and then after taking another look at them, 'I should think you did, I have never seen such grubby-looking things in all my life. But what are they made of?'

D'Onston made no answer to the last question, but simply remarked. 'It is an experiment.'

'What – going into the candle business now?' I retorted jokingly, but he only answered with a surly 'No'.

But two years earlier, in an article on the Whitechapel murders D'Onston had scorned all evasion and revealed that candles 'made from human fat' were essential for the practice of Black Magic. Equally essential, he had revealed, was 'a preparation made from a certain portion of the body of a harlot'.

CHAPTER SEVENTEEN

A Scarlet Woman?

Harlots, murders and grotesque rituals were far from Vittoria Cremers' mind at this time. She was much more concerned with Mabel Collins' sexual reputation which became besmirched in a bitter war of words raging in the Theosophical Society. Blavatsky was now being challenged for leadership of the movement by Colonel Olcott and A. P. Sinett and, although Cremers stood aloof from all this, she was drawn in when Mabel Collins sided with Sinett.

The struggle was fought with cruel, harsh words; malicious charges were thrown recklessly around; and Mabel's character was blackened. It was now alleged that her novel *The Blossom and the Fruit* had once contained an ending endorsing Black Magic of the darkest dye. Blavatsky, herself, had intervened before its publication and had rewritten the final chapters to make it pure in doctrine. Other 'revelations' charged that Mabel was addicted to gross, unmentionable sexual perversions! Cremers only came to know of these smears after Blavatsky decided to purge her staff of all who were disloyal to her. Cremers relates:

> One day Helena Blavatsky sent for me. 'My dear,' she began, 'I must ask you to give up your association with Mabel Collins.'
>
> I told her that I would do nothing of the kind, whereupon she went on to explain that she had been compelled to ask Mabel Collins to leave the Society because of her conduct with the Keightleys. She told me that Mabel Collins was at one time engaged to Dr Archibald Keightley, and that they had taken part in Tantric Worship performing certain sexual Black Magic Rites, as a result of which they had got into serious trouble. 'I had the greatest difficulty in extricating them from the mess into which they had got themselves,' Helena Blavatsky told me.

I promptly told her that I would on no account give up my friendship with Mabel Collins until I myself found her an unfit associate.

Helena Blavatsky shrugged her shoulders. 'Then I am afraid I must ask you also to leave the Society.'

'I shall certainly do so,' I answered, though not without regret, for I was a staunch believer in the faith; but I was furious. At once I sought out Mabel Collins, who, the moment she saw me laughed aloud.

'The old lady's been after you,' she said; and then, 'I knew you'd get it.'

In anger I told her of the accusations Helena Blavatsky had made in giving reasons why I should break with her (Mabel Collins).

It was then the latter's turn to fly into a rage. She began to threaten an action for defamation of character; but things did not go as far as that, although scandal ensued with the result that many of the best people dropped out of the movement.

Only those behind the scenes knew the extent of the bitterness behind the breach. Mabel Collins was not less outspoken about the 'old lady', of whom she wrote:

'She had a greater power over the weak and credulous, a greater capacity for making black appear white, a more ceaseless and insatiable hatred of those whom she thought to be her enemies, a greater disrespect for les *convenances*, a worse temper, a greater command of bad language, and a greater contempt for the intelligence of her fellow-beings than I had ever supposed possible to be contained in one person.'

And from my knowledge of her, this was no exaggeration.

This acrimonious power-struggle brought to light several aspects of Mabel's character that would otherwise have remained undetected. Like D'Onston himself, she had a dual personality. On the surface she was an elegant, beautifully gowned lady of fashion. Intelligent, charming and captivating, she seemed to be above all crudities and lusts. In reality she was quite capable of indulging her uninhibited, unrestrained sexual passions in whatever manner amused and excited her. Today such things are easily understood, even if frowned on a little, but in her time these drives had to be kept as private as state secrets. Even her affair with D'Onston had to be masked as a business relationship.

When we understand this, we can see that Blavatsky's exposure of Mabel's sexual penchants was devastating, especially since charges of 'Tantrism' were involved. The Tantric teachings were originally crafted in India and the followers of these teachings were wedded to secrecy, but with time their secrets became known. They believed that it was possible with mantras and rites to appease, fascinate, bind, drive away, create enmity and even kill. Their doctrines justified the use of all aspects of life. This even involved the deliberate cultivating of repulsive or frightening acts in order to prove that the adept was above fear and disgust. Put into practice this meant that the adept was encouraged to break taboos and allow the sexual drives free range. Group sex, sodomy, incest, bestiality and even necrophilia was acceptable in Tantrism. And now Mabel Collins was identified as accepting such doctrines.

The Blavatsky camp was not short of 'evidence' to throw at Mabel. It was noted that her story *The Idyll of the White Lotus* was based on a period when the Egyptian faith and priesthood '…had already begun to lose its purity and degenerate into a system of Tantric worship contaminated and defiled by black magic, unscrupulously used for selfish and immoral purposes.' Then Blavatsky herself stated that even Mabel's cherished *Light on the Path* contained dangerous teachings, 'whose Occult venom and close relationship to Tantrika Black magic has never been suspected by the innocent and sincere admirers of this otherwise priceless little book…' Then, for the first time, Theosophists were told about Blavatsky's actions in taking over the authorship of the crucial chapters of *The Blossom and the Fruit*.

For Mabel Collins it was humiliating beyond belief to know that from then on the Society was free to picture her in her unbridled, private ecstasies. Her enemies were now able to talk of her indulgence in orgies and imagine her coupling with the traditional rutting goat of the Satanists. In desperation she started an action for libel against Blavatsky. This was lodged in July 1889 but did not reach court until July 1890. It was a very short-lived action; in the opening moments Blavatsky's attorney showed the counsel for Mabel Collins a letter written by Mabel. The action was halted immediately, but the contents of this letter were never disclosed. Had Mabel been indiscreet enough to actually record details of her sexual taboo-breaking? It seems very possible, and her vulnerability in this area makes it easy to understand why D'Onston could exercise such a control and hold over her.

CHAPTER EIGHTEEN

Tongue-Tied by Fear

Both Cremers and Mabel Collins were still angry and seething over Blavatsky's brutality and spitefulness when suddenly, the whole affair was completely overshadowed. Overnight their thoughts became focused on something far graver and much more menacing. This was a supreme turning-point in their lives, as Cremers tells us:

It was a month or so after this scene that an incident happened, fraught with tremendous consequence to all three of us in partnership in the Pompadour Cosmetique Company. It was Mabel Collins who first aroused suspicion in my mind that D'Onston was Jack the Ripper.

One morning she entered the office in Baker Street, and after a nervous glance round the place whispered, 'Where is he?'

'Out,' I replied. 'Why – do you want him?'

She shuddered. In her eyes was the shadow of a haunting fear.

'Vittoria,' she said, 'I believe D'Onston is Jack the Ripper.'

I looked at her in astonishment. 'You must be joking,' I said, but I could see that she was quite serious.

'What on earth makes you say that?' I asked.

'Something he said to me, Vittoria. Something he showed me. I cannot tell even you – but I know it Vittoria – and I am afraid.'

There was no doubt at all about that. Fear reflected in every expression of her eyes and in every shrinking gesture. It was, too, the first occasion on which I had heard the name of Jack the Ripper mentioned since that day in December 1888, when I entered the room at 17 Lansdowne Road, and saw Helena Blavatsky and the Keightleys, crouched over Lord Crawford's article in the *Pall Mall Gazette*. Since then the Ripper had passed almost entirely from my mind, until Mabel Collins blurted out her fears and suspicions to me.

You may wonder, as I have often wondered since, what it was that

D'Onston said to Mabel Collins, or what it was he showed her, which made her so certain that he was Jack the Ripper.

We shall never know now, for she is long since dead. And she never confided in me, as she usually did about anything of great moment. She told me for example of D'Onston's shattered romance with Ada. And this, I should say, was the most intimate revelation he ever made to anyone regarding his private life. Mabel Collins did not hesitate to tell me this story of her lover, readily acknowledging that this inability to forget Ada was the cause of many quarrels between them.

Yet, for some strange reason only known to herself, Mabel Collins never dropped the slightest hint of what D'Onston had said or done to cause her to approach me with that expression of awful dread in her eyes, and say, 'Vittoria, I believe D'Onston is Jack the Ripper.'

Consequently, the whole thing passed from my mind. At the time, I remember thinking that there might have been some misunderstanding between them, and that things would sort themselves out as they so often do under these circumstances. I thought no more about it.

But – there came a day when my own suspicions were awakened by an incident which occurred when I was alone with D'Onston in our office at Baker Street.

We were chatting together about nothing in particular when in a chance remark, he mentioned his wife. This was the first time I had ever heard of the existence of such a person. I had always regarded him as a hard-and-fast bachelor impervious to any emotional or romantic feeling. I pricked up my ears, but as he made no further reference to the lady, I felt impelled – despite my usual practice not to ask questions – to say casually, 'What happened to your wife, D'Onston?'

Whether he sensed that it was no idle question in spite of the manner in which it had been asked, I know not. But I shall never forget the sudden change which came over him. He had been lounging in a chair, and we were talking quietly. But now – he rose to his feet and commenced pacing the room diagonally, from one corner to the other. Backwards and forwards he paced, an expression of restless uneasiness in his eyes. Then as he passed the desk at which I sat, he suddenly paused in his stride, faced me, and raising his head made a dramatic gesture across his throat with one finger. It was just as though he were drawing a knife across it. At the same time he gave an unearthly gutteral groan. Then he resumed his restless pacing, and as I covertly watched and saw him gain control over himself, there came to mind the spoken fear of Mabel Collins when she unburdened herself of her terrible suspicions.

'My God,' I thought, 'he is Jack the Ripper!'

The sinister throat-cutting gesture he made with his finger seemed to confirm what Mabel Collins had confided to me, and at once my brain began a process of speculation. When had D'Onston married, and where? Who was his wife? Had he in fact murdered her? If so, how had he managed to escape suspicion? These thoughts flooded my mind even as D'Onston continued to pace the office.

One could not murder with impunity without arousing some suspicion, I conjectured mentally; and yet – Jack the Ripper had. In fact, had he not murdered woman after woman and got away with it? There flashed through my mind the stories D'Onston had related revealing scant respect for human life. All this passed through my mind in a matter of seconds, but I knew better than to press for any further information regarding the fate of his wife. Instead, in a perfectly casual tone, I asked:

'Any children?'

'No, Vittoria,' with that mirthless smile. 'No encumbrances.'

'Father dead?'

'Yes – curse him!' This with a sudden startling vehemence.

In consequence of this second outburst, I decided to ask no more questions for the time being regarding D'Onston's family life; but in that moment there was born in me a determination to find out all I could about him. I became intent on piercing the aura of mystery with which he had enshrouded himself.

At the very first opportunity I told Mabel Collins of the incident in the office, and she nodded her head.

'Yes, Vittoria,' she said, 'I know he has been married, but he will never talk about his wife. I did not know that he had killed her. He simply said that she had disappeared suddenly – vanished completely, and he had not heard of her for years.'

It struck me at the time, how readily and without surprise Mabel Collins accepted the idea that her lover had murdered his wife. She then went on to express her dread of the man.

'Vittoria, I am terrified of him,' she declared. 'I know he is Jack the Ripper and I want to get away from him, but I am afraid. He has such powers – I wish he would leave me alone – go away – do anything – only leave me alone. I would give him money – anything – if only I could be free of him...'

I had never seen Mabel Collins in such a state of mind as this. Usually calm and equable of disposition, she was now in the throes of something approaching terror. I had of late noticed that the infatuation that once possessed her regarding D'Onston, had cooled; and this cooling of affection coincided with the day she came to me and declared, 'Vittoria, I believe D'Onston is Jack the Ripper.'

And now – here was I, a prey to those very same suspicions; equally convinced with Mabel Collins that D'Onston was indeed the mass murderer of the East End. *I no longer felt governed by the thought that if I was destined to acquire knowledge it would come to me without seeking.* I was determined to probe the secret of D'Onston's origin and satisfy myself of his identity with Jack the Ripper.

I only know that some inner force urged me on. Something compelled me in this matter. I know not what. I was in no hurry, and was prepared to bide my time. And then as if to impress upon me the urgency of my quest, another incident occurred.

Mabel Collins came to my flat late one evening. It was clear that she was in great distress. Her eyes were swollen with weeping, and she looked positively ill. I brewed some tea, and when she had recovered to some extent, she said:

'I'm leaving D'Onston, Vittoria, I cannot stand it any longer, he terrifies me – I must get away from him, or I shall go mad – I am afraid of him Vittoria, I cannot tell you anything – but I want you to help me.'

She paused to get her breath while I poured her out another cup of tea. She drank it eagerly, and then went on:

'I have made arrangements to go to Scarborough and stay for a few months. Nobody but you will know where I am Vittoria, and – I want you to promise that on no account will you let D'Onston know where I am. Promise me Vittoria.'

'Of course I promise you,' I replied, at the same time remarking that I thought she was making too much of a small thing.

'But you don't know, Vittoria,' she insisted, her eyes pleading for some understanding of her plight. 'You don't know him as I do.'

'I'm very glad I don't if this is the state he can reduce one to,' I retorted, adding: 'Well – you get away to the East Coast as soon as you can and forget everything. Otherwise I can see you heading for a nervous breakdown. Let me know when you are settled, and write me poste restante. Then you can be sure your letters will not be intercepted.'

Just as she was leaving me later that evening, I noticed that she walked hurriedly past the room occupied by D'Onston. And then as she bade me goodbye at the door, she whispered to me: 'He is Jack the Ripper, Vittoria.'

I did not know how she knew. I had an idea that one day, later on perhaps, when she got over her fear, she might tell me of her own accord; but that day was never to come, as it happened, for reasons which I shall explain later.

Since Mabel never fully confided in Cremers, what possible fears could have kept her from unburdening herself? The answer lies in her complete acceptance of magical illusions. She really believed in D'Onston's imaginary powers. She really feared the working out of curses. If she was ritually sworn to secrecy, then she would feel herself tongue-tied and helpless to denounce him. He would be mockingly amused to allow her to label him as the Ripper. There was no danger in that, no one would take her mere assertion seriously. Yet the evidence that had devastated her had to be protected. This was only given to her after she had been terrified into accepting it. Her tongue was then stilled by threats of Satanic retribution. Her superstitious frame of mind made her an easy, pliable victim. A frame of mind that made her impotent, and her own worst enemy.

CHAPTER NINETEEN

The Doubts Vanish

Vittoria Cremers' devotion to Mabel Collins was based on much more than homage to intellect. In truth she was in love with the romantic novelist; and this lesbian passion now led to a sudden breach between them. It was a breach cruelly and coldly engineered by D'Onston in a spirit of vengeance, as Cremers reveals:

> Mabel Collins went to Scarborough as intended, and from time to time I received letters from her. Meanwhile D'Onston had taken her departure with a singular lack of interest.
>
> 'So Mabel's gone?' was all he said, and never mentioned her name again for several days. And then one afternoon, he drifted into the office.
>
> At this time the Pompadour Cosmetique Company was not in a very flourishing condition, and as neither D'Onston nor Mabel Collins appeared to be very interested in it, I decided to wind things up and get out of town for a while. I was in the process of sorting out some papers when D'Onston entered the office in his usual soundless way. He perched himself on the table, and I told him what I proposed doing.
>
> 'I quite understand Vittoria,' he said; and then in quiet, unimpassioned tones he began to tell me certain things about Mabel Collins. What they were does not matter. They were of a purely personal nature, and had nothing whatever to do with the Ripper story. They related to details known only to Mabel Collins and myself so that I felt very angry when I realized that D'Onston could only have derived the particulars mentioned from Mabel Collins herself.
>
> That same night I wrote off to Scarborough, repeating what D'Onston had told me. I asked Mabel Collins for any reasonable explanation of her conduct, and informed her that if none was forthcoming then our friendship must cease.

I was hopeful that she would be able to justify her breach of confidence in some way, and awaited her reply with some little anxiety. A day or so later, her reply came. In it she simply said that she 'quite understood'. There was not a word of apology or explanation, no denial, no excuse; nothing but the acknowledgment that she 'quite understood'.

It was a sad moment for me, and I felt a blaze of anger against D'Onston. I called him into the office and told him that he was a swine to have betrayed a woman who had been so kind to him. But he simply smiled that smile which was always so irritatingly expressionless.

It was this attitude on his part which filled me with such disgust, that, in my determination to discover who and what he was, I resorted to a course which, otherwise I should never have entertained. I fully realized that in other circumstances it would have been a low-down thing to do; but, his treatment of Mabel Collins and our suspicions that he was Jack the Ripper, seemed at the time, to justify me in what I did.

I had previously noticed that whenever he went out, he always locked the door of his room. This excited no wonder in my mind, because other people were living in the house. I had also noticed, on the few occasions I entered the room – always when he was present – a black enamelled deed-box as one sees in a solicitor's office. More than once in fact I knocked my shin against it, on one occasion remarking to D'Onston, 'What on earth have you got in that box?'

'A few first editions, Vittoria' he replied, adding, 'Books are very heavy, you know. I also keep some of my private papers in it.'

It was the recollection of this latter remark, which determined me to find out what really was in that box. 'Private papers,' he said, and I wondered whether those papers might yield any clue to his identity, or provide any other information of interest. Both Mabel and I were certain that D'Onston was not his real name, and Mabel Collins once told me that he 'claimed relationship with the Roslyns'. But who the 'Roslyns' were she knew not.

'I have tried all manner of ways to find out who he is,' she once told me when we were discussing the mystery. 'I have tried to trap him into betraying himself. But he is too damned clever, Vittoria – too cunning.'

From time to time, when he went out, I entered his room by means of a key which I had found on an old bunch I always kept. I tried all the smaller keys on this same bunch on the two locks with which the box was secured. They did not fit. I went to another neighbourhood and scoured second-hand shops for old keys, and at length discovered one that fitted.

Armed with this, I seized the opportunity when D'Onston was out, and entered his room. In a few minutes I was on my knees beside the open box, carefully lifting from it the books he had mentioned. I noticed that they were all to do with Magic, one or two of them being written in French. Had I known what I know now I would have looked to see whether the recently published book by Eliphas Levi was among them, but I did not take note of any of the authors. Nor was I particularly interested in the books. It was his 'private papers' that intrigued me, to see what light they might throw upon D'Onston or his family.

But there was not a single paper or document to be seen. Nothing but the books I have mentioned and which I removed with great care so that I could replace them exactly as I found them. Nothing that is, but a few ready-made black ties of the old-fashioned sort that were very popular in that day. These had the knot already tied, with a kind of slot at the back through which one pushed the loose end after placing it round one's collar.

They were the kind that D'Onston always wore.

Frankly I was very disappointed with the results of my burglarious venture. I had hoped for something more informative than those sombre articles of men's wear. Chancing to lift one out of the box, I could not help observe that it was a grubby-looking specimen altogether. I was just about to replace it, when – something caught my eye.

On the underneath side of the flowing end of the tie, and also at the back of the knot, I saw a dull sort of stain. I examined it more closely, and discovered that where the stain was, the tie was quite hard as though something had congealed upon it. I picked up another one, and – on the underneath side of this one I found a similar stain. I examined the others (I do not remember how many), and in each case found a like stain. There were no marks on the outer side of the ties beyond what might have been a smear of something.

I felt completely baffled by my discovery. I could not imagine what the stains could be; nor how they came to be in such a peculiar position; above all – why did D'Onston keep the filthy, dirty things which he could not wear again anyway?

D'Onston, himself, was to supply the answer to these questions at a near future date, but, meantime – I was still as far off as ever from finding out anything about him from the mysterious black-enamelled tin box which I had ransacked.

CHAPTER TWENTY

Confirmed by Confession

In 1890, the *Westminster Gazette* raised the spectre of the Ripper once more. In its July report it claimed that the police had gained advance information about the killer's intentions. A new cycle of horror was about to begin. Cremers read this and decided to mention it to D'Onston to gauge his reaction. But he was one step ahead of her. At the office, he waved the very paper at her while ridiculing the report. Then his mood changed abruptly. *'There will be no more murders.'* He strode across to Cremers' desk and leaning over it, stared down at her and said, 'Did I ever tell you that I knew Jack the Ripper?'

When recalling this incident, Cremers wrote:

> I felt a cold shudder run through me. Anxious to gain time to recover myself, I bent down and opened a drawer. 'Where the deuce did I put that ruler?' I muttered to myself, and continued to fumble in the drawer. But D'Onston was apparently not to be denied, for still leaning over the desk he repeated: 'Did I ever tell you that I knew Jack the Ripper?'

Cremers was now disturbed and uneasy but she struggled to stay calm and gave a noncommittal reply. At that, D'Onston began to pace up and down the room. Cremers was reminded of the time when he'd mimed the throat-cutting of his wife. And then, in a quiet voice D'Onston said:

> 'You know that when Mabel first wrote to me, I was in hospital? That was just after the last of the murders, Vittoria,' he went on, 'and you can take it from me that there were no more Ripper murders after that one in Miller's Court on November 9.'
>
> He paused for a moment, came close to me, and then remarked that he was living in the Whitechapel neighbourhood at the time. I never thought to inquire *where,* nor to ask him *why* he was residing in such a squalid district. It simply did not occur to me, but my brain

registered the fact that he *was* living in the murder area at the time of the crimes.

D'Onston went on to say that he was taken seriously ill and had to enter hospital. Something to do with the 'Chinese slug', was how he put it to me and then he explained:

'It was there that I met him, Vittoria. He was one of the surgeons who operated, and of course when he learned that I had also been a doctor he became more interested in my case, and we became very chummy.

'Naturally we talked about the murders, because they were the one topic of conversation. One night he opened up and confessed that he was Jack the Ripper. At first I did not believe him, but when he began to describe just how he had carried out the crimes I realized that he was speaking from actual knowledge, and – was speaking the truth.'

D'Onston rose from his chair and recommenced his restless pacing up and down the room. Then once more he paused and stood before me.

'At the inquest, Vittoria, it was suggested that the women had been murdered by a *left-handed* man, or at any rate with the left hand.' He smiled in derision. 'It just shows that they could not see an inch before their noses, Vittoria. My surgeon friend explained exactly how the medical witnesses fell into this error. He also told me that he always selected the place where he intended to murder the women. It was for a very special reason, Vittoria, which you would not understand. He took the Whitechapel Road as a sort of base for his operations, and made several journeys before deciding on the spots best suited to fit in with his scheme of things. Then, having got his victims to these particular places, he manoeuvred to get behind them.'

At this point D'Onston paused for some seconds which seemed like hours to me. He seemed as though he were reliving something that had happened some time before. Then he spoke again.

'All those doctor fellows took it for granted that Jack the Ripper was standing in front of the women when he drew the knife across their throats,' he said, and paused again before continuing, 'but he wasn't, Vittoria – he wasn't. *He was standing behind them like this.*'

As he spoke D'Onston crossed over and stood behind my chair. And even at this length of time, I can still recall the uncanny expectant feeling I experienced as I sensed him standing there behind me. I could almost feel a knife at my throat.

But he was talking again, quite calmly, yet with deadly earnestness. 'It was quite simple really,' came his voice from behind as he reached round and placed his left hand over my mouth and nose, pulling my head back. I could scarcely breathe so firm was his grasp. Then his other arm reached round my neck from the right, and again he spoke.

'You see Vittoria,' he said, 'this arm (waving his right arm before my eyes) would be quite free, and all my friend had to do was to make one quick slash with his knife, and it was all over before they could utter a sound.'

As he said this, D'Onston's arm relaxed and he withdrew it from my neck. At the same time he lifted his left hand from my nose and mouth, and I drew a deep and grateful breath. He continued:

'At the inquests, Vittoria, these same doctors made a point of mentioning that the women did not fall but *appeared to have been lain down.* This is about the only thing right about their evidence. They did *not* fall. My friend *did* lay them down, and then – when they were on the ground he carried out the mutilations – so.'

As he spoke he came round to the front of me and made a gesture with his thumb. I remember it striking me at the time – although I must admit to being too shocked to observe very clearly – that the motion was *in the form of a downward triangle,* such as I had often seen him making upon the door of his room on more than one occasion. Meanwhile D'Onston was continuing his narrative of what, he said, happened at the scene of the crimes:

'Everybody, Vittoria, including the police were on the look-out for a man with bloodstained clothing,' he said, 'but of course, killing the women from behind, my doctor friend avoided this, as their bodies offered some sort of protection. *Had* he been in front of them his clothes *must* have been drenched with blood. Once or twice, he told me, he found a spot or two, but soon removed them.'

All D'Onston's revelations were made in a detached fashion; a mood which persisted, even when he revelled in the details of the gory knife-work. Cremers was appalled:

For the first time, I learned how, in two instances, the murderer, after mutilating the bodies, took away the uterus; the mere mention of this fact horrified me, but I can see now the lifeless grin D'Onston gave when relating this part of the story. I was still more horrified when he went on to say:

'He tucked these organs in the space between his shirt and tie, Vittoria,' going through the motions as he did so. I could not repress a shuddering 'Good God!' as, in a flash, there came to my mind the recollection of that black tin box in D'Onston's room containing the ties with their stained underparts. At the time I rifled that box and came upon them, I had wondered why on earth he kept such filthy neckwear, and how they had become stained in such an unlikely spot.

Now I *knew*! D'Onston had, out of his own mouth, provided the *only* explanation. From his own lips he had not only explained *how* those stains could possibly have come upon the underside of his ties, but had also revealed that they came from the blood of his murdered victims.

All this passed through my mind in a flash as I took in the purport of his story; and in that moment one question dominated my mind. 'Who but the murderer himself could possibly know the things D'Onston had told me?'

It was borne in upon me that the 'doctor friend' referred to was nothing more than a figment of D'Onston's imagination, invented to conceal his own identity with Jack the Ripper. I was now convinced beyond all doubt that the man standing before me was in fact the Whitechapel murderer, and that Mabel Collins' fears of her lover were well founded.

During the latter part of his narrative I had been careful to intently watch him. I noticed that the expression on his face never changed except for that one momentary grin when he described the removal of the uterus. Never once did he falter in his recital which was spoken in quiet, unemotional tones. At the end he looked intently at me to see how I was taking it. I endeavoured to assume a calm demeanour; and, to break the spell, as it were, I asked:

'But what did your friend want D'Onston? What was he after?' By this time, I was more than ever anxious to get right into the mind of the man I now regarded as a self-confessed murderer. I was puzzled at the idea of this apparently serene-minded, cultured person, as I knew D'Onston to be, being guilty of the horrors he had just described to me without the quiver of an eyelid. I had not read about the crimes at the time, and it was not until this moment, and from D'Onston himself, that I learned the nature of the atrocities. Hence my desire to discover the motive which impelled him to such gruesome crimes. Why had he murdered so many women, and what was the object of the ghastly mutilations inflicted upon his victims after death?

There was no thought in my mind of any Magical background to the murders. I knew little of Magic beyond Mabel Collins' description of D'Onston as 'a great Magician'. It was the recollection of the ties and his explanation of how they had become stained with blood, which prompted me to ask him, 'But what did he want. What was he after?'

D'Onston was not to be drawn, however. He simply shrugged his shoulders as he answered: 'He *did* tell me, Vittoria, but you would not understand.'

I knew it would be fruitless to pursue the question, so I next ventured: 'But didn't you ever tell the police?'

He smiled. 'Yes,' he replied. 'I told them all right, but by the time they went to arrest him he had gone. You know, Vittoria, the police were awful duffers. Why, they had me in for questioning on two occasions, but of course I was easily able to satisfy them and they had to let me go.'

I proceeded to ask him a question here and there, giving no inkling of my suspicions. Yet, all the time I was paving the way towards a scheme, whereby I hoped to persuade him to set down in fuller detail (with the object of newspaper publication) the story of his mysterious 'doctor friend'. I have already mentioned that I knew he was invariably hard up, and now that Mabel Collins had broken with him, and there was very little coming in from the Cosmetique Company, I felt sure he must be worse off than ever.

Suddenly I put my scheme to him direct, pretending enthusiasm for the idea as though it had just struck me.

'You know D'Onston,' I said, 'that's one of the most amazing stories I have ever heard. There's money in it. Why don't you write it up for the *Pall Mall Gazette*? You are well in with Stead, and he would jump at it.'

'Oh, I don't know,' he began, and for the first time in my experience, it seemed as though he were not anxious to make money. But I kept at him.

'It would create a sensation,' I told him. 'It would pave the way for stories in other newspapers.' He still appeared to be reluctant, but I was determined to make him set down in black and white the terrible story he had told to me.

I got out pen and paper and placed them before him. D'Onston sat down and began to scribble off three or four pages of preamble, handing them to me to read as he did so. The perspiration simply poured from him as he wrote, and he was obviously labouring under some great emotional strain as he scribbled away. I had never before seen him so much affected. Suddenly he rose to his feet, roughly pushed back the chair, and then, quietly, and without a trace of the turmoil which had been so pronounced a few seconds before, he turned to me and said, 'I'll finish it tomorrow, Vittoria, and take it straight round to W. T. Stead in the morning.'

But I knew full well that he would do no such thing. The moment had passed. His excuse was simply a subterfuge to escape writing the story. I realized that he never intended to write it, but had been forced to fall in with my suggestion in order to lull any possible suspicions. I believe now that he knew I suspected him and was trying to elicit how much Mabel Collins had told me.

He left the office and entered his room taking with him the few sheets of paper on which he had begun to write his story.

At the time Cremers had no knowledge of the fact that W.T. Stead already knew about D'Onston's yarn involving Dr Davies. Neither did she know that Stead himself suspected D'Onston of being the Ripper. But because she was certain that D'Onston would remain silent, and because she had such strong suspicions, why didn't she take her story to the police? This is something she dealt with forthrightly when she talked to O'Donnell, saying:

I am a Theosophist. I believe that whatever we do upon this plane we shall reap our deserts in the next incarnation. I believe that we shall be rewarded or punished according to our life on earth. It is not for me to interfere with the laws which govern destiny. I did not do it then, I would not do it now. You will remember that D'Onston had already assured me in the clearest possible terms that *there would be no more Ripper murders* and that the last one had been committed on 9 November, 1888. He had spoken truly. There *were* no Ripper murders during the twenty-one months which had elapsed between that date and the time of our talk. Consequently I felt quite certain that, being the murderer, he *knew* what he was talking about. That there *would* be no more murders by Jack the Ripper. I knew there was no further danger to others.

Cremers' reasoning was sound. D'Onston's illness reduced him to a shadow of his former self. He was now a man of hints and threats and little more; while his so-called magical powers were not even potent enough to bind the three partners together. Inevitably their joint business ended in near farce.

CHAPTER TWENTY-ONE

The Trio Split

Vittoria Cremers saw Mabel as a partner for the last time late in the summer of 1891. It was a brief meeting lasting just under an hour and it only came about because Mabel needed a great favour. D'Onston had a collection of letters from Mabel; compromising letters, so explicitly sexual that they gave him the power of blackmail. She knew where they were kept and even had a key that fitted the lock of the trunk that housed them. But she was far too terrified to enter his room and rifle the trunk, so she pleaded with Vittoria to recover the letters for her. Vittoria took pity on her, gamely extracted the letters and sent them on to Mabel's hideaway. It was some three weeks later before D'Onston discovered the loss of the letters, but he seemed to accept that Mabel herself could have returned to London and taken them. In fact Mabel had stupidly written to him and boasted that he no longer had a hold over her. In the same letter she ordered him out of his room and informed him that all his furniture would be taken away within days.

This marked the end of the Pompadour Company and its name and assets were taken over by a West End consortium. Mabel returned to York Terrace, Cremers went back to Mrs Heilmann's, while D'Onston took out a summons against Mabel demanding the return of the purloined letters. It seemed a foolish act to involve the courts, but D'Onston seemed blinded by hate and the action actually came to a hearing, as Cremers testifies:

The case was heard at Marylebone, and I shall never forget the shock I had on seeing D'Onston. He looked terribly ill, and although he moved in the same silent manner when his name was called and he made his way to the witness-box, he seemed to lack the sanguine calm that was so usual with him. He was not exactly agitated – as he had been when writing the few pages describing his meeting with Jack the Ripper – but he struck me as being uneasy and not sure of himself.

Perhaps he had expected that Mabel would have handed over the letters without daring to appear in court. I don't know! But when he was asked to take the oath, I noticed that while his lips moved mouthing the words of *the ordinary Christian oath sworn upon the New Testament* as is usual, *not a sound could be heard.* Somehow, he must have satisfied the court usher, but although I was sitting not far away I could not hear even a whisper.

D'Onston was represented by a solicitor who asked him to tell the court in his own words the nature of his complaint against Mabel Collins.

He opened his mouth as though to speak, mumbled a few unintelligible words, and stopped, gazing blankly in front of him. It was incomprehensibly eerie to me, who had never found D'Onston at a loss for words. But now he was literally speechless. The solicitor had already outlined the case stating that 'the defendant broke into D'Onston's room and extracted private letters from a locked trunk'. And now, when D'Onston was being invited to substantiate this allegation, he became dumb. It was for all the world as if he were paralysed. The words simply refused to come, and after an interval during which his solicitor went across and spoke quietly to him, D'Onston left the witness-box and the solicitor announced that under the circumstances he could carry the matter no further. Whereupon the case was dismissed.

I left the court hurriedly without even waiting to say goodbye to Mabel Collins. I believed then that both she and D'Onston had passed from my life for ever. It was true so far as Mabel Collins was concerned, for I never saw her again. But as regards D'Onston, I was wrong.

Her very last contact with the man was charged with menace. D'Onston wrote to her asking for money and demanding to meet her on her own. She ignored the note but others followed. Finally she met him at midnight at her lodgings but took care to have two stalwart men waiting in a recess at the foot of the stairs. D'Onston must have caught sight of the men lurking in the dark alcove since he simply took the money offered him and left without even a word of abuse. She felt it an anti-climax but often wondered what might have happened if her allies had not been on hand. Four years later Cremers returned to England after lengthy tours abroad. Awaiting her was a bundle of letters in D'Onston's handwriting, but she resisted the urge to open them and threw them into the fire. In later life she regretted this. What if they'd given further clues to his past and his misdemeanours?

Vittoria Cremers died in 1936 without knowing D'Onston's real name and background and without realizing just how invaluable her testimony would prove to be.

CHAPTER TWENTY-TWO

Blood and Magic

Two different reasons for the murders are included in Vittoria Cremers' memoirs: according to the Earl of Crawford, Black Magic was at play; according to D'Onston, a twisted doctor was at work. Both explanations seem in conflict with each other and yet, as we shall see, there is no clash. We are merely looking at the two halves of one disclosure; both halves fashioned by one man alone. But if the key to the mystery lies in *ritual* murder then we need to understand fully the magical mentality of the Victorians. A superficial or token appraisal is not enough. Only a deep and comprehensive study of their beliefs can show us why murder was enshrined in both White and Black Magic. This does not mean that the ceremonies of the believers unleashed genuine powers. On the contrary, all magical claims are nonsensical. This tragic belief in magic is a burden inherited from the childhood of Man. It is a retrograde view of the Universe and of Man himself. It gains force by using childish dreads and yearnings. It adds to these uncertainties its special heady symbolism and its language of spurious wisdom. All magic deludes by promising unrealizable control; by offering entry into halls of hidden and terrible knowledge. In its most menacing forms it succeeds only by twisting the minds of its dupes, but never by violating the laws of nature. Where it does succeed, this is simply because its devotees have acted out their fantasies, for even the direst nonsense can become a force when people believe in it. So exactly what were the strange beliefs of our forebearers? Beliefs that are even now nurtured by some.

The year is 1888, year of the Ripper. In a London hall a small body of men and women gather to found the Isis-Urania Temple of the Hermetic Society of the Golden Dawn. It is a magical order devoted to so-called White rituals and its Supreme Magus is a solemn-faced, bearded scholar who dresses in splendid robes and wields a heavy, ornate baton. He is also a Queen's Coroner for North London. His name is Dr Wynn Westcott. In recent years some wild fantasists have named him as Jack the Ripper! But this is worthy of a yawn and no more. What is worth noting, though, is his status and the fact that surrounding him were people of intellect, all committed to the belief that they could control people and events by means of signs, symbols, chants and the power of their magically charged wills.

In time the Golden Dawn would count among its members Arthur Machen, Maude Gonne, Florence Farr, Mrs Oscar Wilde, Algernon Blackwood, Sir William Crookes, and W. B. Yeats. Its members would take oaths which threatened them if they disclosed the 'great secrets', declaiming such nonsense as: '…submitting myself by my own consent to a deadly stream of Power, set in motion by the Divine Guardians of this Order, living in the Light of their perfect justice, who can, as tradition and experience affirm strike the breaker of the magical Obligation with death or palsy, or overwhelm him with misfortunes…'

These, remember, were the beliefs of those who labelled themselves as 'Whites'; those whose powers were alleged to be used for the good of mankind. But did these White beliefs go as far as to condone murder for the common good? They certainly did. The supreme example of a·'magical murderess' can be found in the person of Dr Anna Kingsford, a strong influence on Samuel Mathers, one of the founders of the Golden Dawn, and friend of Wynn Wescott.

Anna Kingsford was a doctor of medicine who developed a fanatical hatred of all who practised vivisection. Top of her list of these 'vile practitioners' were three Frenchmen: Claude Bernard, Paul Bert and Louis Pasteur. She absorbed the antique magical belief that one could 'kill by willing'; a belief that she found confirmed by the sixteenth century magician Paracelsus:

> It is possible that my spirit, without the help of my body, may through a fiery will alone, and without a sword, stab and wound others. It is possible for me to bring my adversary's spirit into an image, then double him up and lame him at pleasure…

In Dr Kingsford's case she targeted Claude Bernard as the foremost living representative of the 'vivisection conspirators' and with passionate energy invoked the wrath of God upon him. She later said that she felt as if she had been transformed into a spiritual thunderbolt at the moment of her curse. Shortly afterwards she heard the news of the death of Bernard and was so overwhelmed by her imagined victory that she almost swooned. Then in an ecstatic mood she proclaimed, 'Woe be to the torturers. God willing, what a murrain there shall be among them! I will make it dangerous, nay deadly, to be a vivisector.' And in that state she began to will the death of Paul Bert.

Her diary for 12 November 1886 records:

Yesterday, November 11, at eleven at night, I knew that my will had
smitten another vivisector! Ah, but this man has cost me more toil
than his master, the fiend Claude Bernard. For months I have been
working to encompass the death of Paul Bert, and have but just succeeded. But I have *succeeded*; the demonstration of the power is
complete. The will *can* and *does* kill… Now only one remains on hand
– Pasteur, who is certainly doomed…I have killed Paul Bert, as I killed
Claude Bernard; as I will kill Louis Pasteur, and after him the whole
tribe of vivisectors…'

She was then led to conclude that, 'The White Magician is authorized to
undertake an act of execution in the same spirit and with the same motive,
and in the same frame of mind, as he would entertain in the act of destroy-
ing a noxious beast or a venomous reptile or creeping things.'

If you consider that such a creed was held by a cultured lady who styled
herself a Christian, then it easy to see that an avowed Satanist would have no
problems at all in endorsing murder as a worthwhile pursuit. Indeed Eliphas
Levi, the French occultist who influenced D'Onston, Kingsford, Blavatsky,
and Wescott wrote:

Black Magic is really only a graduated combination of sacrileges and
murders designed for the permanent perversion of the human will
and for the realization in a living man of the hideous phantom of the
demon… The rites of Black Magic have remained revolting like the
impious worships it produced… There was always the same passion for
darkness; there were the same profanations, the same sanguinary
processes. Anarchic Magic is the cultus of death. The sorcerer devotes
himself to fatality, abjures reason, renounces the hope of immortality,
and then sacrifices children. He forswears marriage and is given over to
barren debauch. On such conditions he enjoys the plentitude of his
mania, is made drunk with iniquity till he believes that evil is impotent
and, converting his hallucinations into reality, he thinks that his mas-
tery has power to evoke at pleasure all death and Hades.

Among the self-proclaimed 'elite' drawn to such magical thinking was
a Robert Stephenson from Hull. This was a name which would have meant
nothing to Cremers, or Mabel Collins. Yet it was their partner's name. A
name which now gives us access to many archives and their myriad secrets.

CHAPTER TWENTY-THREE

Man of Secrets

My first verdict on the Whitechapel mystery was an open one. None of the contending theories stood up to close scrutiny, so the killer was probably someone unknown and unsuspected. Study of the FBI material on serial killers led to a slight alteration in emphasis: the killer *could* have been suspected at one time but may well have been able to give a convincing display of total innocence. Then, using the documents of the time and coupling these with our present-day understanding of the serial sexual killer, I was able to draw up a comprehensive profile of the man.

This, in turn, could be realistically reduced to thirteen essential points. The final Master Profile read:

He will not be a person of stature, importance, or fame; however:

1. He will be fit, agile, with an icy control; but at the same time will be inclined to be taunting.
2. Not physically distinguished. Neither a giant nor a dwarf.
3. Nothing about him to repel or arouse suspicion.
4. Able to talk easily with prostitutes.
5. He will have an intimate knowledge of the area.
6. Either still living in the area, or having a retreat there, i.e. a club, institute, friend's or relative's place.
7. Not a surgeon, but with some limited medical knowledge. Maybe a one-time assistant to a GP, or former medical student.
8. Possibly enjoying some form of cover.
9. Possible past record of deviancy. Perhaps even interviewed by the police of the day.
10. May have talked about the killings.
11. A careful planner, but a high-risk taker.
12. His motives? Perverted sexuality.
13. His career ended by death, disablement or leaving the country.

My first book on the murders was planned to end with this profile, leaving the killer as a faceless anonymous blur. But, with a deadline limiting extensive research, a rejected suspect suddenly grew in significance. No published author had ever taken Roslyn D'Onston seriously; the man had been long since dismissed out of hand as a Walter Mitty character. This dismissal arose from blunders made in 1975. D'Onston's birth certificate showed that his father was a 'seed crusher' of Charles Street, Sculcoates.

This was wrongly interpreted. His place of birth was described as a humble one, while his father was pictured as a mere working man toiling in a mill. This, naturally, was at complete odds with D'Onston's claims to have come from a well-off family whose money had allowed him to study in Paris and Munich. So the man became a liar of no importance. His colourful tales of soldiering with Garibaldi, of travels in India and more, were all written off as sheer moonshine. One visit to Hull changed all that.

Hull records showed the address at Charles Street to have been a large middle-class town house. As for the father, he actually *owned* the mills where the seeds were crushed. He was in fact, co-proprietor of the firm of Dawber and Stephenson, bone and seed crushers and linseed oil manufacturers. The mother in turn was from another mill-owning family, the Dawbers. So, it was clear that the Stephensons had ample money, as D'Onston had claimed. And there were other discoveries which showed that D'Onston had a past that simply cried out for full examination.

An autobiographical article of his was located, containing oblique clues to missing years of his life. He spoke of holding a post under the Crown. This was the starting point for a process of gradual elimination which finally led to the discovery of his service records. He was found to have been a customs officer. And there, in those records, was proof of his early entanglements with prostitutes, and proof of his deviancy. Other discoveries came to light. Each one tying the man into the Ripper killings. For the first time ever there emerged an authentic candidate who came to fit the master profile to perfection.

He was born on 20 April 1841 and baptized as Robert D'Onston Stephenson. As a schoolboy he set out to control people and events and believed that he'd found a way through the agency of magic. Of that period he wrote: 'I was always…fond of everything pertaining to mysticism, astrology, witchcraft, and what is commonly known as "occult science" generally; and I devoured with avidity every book or tale that I could get hold of having reference to these arts.' None of this study ever gave him the control he wanted and he stayed frustrated until he tried hypnotism. He recalled: 'I remember, at the early age of fourteen, practising mesmerism on several of my schoolfellows, particularly on my cousin, a year younger than myself. But on this boy…developing a decided talent for somnambulism, and nearly killing himself in one of his nocturnal rambles, my experiments in that direction were brought to an untimely close.'

In his teens he took rooms in Munich and studied chemistry under the renowned Dr James Allan, a Scotsman who had been the former right-hand assistant to Baron Liebig. From there he went on to Paris for further studies in medicine and while there began to revive his old passions:

> …my interest in the effects of mind upon matter once more awoke, and my physiological studies and researches were accompanied by psychological experiments. I read Lytton's *Zanoni* at this time with great zest, but I am afraid with very little understanding, and longed excessively to know its author; little dreaming that I should one day be the pupil of the great Magist, Bulwer Lytton – the one man in modern times for whom all systems of ancient and modern magism and magic, white or black, held back no secrets.

A chance meeting in Paris put an end to his excessive longings. In 1859 he met Bulwer Lytton's son and young Lytton took to D'Onston and willingly furnished him with an introduction to his great father. In the following spring D'Onston met Sir Edward in London and was greeted warmly. D'Onston records: 'I suppose Sir Edward was attracted to me partly by my irrepressible hero-worship of which he was the object , and partly because he saw that I possessed a cool, logical brain, had iron nerve, and above all, was genuinely, terribly in earnest.'

After a brief period D'Onston won complete acceptance. Sir Edward summoned him to a private meeting-place and there began his training. D'Onston wrote:

> I entered, he was standing in the middle of the sacred pentagon, which he had drawn on the floor with red chalk, and holding in his extend-ed right arm the baguette, which was pointed towards me. Standing thus, he asked me if I had duly considered the matter and had decid-ed to enter upon the course. I replied that my mind was made up. He then and there administered to me the oaths of the neophyte of the Hermetic lodge of Alexandria – the oaths of obedience and secrecy.

In later years D'Onston divulged little of the actions of his lodge but he did speak of '…the books of "Black Magic" I had studied under Lytton. Hermetics have to *know* all the practices of the "forbidden art" to enable them to overcome the devilish machinations of its professors.' He must have revelled in writing those hypocritical words, for one thing is certain; in all of his known writings of the nineteenth century there is not a single Christian sentiment. Blood, death, necromancy and deception are his constant themes. Compassion, charity, humanity, are themes always absent.

His initiation provided the first great excitement of the year 1860, then came an unexpected distraction. Like many other reckless, bright-eyed students, he was ensnared by the fire and fury of Garibaldi's rising. In Britain Garibaldi's admirers set out to raise a foreign legion to fight in Italy, but in order not to fall foul of the law they called the legionnaires 'Excursionists'.

From his home in Hull D'Onston offered his services, then he came south to London, stayed at an old school friend's house in Islington and made a second application. This time he inflated his age to twenty-two, in order to escape a veto from his father, and with a background of some military training, became a lieutenant in the Southern Army of Italy. There were no noncombatants in that army. Those with medical training simply swapped their swords for scalpels as the need arose. It was then that D'Onston gained the experience in crude surgery, handling wounds and amputations that only military campaigns provided. Then it was down scalpel and battle order once more. Sword in hand, D'Onston killed and maimed legitimately on the battlefields of Italy. At a totally impressionable age, he became hardened to the sight of blood, death and mutilation. Edward Bowra, one of his colleagues and far less hardened, wrote this of the campaign:

> Only when we came to charge bayonets and form line…would they retreat. And it was well for them that they did so, for so awfully excited and enraged were we that I do not believe we would have given any quarter or spared a single soul. You cannot imagine with what a fierce exulting pleasure, I received with my comrades the order to charge bayonets and clear the ditch. I was heartily ashamed of myself a few hours afterwards…for having allowed such animal and barbarous passions to get the better of me…

Some men, though, treasured the barbarous passions and D'Onston was one of these. But could such passions arouse thoughts of sexual slaughter? Given the right circumstances, such a transition is certain. The whole history of brutal warfare is marked by sexual atrocities. Indeed, a smiling British mercenary with the Croat army recently said this: 'I've always wanted to kill legally…I have that feeling to take people out. I've always wondered what were going through, like, Yorkshire Ripper…Black Panther's mind. These had no compassion. They had no feeling. I want this feel-ing…it's like higher than any drug can get you…'

In D'Onston's case the drug of slaughter was quickly withdrawn. After a victorious few months the conflict was over and a return to England replaced the rough comradeship with infantile student carousings and passive med-ical studies. For him it was empty and arid. Only his magical studies fired his dreams and gave promise of tingling excitements and revelations. His rest-lessness demanded action, so he threw aside his books and set off for the west coast of Africa. There was the lure of the unknown and the chance to view the wonders wrought by witch-doctors. And there, in Africa, he killed his first woman, a fact that he coldly put into print twenty-eight years later. But this was only an interlude; a foolhardy, vagabond existence, hardly like-ly to meet with family approval. When his funds ran out his family put him under pressure and he returned home, reluctantly, rebelliously. In March 1863 he took up a safe, predictable post at the Customs House in Hull. It was a post he came to treat with contempt: 'almost a sinecure', he termed it. And his records show that he gradually antagonised his superior officers. This was to be expected; after all, in his own eyes, he was natural-ly superior to all the mannikins around him, whatever rank they held.

By 1867 his father was not only a prominent manufacturer but held the elected post of Collector of Hull Corporation Dues – a post equivalent to City Treasurer. His elder brother Richard was now a shipowner, partner in the firm of Rayner, Stephenson and Co., Vice-Consul for Uruguay and a Hull City councillor. Yet not all his considerable family influence could shield him from Nemesis. The reckoning came at last in 1868.

CHAPTER TWENTY-FOUR

Reveal and Conceal

At this point our documentary sources begin to intermesh even more closely. The Cremers' memoirs; the service records and D'Onston's own writings, all tell of the same sets of events, and yet there are differences. How then do we evaluate these differences? What standards do we adopt to sort out the evasions from the revelations? Let us take Cremers' writings first. In her case we can show that she has remarkable powers of recall. Many of the things she records can be confirmed from documents she had never seen; documents that, in fact, were not available for public scrutiny until the 1970s. Foremost among these documents are those in the Scotland Yard files directly involving D'Onston.

In D'Onston's writings we meet a very different state of affairs. Here we have to realize that there are complications due to the ancient standards he admired and adopted. These were esoteric traditions that left him free to mingle straightforward truth with parables or illuminating fiction. This is precisely the attitude adopted by his great hero and mentor Lord Lytton who said of his *Zanoni*:

'It is a romance, and it is not a romance. It is a truth for those who can comprehend it, and an extravagance for those who cannot.' Of this same book he said also: 'I love it not the less because it has been little understood, and superficially judged by the common herd. It was not meant for them. I love it not the more, because it has found enthusiastic favourers amongst the Few.'

The same stance was adopted by Mabel Collins who said of her *Light On The Path*: 'The whole...is written in astral cipher, and can therefore only be deciphered by one who reads astrally.' Blavatsky endorsed this view saying: '...only students with spiritual discrimination will most likely discern between symbolic statements, imaginative superstructure and actual facts'.

D'Onston gave clear warning that he worked with these ideas in mind. In his *Pall Mall* article on 'Obeeyahism' (African Magic) he promised that he would go further into the subject in a forthcoming book:

> *Sube, the Obeeyah*, a work of professed fiction. Its readers will have to decide for themselves how much is absolute matter of fact – whether all or none – and how much imagination. It will not be my part to give any clue to the student of occultism; it may convey many new ideas, and indicate the true lines on which his investigations should proceed; to the holiday maker and the simple novel reader it will certainly give a fresh and hitherto unexperienced sensation…

Forewarned is forearmed. We can now put to one side those writings of his which are self-evidently esoteric; that leaves us with a group of articles which refer to real events of his life. Even these have to be treated with caution since the need to reveal has been tempered by the necessity to conceal. By carefully matching all the known writings we can eliminate the misleading passages in his testimony and so grasp the truth.

A document of prime importance was located first of all in the 1931 edition of *Man's Survival After Death* by the Rev. Charles Tweedale. This turned out to be defective and a further search led to the original complete text of 1892. This had appeared in W. T. Stead's *Review of Reviews* (New Year's Extra Number). The authentic, full account read:

Dead or Alive

Mr. R. D'Onston sends me the following communication:
'To those instances in *Real Ghost Stories* of ghosts who have kept promises made in life to appear to those dear to them, may I add my own experience? The incident occurred to me some years ago, and all the details can be substantiated. The date was August 26th, 1867, at midnight. I was then residing in the neighbourhood of Hull, and held an appointment under the Crown which necessitated my repairing thither every day for a few hours' duty. My berth was almost a sinecure; and I had been for some time engaged to a young North-country heiress, it being understood that on our marriage I should take her name and "stand for the county", or rather for one of its divisions.

'For her sake I had to break off a love affair, not of the most reputable order, with a girl in Hull. I will call her Louise. She was young, beautiful, and devoted to me. On the night of the 26th August we took our last walk together, and a few minutes before midnight paused on a wooden bridge running across a kind of canal, locally termed the "drain". We paused on the bridge, listening to the swirling current against the wooden piles and waiting for the stroke of midnight to part forever. In the few minutes' interval she repeated, *sotto voce*, Longfellow's *Bridge*, the words of which, "I stood on the bridge at midnight", seemed terribly appropriate. After nearly twenty-five years I can never hear that piece repeated without feeling a deathly chill and the whole scene of two souls in agony again rising before me. Well! midnight struck, and we parted; but Louise said: "Grant me one favour, the only one that I shall ever ask you on this earth, promise to meet me here twelve months to-night at this same hour." I demurred at first, thinking it would be bad for both of us, and only re-open partially healed wounds. At last, however, I consented, saying: "Well, I will come if I am alive!" but she said, "Say alive or dead!" I said, "Very well then, we will meet, dead or alive."

'The next year I was on the spot a few minutes before the time; and, punctual to the stroke of midnight, Louise arrived. By this time, I had begun to regret the arrangement I had made; but it was of too solemn a nature to be put aside. I therefore kept the appointment, but said that I did not care to renew the compact. Louise, however, persuaded me to renew it for one more year, and I consented, much against my will; and we again left each other repeating the same formula, "Dead or alive".

'The next year after that passed rapidly for me until the first week in July, when I was shot dangerously in the thigh by a fisherman named Thomas Piles, of Hull, a reputed smuggler. A party of four of us had hired his 10 ton yawl to go yachting round the Yorkshire coast, and amuse ourselves by shooting sea-birds amongst the millions of them at Flamborough Head. The third or fourth day out I was shot in the right thigh by the skipper Piles; and the day after, one and a quarter ounce of No.2 shot were cut therefrom by the coastguard surgeon at Bridlington Quay (whose name I forget for the moment), assisted by Dr. Alexander Mackay, at the Black Lion Hotel. The affair was in all the papers at the time, about a column of it appearing in the *Eastern Morning News*, of Hull.

'As soon as I was able to be removed (two or three weeks) I was taken home, where Dr. Kelburne King, of Hull, attended me. The day – and *the* night – (the 26th August) came. I was then unable to walk without crutches, and that for only a short distance, so had to be wheeled about in a Bath chair. The distance to the trysting being rather long, and the time and circumstances being very peculiar, I did not avail myself of the services of my usual attendant, but specially retained an old servant of the family, who frequently did confidential commissions for me, and who knew Miss Louise well. We set forth "without beat of drum", and arrived at the bridge about a few minutes to midnight. I remember that it was a brilliant starlight night, but I do not think that there was any moon, at all events, at that hour. "Old Bob", as he was always affectionately called, wheeled me to the bridge, helped me out of the Bath chair, and gave me my crutch. I walked on to the bridge, and leaned my back against the white painted top rail, then lighted my briar-root, and had a comfortable smoke.

'I was very much annoyed that I had allowed myself to be persuaded to come a second time, and determined to tell "Louise" positively that this should be the last meeting. Besides, *now*, I did not consider it fair to Miss K., with whom I was again negotiating, *en rapport* to a certain extent. So, if anything, it was in rather a sulky frame of mind that I awaited Louise. Just as the quarters before the hour began to chime I distinctly heard the "clink, clink" of the little brass heels, which she always wore, sounding on the long flagged causeway, leading for 200 yards up to the bridge. As she got nearer I could see her pass lamp after lamp in rapid succession, while the strokes of the large clock at Hull resounded through the still night.

'At last the patter, patter of the tiny feet sounded on the woodwork of the bridge, and I saw her distinctly pass under the lamp at the farther end – it was only twenty yards wide, and I stood under the lamp at my side. When she got close to me I saw that she had neither hat nor cape on, and concluded that she had taken a cab to the farther end of the flagged causeway, and (it being a very warm night) had left her wraps in the cab, and for purposes of *effect* had come the short distance in evening dress.

'"Clink, clink" went the brass heels, and she seemed about passing me, when I, suddenly urged by an impulse of affection, stretched out my arms to receive her. She passed through them, intangible, impalpable, and as she looked at me I distinctly saw her lips move, and form the words, "Dead or alive". I even *heard* the words, but not with my outward ears, with something else, some other sense – what, I know not. I felt startled, surprised, but not afraid, until a moment afterwards, when I *felt*, but could not see, some other presence following her. I could *feel*, though I could not hear, the heavy, clumsy "thud" of feet following her; and my blood seemed turned to ice. Recovering myself with an effort, I shouted out to "Old Bob" who was safely ensconced with the Bath chair in a nook out of sight round the corner. "Bob, who passed you just now?" In an instant the old Yorkshireman was by side. "Ne'er a one passed me, sir!" "Nonsense, Bob," I replied, "I told you that I was coming to meet Miss Louise, and she just passed me on the bridge, and *must* have passed you, because there's nowhere else she *could* go! You don't mean to tell me you didn't see her?" The old man replied solemnly, "Maister Ros, there's something uncanny aboot it. I heerd her come on the bridge, and off it, I'd knaw them clicketty heels onywhere; but I'm dommed, sir, if she passed me. I'm thinking we'd better gang." And "gang" we did; and it was the small hours of the morning (getting daylight) before we left off talking over the affair, and went to bed.

'The next day I made inquiries from Louise's family about her, and ascertained that she had died in Liverpool three months previously, being apparently delirious for a few hours before her death, and our parting compact evidently weighing on her mind, as she kept repeating "Dead or Alive! Shall I be there?" to the utter bewilderment of her friends, who could not divine her meaning, being of course entirely unaware of our agreement.'

This one article on its own gives us great insight into his thinking. We can now see that the accounts related by him to Cremers have been rejigged to conceal his true background. For reasons of his own he needed to keep his activities in Hull as secret as possible. Perhaps he had primitive loyalties to some members of his family. One thing is certain, his need to talk about his past later came to overwhelm his caution, and many enigmas now become transparent. He *had* held a military rank, but not in the British army. The '...jaunts with some brother officers...' were with fellow Customs Officers, not army men. The events that put him in a bath-chair were not the result of the death of his loved one but involved a suspicious shooting affair. The phantom footsteps on the bridge were heard in Hull, not in London. What then *can* we believe in this account? Surprisingly the answer is: everything. When first researched though, many things failed to find support. The claim about his post was true, but his service records showed no mention of the grave shooting incident. And the Hull newspapers printed no reports either, though logically the event should have made front page. All very puzzling. But the doubts were resolved when misplaced service papers came to light. There, in the records for 26 August 1868 is confirmation: '...Mr Stephenson accidentally received a gunshot wound, which quite incapacitated him for duty...' (this referred back to 7 July). Spurred by this, new searches were made in the newspapers, but their columns held no records. The area of search was then broadened until finally, my colleague Andy Aliffe, focused his tired eyes on a gem of a report. Weary days spent peering at microfilm had paid off. The find was the 16 July issue of the *Bridlington-Quay Observer*, and it carried this text:

Serious Accident to a Hull Gentleman

On Tuesday afternoon, Mr. R. D'O. Stephenson, of Her Majesty's Customs, at Hull, while cruising off Flamborough, on board the yacht *Flying Scud*, met with a serious accident. The party on board were shooting sea birds, and Mr. Stephenson was standing just abaft the mast, waiting for a shot, when a boatman belonging to the yacht, who was behind him, took up one of the guns to fire, and managed to explode it prematurely, sending the whole charge into the back of Mr. Stephenson's thigh. The heavy charge (1.25 oz of No. 2 shot), at a distance of about two yards, tore a jagged hole, about 1.5 inches wide, and the same depth, and lodged itself in a lump near the bone, which, however, it miraculously failed to injure. Fortunately a gentleman was on board who had had some surgical experience, and immediately applied temporary bandages. The unfortunate gentleman was landed at Flamborough as soon as possible, and carried to the top of the cliffs by a stalwart young fisherman. The only available conveyance being a fish-cart, belonging to the landlord of the inn, it was filled with clean straw, and the patient removed in it to Bridlington, where, under the skilful hands of Drs. Brett and Mackay, the greater part of the shot was removed. We are informed by eye witnesses that the *sang-froid* with which the sufferer treated his terrible and painful wound was something remarkable, and excited the warmest admiration and sympathy in the bystanders. We understand that there is every hope of saving the limb, provided that neither erysipelas nor gangrene (the two great dangers in gun-shot wounds) make their appearance. Mr. Edwin Gray, timber merchant, Hull, very kindly superintended the landing at Flamborough.

A second report in the *Bridlington Free Press* for July 11 confirmed that the surgical aid was was given at the Black Lion Hotel. So every verifiable detail stood up, even to the size and weight of the lead shot. Given the extent of his injuries it became easy to see that the phantom footfalls on the bridge were simply night sounds hallucinated into a ghostly experience. When operating on his thigh, the surgeon would have made free with his injections of pain-killing morphia. In that year, as articles in the *Practitioner* show, doctors held that there were no dangers involved in injecting morphia, even over long periods. So the drug would have been at D'Onston's daily disposal during his recovery. His capacity for hallucinating was thus at a peak.

Remarkably the Bridlington reporter confirms the observations made by others in later years. They all noted D'Onston's icy control. This reporter drew special attention to D'Onston's coolness, cold-bloodedness, *sang-froid*, when coping with his terrible injury. This is the Ripper of my profile.

One mystery still remains though. Why did the Hull papers ignore the story, for D'Onston's recollection is here at fault? The only sensible explanation seems to be that the story was hushed up. Family pressure may have been strong enough to have achieved this, especially since one of the leading papers was owned by a branch of the Stephensons.

There were pressing reasons for avoiding any type of scandal at that time, for the Stephenson family were still desperately trying to save the proposed alliance with the heiress. D'Onston's conduct, on the other hand, had gradually placed their well-laid plans in dire jeopardy. And 1868 had already been crises-ridden from its very first months.

CHAPTER TWENTY-FIVE

The Death of Love

Before D'Onston became utterly corrupted he suffered from a peculiarly Victorian malady. He believed that he could redeem a prostitute by the sheer force of love. Novelist George Gissing, a fellow Yorkshireman, also suffered from this malady. In Gissing's case he threw away his academic future by stealing from the men's locker rooms in Owens College. None of these thefts were for personal gain, they were desperate attempts to provide a prostitute with money and wean her away from the streets. He adored this girl, Nell Harrison, and after a term of imprisonment and wanderings in America, Gissing actually married her. The union was a disaster. The girl proved to be a shrew, unable to meet his standards and she drifted back to the streets, leaving Gissing drained and desolate. D'Onston too staked everything on an idealized union between himself and a prostitute. This was the girl he called 'Ada-Louise'; the girl of his hallucinations; the one he was forced to reject.

Naturally, a woman of the streets was quite unacceptable to his family and he knew this; yet, in his determined, egocentric fashion he intended to push through with his plans. But the family was able to enforce its will after D'Onston ran up huge gambling debts. His father agreed to pay off the debts on condition that all contact with this street-woman ended. D'Onston gave in and promised to break with Ada-Louise, but secretly he arranged a poignant once-a-year tryst with her. And there may well have been some extra meetings, for on 25 February 1868 he was warned that the heiress had found out about this love-affair, '…not of a most reputable order…' as he put it. He dealt with this crisis by taking unauthorized leave and was summoned to face an internal disciplinary hearing by the Customs.

Records of this hearing show how a letter was involved that could have seriously affected his prospects and character, if not dealt with at once. The Hull disciplinary board seemed quite happy to accept this generalized statement, but the London HQ insisted in knowing more. The Hull Collector then reported: '…his absence was caused by information given to him that certain matters prejudicial to his moral character had been communicated to the lady he is about to marry, and it was of great importance to his future welfare, that he should at once refute them.'

But things had now gone too far. His excuses failed to placate the lady and the marriage hopes were ended. From then on it was a downwards track. He began seeking comfort from the dockside ladies of pleasure and for his pains contracted a veneral disease which left him in a feverish state.

The official report on his condition states '…there is little or no doubt that the illness from which he is now suffering is the result of the discreditable life he leads.' And while he was still on sick leave, came the shooting incident; an event which must have raised serious doubts about his reliability. There were many boats available for hire in the area, but D'Onston had opted for one owned by a man with a reputation as a smuggler. That man had then shot him. An accident it was said, but was it?

What on earth was a Customs Officer doing in the company of such a man? Was this smuggler benefiting from inside knowledge of Customs plans? Was this wounding the result of a quarrel between knaves? Or were gambling debts involved?

Whatever the Hull Customs discovered about this shooting is still unknown – the records are infuriatingly incomplete, but on his return to duty he was dismissed from the Service: 'Struck off the establishment' is the official wording. This in itself was a severe disgrace and a blow to his prominent family with its aura of respectability. What is more this dismissal raised doubts about his basic honesty and stability. It even hinted at criminality.

Shortly after this ignominy he left Hull for London and covered up all traces of his past life as a servant of the Crown. From now on, his hometown was linked with sorrow and failure. And most tragic of all for him, it was dark-shadowed by the death of the only woman he would ever love. A death which he would always blame on the profession of harlotry. But for that stigma, he would have unfailingly made her his wife. Instead, all the love within him died with her. In later years the harlots themselves would pay for the cruel death of his last streak of humanity. In the meantime, he hit back at his family and its respectability by marrying his mother's illiterate servant girl.

His marriage to this Anne Deary took place on 14 February 1876 in the North London Church of St James in Holloway. Ironically it was in this very same church that Frederick George Abberline was married. The two men may even have known each other at this time, since D'Onston worked

No. 1423.—Vol. 55

SEPTEMBER 8, 1888

THE PENNY
ILLUSTRATED PAPER
AND ILLUSTRATED TIMES

REGISTERED AT THE GENERAL POST-OFFICE AS A NEWSPAPER.

London : Printed and Published at the Office, 10, Milford-lane, Strand, in the Parish of St. Clement Danes, in the County of Middlesex, by THOMAS FOX, 10, Milford-lane, Strand, aforesaid.

P.C. NIEL J.97.   DR LLEWELLYN   INSPR HELSON   THE CORONER

SKETCHES AT THE INQUEST

EAST London has a terror that must be stamped out. We illustrate on this page, and describe in another, Police-Constable Niel's discovery of murdered Mary Ann Nicholls in Buck's-row, Whitechapel, on the early morning of August the Thirty-first. This crime has so many points of similarity with the murders of the two other women in the same neighbourhood—one, Martha Turner, as recently as Aug. 7, and the other less than twelve months previously—that the police admit their belief that the three crimes are the work of one individual. All three women were of the same class, and each of them was so poor that robbery could have formed no motive for the crime. The three murders were committed within a distance of 200 yards of each other

THE WHITECHAPEL MYSTERY.

The popular illustrated papers immediately saw the dramatic appeal of the first Ripper murders

Mary Kelly – the fairest and most brutally butchered of all the victims

Above: James Kenneth Stephen, one-time tutor to the Duke of Clarence, was accused of being the Ripper in 1972. He was more of a joke candidate than a serious one and yet he has been named as the Ripper in at least three recent books. In fact, Stephen had no involvement in the murders

Above right: The Duke of Clarence ('Eddy'), Queen Victoria's grandson, died young in the 'flu epidemic of 1892. Until the 1960s he was remembered only as a weak, gentle creature but since then he has been dragged into eight different books about the Ripper despite there being nothing to connect him with the murders

Right: In 1894, Sir Melville Macnaghten, Chief Commissioner of the Metropolitan Police, named his three prime Ripper suspects in order to deflect the accusation of a cover-up involving the lunatic nephew of a high-ranking police officer

Left: Montague James Druitt committed suicide in December 1888. He is a Ripper suspect simply because he was named by Macnaghten in 1894 but years of research by a number of authors have failed to bring a single worthwhile piece of evidence to light to support the idea that he was a killer

Right: William Le Queux, author of highly successful thrillers, was the man behind the myth of a Russian Ripper. His nominee was Alexander Pedachenko, a fictitious character, who has taken in a good many writers since

Above: The painter, Walter Sickert, whose interest in the murders led to him being falsely 'identified' as the Ripper

Above right: Alois Szemeredy, the false Ripper from Vienna. He was the subject of the first book on the Ripper murders written in Danish by Carl Muusmann in 1908

Right: Algernon Charles Swinburne – yet another false face of Jack the Ripper. This remarkable poet has been implicated simply because he had strange erotic interests

Above left: Sir William Gull, royal physician. In the 1970s, he became besmirched by a fantasy which labelled him 'a masonic madman' who organized the Ripper murders

Above right: Dr William Wynn Westcott, dressed in his 'magical' robes. Westcott was coroner for northwest London but also a firm believer in magic and the founder of 'The Society of the Golden Dawn'. He, too, has been falsely accused of being the Ripper

Left: Robert James Lees, the spiritualist who depended heavily on his 'spirit guides', figured prominently in the monumental Chicago Ripper hoax of 1895. In later years he actually came to believe some of the fairy tales woven around his name

Above left: Dr Lyttleton Forbes Winslow, owner of two private asylums and an authority on criminal lunacy, claimed that he was responsible for the end of the Ripper's reign of terror. The Ripper, he said, left the country when he realized his identity had been discovered. Unfortunately, this egocentric, devious doctor faked evidence in an effort to make his own dreams come true

Above right: James Maybrick, Liverpool cotton-broker, was allegedly poisoned by his wife Florence in 1889. In 1992, a diary emerged supposedly written by Maybrick confessing that he was Jack the Ripper

Left: Severin Klosowski (alias George Chapman), the Polish barber who poisoned three of his wives. He lived in Whitechapel in 1888, but was never associated with the Ripper murders until 1902, when he was falsely 'identified' as the Ripper by ex-Chief Inspector Abberline

Dr Thomas Neill Cream was found guilty of poisoning prostitutes and was executed in 1892. His nomination as the Ripper ignores the fact that he languished in prison in the USA at the time of the Whitechapel murders

Sir Robert Anderson, head of the C.I.D. in 1888, left for a rest-cure in Switzerland on the eve of the first Ripper murder. In later years he claimed that he 'knew' the Ripper was a Polish Jew

GHASTLY MURDER

IN THE EAST-END.

DREADFUL MUTILATION OF A WOMAN.

Capture : Leather Apron

Another murder of a character even more diabolical than that perpetrated in Buck's Row, on Friday week, was discovered in the same neighbourhood, on Saturday morning. At about six o'clock a woman was found lying in a back yard at the foot of a passage leading to a lodging-house in a Old Brown's Lane, Spitalfields. The house is occupied by a Mrs. Richardson, who lets it out to lodgers, and the door which admits to this passage, at the foot of which lies the yard where the body was found, is always open for the convenience of lodgers. A lodger named Davis was going down to work at the time mentioned and found the woman lying on her back close to the flight of steps leading into the yard. Her throat was cut in a fearful manner. The woman's body had been completely ripped open, and the heart and o b r organs laying about the place, and portions of the entrails round the victim's neck An excited crowd gathered in front of Mrs. Richardson's house and also round the mortuary in old Montague Street, whither the body was quickly conveyed. As the body lies in the rough coffin in which it has been placed in the mortuary —the same coffin in which the unfortunate Mrs. Nicholls was first placed—it presents a tearful sight. The body is that of a woman about 45 years of age. The height is exactly five feet. The complexion is fair, with wavy dark brown hair; the eyes are blue, and two lower teeth have been knocked out. The nose is rather large and prominent.

One of the broadsheets that whipped up hysteria in the East End

HOUSE TO HOUSE SEARCH BY THE POLICE. EASTEND.

A SUSPECTED LODGER.

Left: The house-to-house searches fell heaviest on the Jewish population. Few believed that the murderer could be English. It was much easier to assume he was 'foreign'

Below: A journalists' 'Tall Story Club' in Chicago was so taken with the horror and gore of the Whitechapel murders that it styled itself 'The Whitechapel Club'. In 1895 its jokers perpetrated one of the most potent Ripper hoaxes

James Sadler, seaman, the first man wrongly accused of being the Ripper to reach court

PUNCH TO THE PEELERS,

All honour to your management, my WARREN
   All honour to the Force you featly led!
And that honour, *Punch* opines, should not be barren
   (May he hear hereafter more upon *that* head).
'Midst the Jubilee's joyous pageantry and pother,
   (Though 'tis common of our Bobbies to make fun)
"Taking one consideration with another,"
   The Policemen's work was excellently done.

Mr. *Punch* from post of vantage proudly viewed them;
   They combined unshrinking toil with ready tact,
Whilst the sultry summer sunshine broiled and stewed them,
   Showing judgment when to act or not to act.
Their thin blue line kept order; firm yet kindly,
   They stood with faces flushed, but pulses cool,
Whilst the multitude around them crowded blindly,
   True type of a free people's civic rule!

By Jingo, how they worked amidst the jostle
   With steady backs and ever ready hands!
When the whistle sounded, mellow as a throstle,
   How they helped the Ambulance's helpful hands!
Fainting woman, shrieking girl, or panting 'ARRY,
   All with equal care and courtesy they served,
With ready arm to cover or to carry
   From the press where the packed people swayed and swerved.

How many lives and limbs they saved, those Peelers,
   And the Ambulance with which they worked so well,
Unless the rescued all should turn revealers,
   No record will declare, no story tell.
But Mr. *Punch's* vigilant observation
   Marked their hard toil amidst the mob's wild fun,
And, filled with genuine pride and admiration,
   He publicly awards his warm " Well done!"

Above: Punch caricature of Sir Charles Warren, controversial Chief Commissioner of Police. He
resigned at the close of the Ripper murders, and few shed any tears

Above: Mabel Collins, novelist and fashion editor, who was fascinated by 'magic'. She became obsessed with D'Onston, as did her colleague Baroness Cremers. Both eventually came to believe that D'Onston was the Ripper

Below: York Terrace, Regent's Park where Mabel Collins lived. Her belief in magic led her to be ensnared by D'Onston

YORK TERRACE, REGENT'S PARK.

Above left: William T. Stead (who was drowned when the *Titanic* went down) was the crusading editor of *The Pall Mall Gazette.* He led a successful campaign against child prostitution and was familiar with London's underworld. He not only employed D'Onston but also came to suspect him of being the Ripper

Above: Bulwer Lytton (Lord Lytton) – the novelist whose works on black magic energized and terrorized D'Onston

Left: Edward Robert Lytton, son of the famous novelist Bulwer Lytton, and later Viceroy of India. His early friendship with the man who became the Ripper had dire consequences

Roslyn D'Onston was a cold-blooded killer at the age of 18. A traveller, adventurer, a man with a grudge against prostitutes. His is the true face of Jack the Ripper

Three years after the murders ended, the Ripper was still being blamed for similar crimes and the number of victims became grossly exaggerated

as a journalist for one of the papers covering the district, and Abberline worked and lived in the same area until 1873, when fate first took him to Whitechapel.

D'Onston's marriage certificate has an added significance since it shows his first known use of *Roslyn* as a forename. This use marks a new stage in his thinking. It is an open avowal of his dedication to magic, for the name has Rosicrucian and occult masonic origins. And to understand fully the importance of such a name-change we have to look again at the Victorian hermetic traditions. These traditions held that allegories, even single words, had powers of their own and became channels of esoteric communication. This may sound highflown and foolish to us, but here our own reactions are of little account. What matters is that believers in such teachings were influenced, moved and energized by these ideas. There are many examples to prove this but just two will be enough.

Take the case of George Russell. He came to write and paint under the name Æ, and when he did so, it was as if a secondary personality took over control. But his Æ is not a display of initials, as most people thought, it is short for 'Æon', a mystic Gnostic name; the name, in fact, of the solar-phallic God of the Gnostics. It was a name that he swore had been whispered to him in a vision. As with D'Onston's choice it was heavy with sexual symbolism. So it is hardly startling to find that Russell, like D'Onston, felt himself drawn to forbidden rites:

> I was one of the Children of Light…I became aware of a dark presence beside me, and I trembled because I knew it was one of the Children of Darkness. But this being whispered gently to me, 'We of the Darkness are more ancient than you of the Light', and at the saying of that, I forsook my allegiance to the Light, and my whole being yearned to lose itself in that Divine Darkness.

At this time Russell was a member of the Hermetic Society in Dublin along with W. B. Yeats, who, on joining the Golden Dawn, showed signs of the same duality of thought by taking this magical motto for himself: 'Demon Est Deus Inversus' (The Devil is the Reverse Side of God).

This was a motto that D'Onston himself could have easily found apt and acceptable, but in picking 'Roslyn' he had chosen a name that in a way foreshadowed his future; its Rosicrucian echoes spoke of a cross and a five-petalled rose. In the warped traditions dear to him the five-petalled rose came to stand for Babylon, the Scarlet Woman, the Great Whore.

Once again, these ideas may seem infantile and hard to take seriously, yet we have to disregard such judgments, and recognize that what is *real* for the believer is the only thing that matters. Illusions, fantasies, hoaxes and mis-conceptions can all lead to real-life actions, for better or worse. In D'Onston's case his illusions even led him to make a gruelling journey through India in search of real magic. He was then thirty-seven.

In 1896 D'Onston wrote a full account of these experiences in India. His journeyings took place in 1878, at a time when Bulwer Lytton's son, Edward held the post of Viceroy of India. The old friendship with Edward (begun in Paris), stood him in good stead. Many doors opened for D'Onston and in the company of several high-ranking army officers he witnessed a fantastic display of 'real magic' invoked by a wealthy diamond merchant, Mr Jacob of Simla.

He saw a barren walking-stick put out green shoots, then twigs and branches which burst into flowers, which then in turn changed into bunch-es of fine black grapes; and this was only the beginning. Next, he took part in a ceremony which culminated in a sword being thrust right through his body. He felt not the slightest pain. After that the whole company were treated to an amazing series of visions including a re-run of the Charge of the Light Brigade. The entertainment ended when Mr Jacob waved a wand and summoned up thousands of butterflies from the air.

When his account of these wonders was first published, D'Onston was written off as a second Baron Munchausen. His stories were branded 'tall tales'. But within months, the scoffers had to eat their words. Mr Jacob of Simla was still alive and in an interview published in *Borderland* in 1897 he testified that D'Onston's visit *had* taken place and his narrative was sub-stantially correct.

Having said that, Mr Jacob then confessed that he had cleverly staged a series of tricks to deceive D'Onston and the others. It had all been done with the greatest of skill and Mr Jacob even disclosed some of the secrets lying behind his elegant illusions. The rod that had blossomed was a specially prepared stick. The sword was driven through at a safe place, only after much pinching had left the flesh bloodless and numb. It was a trick worked daily by many showmen in India. The rest of his magical act Mr Jacob pre-ferred to keep secret.

Three points of importance arise out of these reminiscences of India. We can see that D'Onston was driven to great lengths by his beliefs; we can prove that his writings were extremely accurate; and we can note that despite his experience, he readily accepted skilled trickery as proof of the paranormal. In short he was both gullible and open to massive self-deception. This is a dangerous combination for any man; in his case the danger grew to deadly proportions.

Until the Ripper terror opens we can only chart many stages of D'Onston's life in a sketchy manner. His callous ventures in America in the 1870s can be found only in Cremers' all-too-brief account. Yet everything we can glean about him points to a steady decline in his fortunes. It wasn't poverty, at first. He simply became more and more of a loner, his brain tormented by delusions of grandeur which were fired by drugs and drink; and his unshakeable belief in the power of magic.

Set in his mind was the eternal dream, that one day he would make the great breakthrough. Then, his knowledge of the occult would change his fortunes and status and astonish the sheep-like masses.

There is some evidence in police files, though, that at one point realism overtook dreaming. Belatedly, D'Onston once made a totally different bid for status. He was even prepared to discard all Bohemian ways and commit himself to a regular, responsible post. Ironically, it was a post serving, and controlled by, *the police*. In July 1886 the Secretaryship of the Metropolitan and City Police Orphanage fell vacant and was advertised. The salary was £200 a year, but the successful candidates had to give security for the sum of £500. Among the candidates was Roslyn D'Onston. The man who remained convinced of his own intellectual superiority was not even short-listed. Had he reached that list he would have found himself face to face with Sir Charles Warren, who chaired the selection board. Had he been chosen, the Whitechapel murders would never have happened: the post offered long-term stability and recognition; it also involved living over the orphanage at Wellesley House in Twickenham – far from the dark alleys and slum rooms and hideaways of the East End. The post went to Arthur Kestin, a respectable managing clerk, the sort of man D'Onston would despise. D'Onston could only see this rejection as a personal affront – he had no means of knowing that the post had attracted 372 candidates. He put all thoughts of conformity behind him and resigned himself to an increasingly vagabond existence and the seamy pleasures of the East End. From then on there was only one obstacle in his way – his wife.

CHAPTER TWENTY-SIX

Sacrificial Rites

D'Onston's wife is a woman of mystery. We know where she came from. We know she once served as personal maid to D'Onston's mother in Hull. We know where she married, and when. And we know that she was still alive in 1886. And there our knowledge ends. Here we need to refer back to Cremers' testimony. She has told us that she knew of the wife's existence only through a chance remark made by D'Onston. It was after this, that Mabel Collins revealed that as far as she knew, the wife had 'disappeared suddenly – vanished completely'. But Cremers drew a very different conclusion. She had questioned D'Onston about his wife, but he had never given a straight answer. Instead he reeled as from an emotional shock. His agitation at that time; his pacing about the room, his throat-cutting gesture; led her to accept that the wife had been killed by him.

Cremers could not have checked on the story; to search she needed D'Onston's full name. But even that name would have yielded nothing. The records are mute. All our searches have failed to find a death certificate for Mrs Stephenson. What we can find,though, are reports in 1887 of the discovery of various parts of a dismembered woman's body in the Thames and the Regent's Canal.

The first find was of a trunk section floating near the Thames ferry landing at Rainham in Essex. These remains were thought to be those of a woman aged about twenty-eight or -nine; later on, the age was revised upwards. This horror of 11 May, was followed by five further finds in June. first came the discovery of a thigh in the Thames, near Temple Steps; then two arms and two legs were fished out of the St Mary's Lock section of the Regent's Canal. The body had been dissected with knife and saw by someone 'having a knowledge of a human body' – this was the conclusion of Dr Edwin Calloway. Although this corpse was never identified, it was the body of a woman who had never been a mother. The head, that might have provided important clues, was never found. So, could this butchered woman have been D'Onston's childless wife; the woman he 'killed' in his mime show?

All we know for certain, on this score, is that D'Onston was very familiar with the Regent's Canal. He had lodged just yards away from it in 1860; then in later years had actually lived near it; and visited two mission houses on the very edges of the canal. This was an ideal dumping spot for D'Onston if he wished to dispose of a dissected corpse. Remember, the canal fed south into the Regent's Dock, which in turn opened up into the Thames itself.

One other fact is worth noting: after these discoveries and the final inquest in August, D'Onston began to describe himself as 'unmarried'. *And this signifies that he knew that his wife was not going to return.* At this point he could afford to be both complacent and blatant, since the investigation into the identity of the body was never taken any further. This was the result of the inquest jury returning a quirky verdict of 'insufficient evidence to show cause of death'.

What we do know for certain is that shortly after his wife's vanishing act, D'Onston changed his life-style and – quite out of character – deserted London. Very strange. Since 1869, he'd been virtually ensnared by London. Even after trips abroad he'd always returned to the capital. It was always his home base; first in Holloway, then in different parts of the East End. Now he turned his back on the old haunts and delights, to take up residence in Brighton, in Black Lion Square, as a boarder at The Cricketer's Inn. There he described himself as 'unmarried', 'single', but never as a 'widower'; though that description would have won him sympathy.

So why did he change? Was it because the secure post at the police orphanage had eluded him. Was this the final blow that led to a massive crisis of confidence? After all, he was forty-five and all his cherished, magical rituals had failed him utterly. Was this enough to impel him to try something stronger, and push him into *advanced* Satanic practices? Were his victims doomed by his infantile need to revenge his lost love?

We now know that serial killers will go to extreme lengths to make their fantasies come true. Careful prior planning is one of the hallmarks of such killers, and in D'Onston's case we now have evidence of his bizarre, calculated moves. We can now show how he engineered a safe bolt-hole for himself right in the heart of Whitechapel.

In 1888 Brighton was renowned as a supreme place for rest-cures in its own right. As the *Penny Illustrated Paper* put it in its 21 January 1888 issue:

Are you suffering from 'the blues', down with 'the dumps', afflicted with 'vapours', neuralgia, rheumatism, pains in the back, or *tic doloreux?* Then, try my prescription! Go in for a Brighton Brightener! Remember that many a time and oft when it's foggy and gloomy in town, the Sun shines gaily in Brighton, chasing away Dull Care, and infusing some of the salubrious sparkle of good champagne into your veins… A Brighton Brightener! Elixir of Life! The dose for longevity and vigour!…

Clearly, an ideal place to rest. But for those wanting special care and comfort Brighton could also offer its outstandingly fine Royal Sussex County Hospital, sited in a place where the fresh country air circulated day and night. A private bed could be secured in these ideal surroundings by anyone, with money. It was the perfect place for someone seeking tranquillity. Given that understanding, consider this strange state of affairs. It is July 1888. D'Onston is living there in Brighton, just minutes from the sea-front, when he suddenly puts on an act that he is suffering from neurosthenia. Now this describes a state of *excitability* and should not be confused with neurasthenia, its very opposite. The treatment for neurosthenia was simple: a light diet, plenty of rest, no stimulants, and *fresh air*. In other words: a rest-cure. It was the perfect condition for a Brighton-based treatment. So in all logic D'Onston should have stayed put; that is, if there *had been* anything wrong with him.

Instead, he left Brighton and chose to go to the London Hospital in Whitechapel, with its grim reputation of pain and death. There, on 26 July 1888 he booked into a private bed, registered as a neurosthenic and began his rest-cure. Illogically, he chose to breathe the acrid, sooty, sulphur-laden air of the East End, for month after month after month. His complaint was certainly faked. The symptoms: excitability, tension, sleeplessness, are easy to assume or induce. And this man, with his medical training, knew a great deal about inducing bodily reactions.

Once inside, with his aristocratic bearing and his private bed, he is privileged and uncircumscribed. He has ample time to prepare. First he needs to make himself 'invisible'. This is easily done, simply by being seen around often and everywhere. At all hours he can be spotted slowly walking the corridors and the grounds; pausing to talk to surgeons, physicians, orderlies, anyone he meets up with. In a short while he is accepted as that nice, mild-mannered man, who is ever restless; who finds it hard to sleep; who paces wearily around in order to become quite fatigued. Nocturnal prowling on his part becomes accepted as unremarkable, even expected; like those nocturnal excursions of the Elephant Man, who was there at the very same time. But, at no point does D'Onston display any energetic movements. His swiftness of foot, his innate agility has to be disguised – at all times.

In 1888 the grounds of the London Hospital were extensive, they were also dotted around with temporary huts and sheds left over from the erecting of a nurses' home and the enlargement of the medical college in 1887. At the side of the west wing was the large House Governor's garden; to the rear was a huge open garden field. Around the perimeter mature trees and bushes abounded. For the most part, simple railings set in low brick walls surrounded the hospital grounds and its college. These could be easily scaled in seconds by anyone with agility and determination. With the greenery as quick cover, entry and exit was an easy matter. This made the hospital an ideal staging-post for D'Onston's series of premeditated killings.

His first killing was staged just two minutes' walk from the hospital entrance. The second was to the north-west of the hospital, but still within easy walking distance. The third was to the south-west of the building, roughly the same distance away as the second. The Mitre Square murder was the one most distant; but for someone in a hurry, still within quick reach of the hospital.

The Kelly murder was in a class of its own. The four others were quick 'taunt and display' killings; Kelly's was meant to be the peak of visual horror, and a leisurely indulgence in rituals of the blackest hate. The butchery was concealed within the privacy of a house, so an exit could be made at any time. No need to rush along back streets to the hospital. The return to base could be taken at a brisk walk. And, as always, the hospital grounds provided plenty of cover for a clean-up, even a change of clothing if needed.

D'Onston's stay at the hospital ended on Friday 7 December 1888, his 'rest-cure' had lasted a remarkable 134 days. But while in the hospital he had written two intriguing pieces: one a letter, the other a newspaper article. These were used as smokescreens, meant to mislead by diverting any suspicion away from him. By being obvious he hoped to be ignored. The letter came first. It was sent by him to the City of London Police on 16 October 1888. It read:

The London Hospital,

> Sir, Having read Sir Charles Warren's Circular in yesterday's papers that 'It is not known That There is any dialect or language in which The word Jews is spelt JUWES.'
>
> I beg to inform you That The word written by the murderer does exist in a European language, Though it was not JUWES.

Try it in script – Thus,

The Juwes. &c

Now place a dot over The Third upstroke (which dot was natural-ly overlooked by lantern light) and we get, plainly The *Juives* which, I need not tell you, is the French word for Jews.

The murderer unconsciously reverted, for a moment, To his native language.

Pardon my presuming to suggest That There are Three parts indu-bitably shown (2 another, *probably*) by the inscription.

1. The man was a Frenchman.

2. He had resided a long time in England To write so correctly; Frenchmen being, notoriously, The Worst linguists in the World.

3. He has frequented The East End for years, to have acquired, as in The sentences written, a purely East End idiom.

4. It is *probable* (not certain) That he is a notorious Jew-hater: Though he *may* only have written it To Throw a false scent.

May I request an acknowledgment That This letter has safely reached you, & That it be preserved until I am well enough to do myself The honour to call upon you personally.

I am Sir,

Yr. Obedt. Servant

Roslyn D'O. Stephenson

PS. I can tell you, from a French book, a use made of the organ in question – 'd'une femme *prostituée*', which has not yet been suggested, if you think it worth while. R.D'O.S.

We can now see that this letter was one of the utmost cunning. He has a need to talk about the murders, but he is taking the precaution of shielding himself from too close a scrutiny. He creates a shield by first giving advance notice of a newspaper piece he has in mind. Then he gives the false impres-sion that he is an invalid, scarcely mobile, who will call upon them when he is 'well enough'. This man has no intention of letting his conceit endan-ger him; his instinct for self-preservation is far too powerful to allow the hunt to centre on him.

The article, he then had in mind, appeared *after* the last victim was cho-sen and despatched. It was the strangest of all the accounts of the day. Its slant was new. But was it more than pure fantasy?

CHAPTER TWENTY-SEVEN

The Veil Lifts

From the comfort of his hospital bed D'Onston had put together the article that had begun to germinate in his mind in October. It appeared on the 1 December 1888, on the front page of W. T. Stead's *Pall Mall Gazette*. It was a masterpiece of deception designed to make the author look both like a genius and a wild extravagant theorist simultaneously. Its lengthy title read: THE WHITECHAPEL DEMON'S NATIONALITY: AND WHY HE COMMITTED THE MURDERS.

In calmly reviewing the whole chain of facts connected with these daring and bloodthirsty atrocities, the first thing which strikes one is the fact that the murderer was kind enough to (so to speak) leave his card with the Mitre-square victim. But this most important clue to his identity, which 'he who runs may read', seems to have baffled the combined intellects of all grades of the police. This admits of no question, because we find in all the journals a note from Sir C. Warren to the effect that 'no language or dialogue is known in which the word "Jews" is spelt "Juwes".'

O! most sapient conclusion! Let us see what *we* can make of the word.

It will be remembered that a chalk inscription (which it is not denied was written by the murderer) was found on the wall in Mitre-square, just above the body of the murdered woman. It ran as follows: 'The Juwes are the men who will not be blamed for nothing', and was evidently intended to throw suspicion on the Jews. This writing was seen by the police by means of artificial light, and was unfortunately obliterated by them before daylight. *Hinc illae lachrymae!*

Why did the murderer spell the word Jews 'Juwes'? Was it that he was an uneducated Englishman who did not know how to spell the word; was he in reality an ignorant Jew, reckless of consequences and glorying in his deeds; or was he a foreigner, well accustomed to the English language, but who in the tremendous hurry of the moment unconsciously wrote the fatal word in his native tongue?

The answers to these three queries, on which the whole matter rests, are easy. Juwes is a much too difficult word for an uneducated man to evolve on the spur of the moment, as any philologist will allow. Any ignorant Jew capable of spelling the rest of the sentence as correctly as he did, would know, certainly, how to spell the name of his own people. Therefore, only the last proposition remains, which we shall now show, in the most conclusive manner, to be the truth.

To critically examine an inscription of this kind, the first thing we naturally do is not to rest satisfied with reading it in print, but to make, as nearly as we can, a facsimile of it in script, thus:-

Juwes

Inspection at once shows us, then, that a *dot* has been overlooked by the constable who copied it, as might easily occur, especially if it were placed at some distance, after the manner of foreigners.

Juives

Therefore we place a dot above the *third* upstroke in the word Juwes, and we find it to be *Juives*, which is the French word for Jews. Strictly Juives and grammatically speaking, of course, it is the feminine form of *Juifs* and means 'Jewesses.' But in practice it will be found that (Frenchmen being notoriously the worst linguists in the world) most Frenchmen who are not either litterateurs or men of science are very inaccurate as to their genders. And almost all the ouvrier and a large majority of the bourgeois class use the feminine where the word should be masculine. Even the Emperor Napoleon III was a great sinner in this respect, as his voluminous correspondence amply shows.

Therefore, it is evident that the native language – or, to be more accurate, the language in which this murderer *thinks* – is French.

The murderer is, therefore, a Frenchman.

It may here be argued that both Swiss and Belgians make French almost their mother tongue; but Flemish is the natural and usual vehicle for the latter, while the idiosyncrasy of both those nationalities is adverse to this class of crime.

On the contrary, in France, the murdering of prostitutes has long been practised, and has been considered to be almost peculiarly a French crime.

Again, the grammatical construction of the sentence under examination is distinctly French in two points – first, in the double negative contained; and, secondly, in the employment of the definite article before the second noun. An Englishman or an American would have said, 'The Jews are men who, &c.' But the murderer followed his native idiom 'Les Juifs sont *des* hommes' in his thoughts, and when putting it into English rendered *des hommes* '*the* men'.

Again, neither Belgians nor Swiss entertain any animosity to the Jews, whereas the hatred of the French proletarian to them is notorious.

The ground for research being thus cleared and narrowed, the next question is, what is the motive? Speculation has been rife, the cries are many; almost every man one meets, who is competent to form an opinion, having a different one.

And in endeavouring to sift a mystery like this one cannot afford to throw aside *any* theory, however extravagant, without careful examination, because the truth might, after all, lie in the most unlikely one.

There seems to be no doubt that the murderer, whether mad or not, had a distinct motive in his mutilations; but one possible theory of that motive has never yet been suggested. In the nineteenth century, with all its enlightenment, it would seem absurd, were it not that superstition dies hard, and some of its votaries do undoubtedly to this day practice unholy rites.

Now, in one of the books by the great modern occultist who wrote under the *nom de plume* of 'Eliphaz Levy', 'Le Dogme et Rituel de la Haute Magie,' we find the most elaborate directions for working magical spells of all kinds. The second volume has a chapter on Necromancy, or black magic, which the author justly denounces as a profanation. Black magic employs the agencies of evil spirits and demons, instead of the beneficent spirits directed by the adepts of *la haute magie.* At the same time he gives the clearest and fullest details of the necessary steps for evocation by this means, and it is in the list of substances prescribed as absolutely necessary to success that we find the

link which joins modern French necromancy with the quest of the
East-end murderer. These substances are in themselves horrible, and
difficult to procure. They can only be obtained by means of the most
appalling crimes, of which murder and mutilation of the dead are the
least heinous. Among them are strips of the skin of a suicide, nails
from a murderer's gallows, candles made from human fat, the head
of a black cat which has been fed forty days on human flesh, the horns
of a goat which has been made the instrument of an infamous capital
crime, and a preparation made from a certain portion of the body of a
harlot. This last point is insisted upon as essential and it was this extraordinary fact that first drew my attention to the possible connection of
the murderer with the black art.

Further, in the practice of evocation the sacrifice of human victims
was a necessary part of the process, and the profanation of the cross and
other emblems usually considered sacred was also enjoined. In this
connection it will be well to remember one most extraordinary and
unparalleled circumstance in the commission of the Whitechapel murders, and a thing which could not by any possibility have been brought
about fortuitously. Leaving out the last murder, committed indoors,
which was most probably not committed by *the* fiend of whom we
speak, we find that the sites of the murders, six in number, form a
perfect cross. That is to say, a line ruled from No. 3 to No. 6, on a
map having the murder sites marked and numbered, passes *exactly*
through Nos. 1 and 2, while the cross arms are accurately formed by a
line from No. 4 to 5. The seventh, or Dorset-street murder, does not
fall within either of these lines, and there is nothing to connect it with
the others except the mutilations. But the mutilations in this latter
case were evidently not made by any one having the practical knowledge of the knife and the position of the respective organs which was
exhibited in the other six cases, and also in the mutilated trunk found
in the new police-buildings, which was probably the first of the series
of murders, and was committed somewhere on the lines of the cross,
the body being removed at the time. Did the murderer, then, design-
ing to offer the mystic number of seven human sacrifices in the form
of a cross – a form which he intended to profane – deliberately pick out
beforehand on a map the places in which he would offer them to his
infernal deity of murder? If not, surely these six *coincidences(?)* are the
most marvellous event of our time.

To those persons to whom this theory may seem somewhat far-
fetched, we would merely remark that the French book referred to

was only published a few years ago; that thousands of copies were sold; that societies have been formed for the study and practice of its teachings and philosophy; and, finally, that within the last twelve months an English edition has been issued. In all things history repeats itself, and the superstitions of yesterday become the creeds of today.

This article was unsigned, attributed only to: 'One Who Thinks He Knows'. Its authorship would have astonished Vittoria Cremers, for *this* was the very same piece that had excited Blavatsky, and her companions so much. This is the piece that they had all wrongly imagined was written by the Earl of Crawford. But it was by D'Onston, who was paid the glorious sum of £4 for it. Four pounds, for an article which is at once a veiled confession and a tantalizing exercise in misdirection! His authorship was partly revealed in an amusing fragment written by W. T. Stead, on 3 December 1888:

> Mr. Arthur Diosy is aggrieved. The ingenious contributor who discovered the nationality of the Whitechapel murderer said that no one had hit upon the suggested necromantic motive. Mr. Diosy says he told the police all about it on Oct 14, which of course is news to everybody else. He also darkly hints that the dates of the crimes have some occult relation to magical astrology. It would be more to the point if Mr. Diosy would tell us where the next murder ought to occur according to the dates of magical astrology.
>
> 'One who Thinks he Knows' – the contributor in question – is an occultist of some experience. When he was a lad of eighteen he studied necromancy under the late Lord Lytton at Alexandria. It would be odd if the mystical lore of the author of 'Zanoni' were to help unearth Jack the Ripper.

Here Stead is slightly confused, since Lytton's Lodge of Alexandria was based in London, not Egypt, but this is of minor importance. This same article also brought to light details of a series of sexual serial murders even more hideous than those recorded in Austin, Texas. These details came in a letter published in *Pall Mall* on 12 December 1888. The writer had seen the reprint of the article in the *Pall Mall Budget* of 6 December 1888, and wrote:

'Jack the Ripper's' Motive

Sir, – Although the anxiety to solve the Whitechapel mystery is, for the nonce, allayed, if not extinct, it may interest students of human nature

to hear of a somewhat similar case in which the murderer, when discovered, was found to be actuated by a less extraordinary motive than
that of solving necromantic problems, attributed to the Whitechapel
monster by the writer of 'Who is the Whitechapel Demon', published
in your issue of the 6th inst. Forty or fifty years ago, my grandfather,
a Portuguese judge at Coviltra, convicted a man for the murder of
sixteen women by stabbing them in the abdomen. For the space of
twelve months the inhabitants of the town had been in a state of wild
panic at the periodical repetition of such hideous and objectless crimes,
as in no case could pillage or lust be ascribed as cause; the victims, in
many cases, being penniless octogenarians. At last the miscreant was
caught *in flagrante delicto,* and on trying him for wilful murder Judge
Joao de Campes received from him the confession that he had done it
solely to enjoy the fun of watching the grimaces the poor women
made in their agony! I have no details of the criminal's *modus operandi,* as it occurred long before my time; I had in fact forgotten this
episode in my grandfather's judicial career until the accounts of the
London ghastly tragedies brought to my mind the conviction that
should the East-end murderer ever be brought to justice, which I do not
anticipate, it will be ascertained that his motive has been either a morbid taste of the very same kind, or an exaggerated longing for notoriety,
coupled with the love of excitement that feeds on perusing the different versions of his deeds, his intentions, and the means he employs
to defeat the combined intellects of the detective administrations of
London, which last feat, be it said, might make anybody a little proud.

Yours faithfully,
Esther Delaforce
9, Courthope-villa, Wimbledon

Esther Delaforce drew some shrewd conclusions in her letter, but it is
doubtful if anyone at the time realized the mocking nature of D'Onston's
article. Indeed its full significance can only be fully grasped today. Only
now are we able to cross-reference his various statements. Only now can
we match his conduct with that of the many other serial killers whose patterns have been assessed and profiled.

What, then does he have to say for himself? What lies behind the taunts?

CHAPTER TWENTY-EIGHT

The Tangled Truth

The *Pall Mall* article shows D'Onston in an arrogant, mocking mood. He sets off to unfold a freshly developed theory and writes as if the Black Magic aspect is something new to him. Yet we now know that he had studied the subject for well over twenty years. Then he rules out English villainy and points the finger at a Frenchman. So what is he is up to?

Behind the smokescreen of words is the simple boast: 'You are deceived by a man devoted to Black Magic; a man who is a linguist; an educated man; a Frenchman'. Had he placed his name to the article, readers would have seen the French connection at once. Had they glimpsed his letter to the City Police they would have known that he was alluding to someone who '...has frequented the East End for years...' Someone who may well have '...written [the message] to throw a false scent'. He is in fact pointing the finger at himself, but in a safe way. By placing absurdities in his account he makes it look like the musings of an inept armchair detective. It ceases to look like the work of an insider. And yet his absurdities are grotesque. He states that the writing on the wall was written '...just above the body of the murdered woman...' None of the papers he read at the time made that blunder. Then he adds in the Tabram killing, strikes the Kelly murder out of the reckoning and fools around by introducing the body 'found in the new police-buildings'. Now these are not his *real* views. We know from Cremers that he gave the true number of murders as five. We know from her that he was adamant that these murders had ended with Kelly. We know further that he insisted that there were no more murders to come. And there speaks *the insider*. All around him people were inflating the figures: seven, nine, twelve, fourteen. But he knew there were five only. We can now recognize that this article was simply the second stage in a planned campaign of misinformation.

The third stage was reached after he left the London Hospital on 7 December 1888. From his hospital bed he had written to Editor Stead and asked for financial assistance to hunt down the Ripper. That was in November. He then made contact with the City police and wrote his notable Whitechapel piece. So he was, on the surface, eager and keen to cash in on the murders. Any good journalist would have been. But on 7 December, at the very time when a new murder could have been expected, D'Onston *left* the East End! Every other journalist stayed put, waiting for the next horror, but not him. On leaving the hospital he moved away from White-chapel and moved to quarters just off St Martin's Lane, north of Trafalgar Square. His new-found indifference to the murder area showed that no further murders were planned – just yet. His actions were exactly those of someone who dealt in certainties.

Once settled into his new rooms, he began to engineer the boldest part of his plan. He decided to add to the confusion and bring matters to a head. This decision may well have been forced on him by an odd story that fellow-journalists were working on at this time. The basic elements of this story involved a letter sent by a patient at a London hospital. The writing was said to resemble that of the original Ripper missives. The sender was a man well acquainted with the East End, with contacts among the rescue and mission workers there. These things, and more, had led to a police interest and a look-out for the man.

Now, this outline description fitted D'Onston easily. His contacts among the mission workers began when he edited sermons for the late Rev. Alex McAuslane; and his handwriting did look similar to that on the two original Ripper items. But though he knew those Ripper pieces were hoaxes, he also knew that many took them seriously. So it was now time to disengage him-self from all danger. Time to make the first move, and deliberately court suspicion. Time to involve himself in a time-wasting charade so that the police would dismiss him completely. Time to meet the police face to face.

His plan was simple. First find a gullible dupe who would take in every lurid tale told him. Talk to him often and vividly enough and let him feel that the talker knew just too much. Such a dupe would fly to the police and unburden himself quite soon. In seeking out such a dupe D'Onston struck good fortune; he met impressionable George Marsh.

Marsh was an unemployed man with dreams of becoming a private detective, but he was no match for D'Onston's cunning. They drank together almost nightly and D'Onston fed him a strange tale about the murders. He said he knew the killer well, and even named him as a Dr Davies. Then he described the techniques used in the murders, and revelled in his descriptions.

But D'Onston knew all about suggestibility and he saw to it that Marsh would soon reject the idea of Davies as the killer. His subterfuge was rewarded. Marsh was swayed by the sheer realism of D'Onston's descriptions and drew his own conclusions; he came to believe that he was talking to the killer himself. Only an 'insider' could have such such a feel for the murders and radiate such certainties about them. This was no overnight conviction, but when it came it was all the stronger for the delay.

D'Onston proved to be an astute psychologist and judge of men. Marsh became so excited by the encounters that within three weeks he went to Scotland Yard and fingered *D'Onston* as the Ripper. This fitted D'Onston's plans exactly. Marsh's statement, dictated to Inspector J. Roots on Christmas Eve 1888, read:

About a month ago at Prince Albert public house, Upper St Martin's Lane, I met a man named Stephenson and casually discussed the murders in Whitechapel with him. From that time to the present I have met him there two or three times a week and we have on each occasion discussed the murders in a confidential manner. He has tried to tell me how I could capture the man if I went his way to work. I simply told him I should go my own way about it and sooner or later I'd have him. I told him I was an amateur detective and that I had been for weeks looking for the culprit. He explained to me how the murders were committed. He said they were committed by a woman-hater after the forthcoming manner:-

The murderer would induce a woman to go up a back street or room and to excite his passion would 'bugger' her and cut her throat at the same time with his right hand, holding on by the left.

He illustrated the action. From his manner I am of the opinion he is the murderer in the first six cases, if not the last one.

Today Stephenson told me that Dr Davies of Houndsditch (I don't know the address although I have been there and could point it out) was the murderer and he wished me to see him. He drew up an agreement to share the reward on the conviction of Dr Davies. I know that agreement is valueless but it secured his handwriting. I made him under the influence of drink thinking that I should get some further statement but in this I failed as he left to see Dr Davies and also to go to Mr Stead of the *Pall Mall Gazette* with an article for which he expected £2. He wrote the article in the *Pall Mall Gazette* in relation to the writing on the wall about Jews. He had £4 for that. I have seen letters from Mr Stead in his possession about it; also a letter from Mr Stead refusing to allow him money to find out the Whitechapel Murderer.

Stephenson has shown me a discharge as a patient from the London Hospital. The name Stephenson is obliterated and that of Davies is marked in red ink. I do not know the date.

Stephenson is now at the common lodging house No. 29 Castle St., St Martin's Lane, WC, and has been there three weeks. His description is: Age 48, Height 5ft 10in, full face, sallow complexion, moustache heavy – mouse coloured – waxed and turned up, hair brown turning grey, eyes sunken. When looking at a stranger generally has an eyeglass. Dress, grey suit and light brown felt hat – all well worn; military appearance: says he has been in 42 battles: well educated.

The agreement he gave me I will leave with you and will render any assistance the Police may require.

Stephenson is not a drunkard: he is what I call a regular soaker – can drink from 8 o'clock in the morning until closing time but keep a clear head.

The 'agreement' referred to by Marsh is a tongue-in-cheek missive scribbled out on a scrap of paper by D'Onston. It reads ' I hereby agree to pay to Dr R. D'O. Stephenson (also known as 'Sudden Death') one half of any or all the rewards or monies received by me on a/c of the conviction of Dr Davies for wilful murder.'

It should be noted that this was one of the rare occasions when D'Onston used his real family name, and he had a good reason for this, since he knew the document would land on the desk of an old friend of his at the Yard. As for the use of the nickname 'Sudden Death', this was a minor stroke of genius. It has no bearing on the murders. It is nothing but a weird card-gambling term along with others like 'Suicide Squeeze' and 'Cannibal Squeeze' and its use simply confirms that, like his mentor Lord Lytton, he was addicted to the card-tables. But by using it on that agreement he made the whole transaction look childish and foolish; like a game of solemn make-believe between two reeling drinkers.

Two days after Marsh made his move, D'Onston went in person to the Yard and wrote out his own lengthy statement implicating the unfortunate Dr Davies:

I beg to draw your attention to the attitude of Dr Morgan Davies of…Houndsditch, E. with respect to these murders. But my suspicions attach to him principally in connection with the last one – committed indoors.

Three weeks ago, I was a patient in the London Hospital, in a private ward…with a Dr Evans, suffering from typhoid, who used to be visited almost nightly by Dr Davies, when the murders were our usual subject of conversation.

Dr Davies always insisted on the fact that the murderer was a man of sexual powers almost effete, which could only be brought into action by some strong stimulus – such as sodomy. He was very positive on this point, that the murderer performed on the women from behind – in fact, *per ano*. At that time he could have had no information, any more than myself, about the fact that the post-mortem examination revealed that semen was found up the woman's rectum, mixed with her faeces.

Many things, which would seem trivial in writing, seemed to me to connect him with the affair – for instance, he is himself a woman-hater. Although a man of powerful frame, &, (according to the lines on his sallow face) of strong sexual passions. He is *supposed*, however, by his inmates, never to touch a woman. One night, when five medicos were present, quietly discussing the subject, & combatting his argument that the murderer did not do these things to obtain specimens of uteri (wombs) but that – in his case – it was the lust of murder developed from sexual lust – a thing not unknown to medicos, he acted (in a way which *fairly terrified* those five doctors) the whole scene. He took a knife, 'buggered' an imaginary woman, cut her throat from behind; then, when she was apparently laid prostrate, ripped and slashed her in all directions in a perfect frenzy.

Previously to this performance I had said: 'After a man had done a thing like this, reaction would take place, & he would collapse, & be taken at once to the police, or would attract the attention of the bystanders by his exhausted condition?' Dr D— said 'NO! he would recover himself when the fit was over & be as calm as a lamb. I will show you!' Then he began his performance. At the end of it he stopped, buttoned up his coat, put on his hat, and walked down the room with the most perfect calmness. Certainly his face was as pale as death, but that was all.

It was only a few days ago, after I was *positively* informed by the Editor of the *Pall Mall Gazette* that the murdered woman last operated on had been sodomized – that I thought – 'How did *he* know?' His acting was the most vivid I ever saw. Henry Irving was a fool to it. Another point. He argued that the murderer did not want specimens of uteri, but grasped them & slashed them & slashed them off in his madness as being *the only hard* substance which met his grasp, when his hands were madly plunging into the abdomen of his victim.

I may say that Dr Davies was for some time House Physician at the London Hospital Whitechapel, that he has lately taken this house in Castle St., Houndsditch; that he has lived in the locality of the murders for some years; & that he professes his intention of going to Australia shortly should he not quickly make a success in his new house.

Roslyn D'O Stephenson

PS I have mentioned this matter to a pseudo-detective named George Marsh of 24 Pratt St., Camden Town NW, with whom I have made an agreement (enclosed herewith) to share any reward which he may derive from my information.

There is no record of the inquiries prompted by this statement, once again the records are incomplete. But, as we have seen, there is nothing sinister in this. What we do know is that no action was taken against Dr Davies. After checking the tale the police most likely concluded that the account was simply drawn from fevered memories brought on by hospital medication. That, naturally, is what they were meant to conclude. But we do learn one important thing from this visit. We discover that Marsh had actually been interviewed by a long-time friend of D'Onston's, Inspector Roots.

This is too much to explain away by a mere coincidence. The Inspector's name must have been brought to Marsh's mind during one of the drinking bouts. By leading Marsh to ask for the right man, D'Onston minimized the difficulties for himself. As Roots' own statement shows, he had a sneaking admiration for the Bohemian journalist; he may well have been one of D'Onston's referees at the time of his Orphanage application. Inspector Roots' report is short but of great interest and value:

> With reference to the statement of Mr George Marsh of 24th inst., regarding the probable association of Dr Davies and Stephenson with the murders in Whitechapel.
>
> I beg to report that Dr Stephenson came here this evening and wrote the attached statement of his suspicions of Dr Morgan Davies, Castle St., Houndsditch; and also left with me his agreement with Marsh as to the reward. I attach it.
>
> When Marsh came here on 24th I was under the impression that Stephenson was a man I had known 20 years. I now find that impression was correct. He is a travelled man of education and ability, a doctor of medicine upon diplomas of Paris & New York: a major from the Italian Army – he fought under Garibaldi: and a newspaper writer. He says

that he wrote the article about Jews in the *Pall Mall Gazette*, that he occasionally writes for that paper, and that he offered his services to Mr Stead to track the murderer. He showed me a letter from Mr Stead, dated Nov. 30 1888, about this and said that the result was that the proprietor declined to engage upon it. He has lead a Bohemian life, drinks very heavily, and always carries drugs to sober him and stave off delirium tremens.

He was an applicant for the Orphanage Secretaryship at the last election.

All these important papers on D'Onston were not unearthed until 1974, when BBC programme-makers were allowed to view many of the then-closed files. But they were just a few sheets among many and were regarded as oddities; their full significance was not realized until I put the first unfettered enquiry on foot. Their dates show that D'Onston made his move just in time, for on 30 December 1888, the *Sunday Times* revealed some of the details of the investigation that had alerted and alarmed D'Onston. As summarized by *Pall Mall*, this story ran:

> …a gentleman who has for some time been engaged in philanthropic work in the East-end recently received a letter, the handwriting of which had previously attracted the attention of the Post-office authorities on account of its similarity to that of the writer of some of the letters signed 'Jack the Ripper'. The police made inquiries, and ascertained that the writer was known to his correspondent as a person intimately acquainted with East-end life, and that he was then a patient in a metropolitan hospital. It is stated that on an inquiry at the hospital it was discovered that the person sought had left without the consent or knowledge of the hospital authorities, but that he has been subsequently seen, and is now under observation. The police are of the opinion that the last five murders were a series, and that the first two were independently perpetrated.

Was the suspect mentioned in that article D'Onston himself? Or were the resemblances purely coincidental? There is no sure answer to those questions, but we do know that D'Onston was taken in for questioning on two occasions. Yet he was more than a match for the police. As we have seen, they were looking for the proverbial madman, not for a quiet-spoken, cultured gentleman, well accustomed to using words to conceal and reveal. He may well have seemed an oddity to them, but never for a moment did he look like a gory knife-man. And yet, had they but read his later articles in *Pall Mall* they would have seen something of his darker side. They would have read the words of someone who openly admitted killing a woman.

CHAPTER TWENTY-NINE

From the Pen of the Ripper

The black year of 1888 ended with some false alarms but no dramatic arrests. For a while D'Onston lay low and provoked no further mischief. Then, in January 1889, he was commissioned to write an article for *Pall Mall*, dealing with the real-life background of Rider Haggard's book *She*. It appeared on 3 January, and in it, he dealt with the magical cults of the West Coast of Africa. In particular he wrote: '..whatever you have read of magical powers – especially those of necromancy – are absolutely possible; absolutely true; absolutely accomplished!'

These words from a complete believer attracted so much interest and correspondence that Stead commissioned a second article, which he ran front page on 15 February 1889. In this new piece D'Onston first amplifies his dramatic views on devil worship:

> …that is, the use of rites, ceremonies, adjurations, and hymns to the powerful and personal spirit of evil, whose favour is obtained by means of orgies which for horror, blasphemy and obscenity cannot have ever been exceeded – if indeed they have ever been equalled, in the history of the world. These things are too utterly horrible even to be hinted at. It is the fashion at present to deny the existence of Satan, Shaitan, Ahrimanes (or whatever you please to call the incarnation of all evil. But all occults, of whatever school, know that everything in Nature has its counterpart, that you cannot have light without shadow, heat without cold, good without evil, nor yet a personal Deity without an equally personal evil principle.

Later in this article he describes the amazing powers of a malevolent woman witch-doctor in the Cameroons, who imprisoned him. Then he claims that he eliminated her; that he was the means '…not only of her death, but of her absolute annihilation'.

How he killed the woman is not clear. Yet the *manner* of her death is of small account. What is of importance is his cold-blooded recording of the deed, and the fact that he revelled in it. Few normal men would have boasted of such a deed *in print*, but this was a man without guilt or remorse.

His confession to killing a woman was made in such a casual fashion that its impact was smothered. But this was his style. This is what he wanted. Think back to his revelations to Cremers. Remember how he spoke of his brutalities in America, and his butchery in Italy. Everything, then, was delivered in a superior throw-away manner, hiding all signs of any gloating pleasure.

This is exactly how he revealed the killing in his article. There he dismissed his guilt by arguing that the witch-doctor was intent on killing him. Her death then and her 'absolute annihilation' was a necessary evil. So, with a single master-stroke he justified his actions, and satisfied his burning drive to confess and savour his crimes. All this without one word of regret; a man without a soul.

Since no reader protested against his presentation, it seems that his tactic worked. But for us, this confession further illuminates his character. It is a public affirmation that he *was* prepared to kill a woman any time it suited his interests, and without pangs of conscience.

Later, in November 1890, another of his articles on 'African Magic' appeared in *Lucifer,* a magazine meant for a quite restricted readership. This encouraged D'Onston to open up in a bolder way for in his piece he spells out the differences between White and Black Magic. his words apply not just to Africa, but universally; in particular they embrace the Whitechapel killings, for he states:

> ...the necromancer must outrage and degrade human nature in every way conceivable. The very least of the crimes necessary for him (or her) to commit to attain the power sought is actual murder, by which the human victim essential to the sacrifice is provided...Yet, though the price is awful, horrible, unutterable, the power is real. There is no possibility of mistake about that.

Murder to gain power; this is the message straight from the pen of a man steeped in the traditions of Black Magic. But these are the ideas he had nursed for years; the very ideas that had fired the sexual lusts behind his killings. For ultimately, all lust-murder is an exercise of supreme merciless power. But whatever dynamic powers he sought to draw on 1888, they had failed him totally in the year following the murders. 1889 began for him on a hateful note. On 5 January his father died and left him nothing at all; the hate he had felt for his father had been returned with full bitterness.

Then, on Monday 13 May, D'Onston was taken into the London Hospital seriously ill, suffering from an acute bout of 'chloralism'; not surprising for a man who had pushed himself to the limits. Chloralism is a paralysed state of the system brought on by the immoderate or prolonged use of chloral hydrate. This drug is little used today in medicine, though it is still slyly introduced into drinks in the underworld; in fact, it is the basis of 'knockout drops' or 'Mickey Finns'. Used in large and repeated doses it causes delirium, hallucinations, and a state of coma which can lead to cardiac failure.

At the time of his collapse D'Onston was back in the East End. He had moved into the headquarters of the London Cottage Mission in Burdett Road. What special role he played there is unknown. What we do know is that his need for choral hydrate shows that sleep had deserted him. Now the black pit of despondency had opened up. All the hideous killings had taken their toll. Nothing had been gained but wild excitements and tortured memories. And there he was, a bleak nonentity, with his funds draining away and all his dreams of grandeur vanishing. It was then he reached his lowest point ever. Weak and demoralized, he was now incapable of even imagining a new autumn of terror.

It was a grim irony, that the London Hospital, once the nerve-centre of his triumphs and ruthless plans, now became a cold, clinical refuge for his exhausted mind and body. One event only was to brighten up his seventy-four dreary days spent there; it was a totally unexpected and glowing letter written by Mabel Collins. She was so excited by his African reminiscences that she now ached to meet the author. A meeting was arranged the moment D'Onston was fit. Then the two met as equals, and soon blended as lovers.

It was a fateful encounter for Collins. Early hero-worship and elation died fast. Euphoria was quickly overshadowed by remorseless despair as her 'great magician' revealed himself as rotten to the core. Stark fear then gripped her. A sadistic killer had ensnared her and enforced her silence. A blind hunger for love had bedded her down with a ghoul.

At the end of the affair and the break-up of the cosmetic business, D'Onston stayed on for a while in Upper Baker Street. He was no longer a kept man and had to fall back on his own resources. It was at this time he began using his full name and his New York medical diploma; whether this implies some type of consultancy is uncertain. His shadowy lifestyle still veils our understanding. But a curious and notable coincidence occurred at this time.

Going south from his Baker Street rooms D'Onston would have reached the doorstep of 14 York Place within minutes. This was the home of the flamboyant Dr Forbes Winslow, the man *totally* convinced that he knew who the Ripper was. It is bizarre to realize that these two men may well have met each other; and may even have talked about the murders. How the Ripper would have enjoyed egging the 'Ripper expert' on to new heights of verbal folly; for D'Onston would have recognized the doctor at once. Indeed every London journalist knew the vocal and dogmatic doctor. His bombastic words were a treasure for them. So the chance to taunt the pompous poseur would have proved irresistible.

But how long did D'Onston stay in Baker Street? No answer is yet possible. The missing five years baffle us. There is not the slightest trace of the man until 1896. In that year we learn for the first time that Cremers and Collins were not alone in thinking of him as the Ripper. In his quarterly magazine *Borderland*, W. T. Stead introduced some articles by D'Onston with these telling words:

> He has been known to me for many years. He is one of the most remarkable persons I ever met. For more than a year I was under the impression that he was the veritable Jack the Ripper; an impression which I believe was shared by the police, who at least once had him under arrest; although, as he completely satisfied them, they liberated him without bringing him into court.

Note those words well. Dwell on them. They prove that D'Onston had lowered his guard with Stead and said a little too much. Stead, in turn, began to probe. He must then have uncovered things that showed D'Onston quite capable of murder. And not just ordinary murder, but the grotesque knife-killings that were the hallmark of the Ripper. This conviction stayed with Stead for over a year and made such a deep impression, that eight years later he felt impelled to record it.

What caused Stead to abandon his view? Since no one ever asked him, we have to guess at the reason and it probably stems from the idea that the Ripper went on killing *after* 1888. This belief was held by many newspapers and even Police Commissioner Monro was uncertain.

At first, Monro viewed the McKenzie murder, of July 1889, as 'identical with the notorious Jack the Ripper of last year'. Two months later came the finding of the body under the railway arch, and again Monro speculated that it might be another Ripper victim. Given this confusion, it is likely that D'Onston had an unbreakable alibi for the time of one of the pseudo-Ripper events, and that was enough for Stead to back down.

But is there nothing in D'Onston's actions and claims that give us legitimate cause for doubt? To answer that we need to look at some of the problems that appear to be raised by his statement made on Boxing Day 1888 at Scotland Yard. In that statement we find two unexpected claims.

These appear where D'Onston comments on the Kelly murder. He first writes that a post-mortem examination had '...revealed that semen was found up the woman's rectum...' That seems a clear enough statement by any standards. One woman, Kelly, had been shown to have been sodomized. At the end of this document, he reinforces this initial claim by elaborating further, and giving his source: 'It was only a few days ago...I was positively informed by the Editor of the *Pall Mall Gazette* that the murdered woman *last* operated on had been sodomized...' Again, another clear reference to Kelly, the last to die, and a clear reference to W. T. Stead.

It is hard to see how these two extremely clear statements could ever be misunderstood, yet they have been. Faulty research by the three authors of *The Jack the Ripper A to Z* has lead them into error. In their book they offer *misreadings* of the original, unambiguous text. They alter D'Onston's meaning and make him seem to refer to a number of victims, instead of just one. Then having done that, they are able to draw false conclusions, leading to the assumption that D'Onston is quite unreliable.

Consider their page 276. It says this of D'Onston: '...he learned (erroneously) from W. T. Stead that the Ripper habitually sodomized his victims'. This misrepresents the basic texts. They appear in full, here, in my book. Anyone can immediately check and see what Stead actually said; that he spoke only of one victim.

The same basic error is repeated in substance on their page 274, which says: 'Stead...accepted articles on the case from Robert D'Onston Stephenson, according to whom he also supplied the information that the victims had been sodomized.'

This misrepresentation is further compounded by a passage on page 64: '...he [D'Onston] learned from W. T. Stead that medical reports showed that the victims had been sodomized (they didn't)...'

If the D'Onston statement is now re-read with due care, it will be seen at once that his claim about Stead is tied to ONE case, and one case only, namely '...the last one – committed indoors...the murdered woman last operated on...' In other words he is talking about Kelly and Kelly alone. Note that.

Note further, that at no point does D'Onston make mention of any 'medical reports', in truth he does not even speak of a single report; he does no more than state that Stead had informed him that Kelly had been sodomized, and that this was a discovery made in the course of the post-mortem examination.

Now a post-mortem examination can lead to a written report or reports, but it can also involve *discussion* of facts never committed to writing. And it can result in leaks to trusted or valued outsiders. Such leaks can involve information not generally known. Stead had many contacts who gave him this type of information with regularity. This is well known.

Having established that, reconsider Bond's written report on Mary Jane Kelly. No mention of sodomy, certainly, but equally no mention of vaginal intercourse, and no mention of a search for any 'signs of connection'. There is not even a mention of seminal fluids anywhere. But in all logic, sexual activity of one kind or another would have taken place. So the very absence of all mention of sexual traces means that Bond chose not to put his findings in writing. He had the latitude to do this. There were no rigid rules governing the writing of such reports – they could be curt, or highly elaborate and still be acceptable. The contrast between Brown's detailed report on Eddowes, and Bond's terse report on Kelly illustrates this perfectly.

Let this be emphasized: Bond's report neither confirms nor negates the information said to have been known to Stead. On this score his report is neutral. On the other hand, though, Bond's very silence makes it possible, indeed highly probable, that he would have extra knowledge to share with confidants.

I accept D'Onston's claim relating to Stead for the very good reason that Stead was the last person that D'Onston could afford to offend. He could not invoke Stead's name in connection with *any* bogus statements, since Stead was his sole source of income and prestige at the time. Once Stead was drawn in, D'Onston had no control over subsequent developments. So his confidence in naming Stead has to rest on firm ground; there would be no comeback. And in fact there wasn't. Far from it. Following the statement and enquiries by the Yard came two good commissions from Stead – a vote of confidence if anything ever was.

As for D'Onston's claim that the victims were 'performed on from behind – in fact, *per ano*' – in police terms, this is a perfectly acceptable *modus operandi* with nothing in the records to refute it. We need to remember that the sexual rituals will vary in degrees, even if they are staged along similar patterns with predetermined sequences. An act of penetration alone, without orgasm, can count as the symbolic exercise of power. Withdrawal; delayed gratification; onanism proper; all these things can be present at one time and absent at another. That is why I regard Dr Brown's report on Eddowes as equally neutral on the issue of sodomy.

Unlike Bond, Dr Brown did write about his *sexual* findings and stated that he found no traces of recent connection or secretion of any kind on the thighs. Yet, even if he had made such a probe, he would still be in the dark if no semen had been ejected. So 'neutral' is the only sound and just verdict possible.

Having disposed of those meritless objections, what else do we need to clarify? One of the obvious puzzles seems to be the clash between his article with its description of the killings as purely ritual murders, pre-planned to profane the cross; and his later contention when speaking to Marsh, Inspector Roots, and Cremers, that the prime motive was sexual. But these two explanations in fact, harmonize with each other, as we shall see.

D'Onston knew full well that the driving force behind his crude rites and beliefs was a warped sexual impulse. You have only to study the numerous works on magic to see that all sexual yearnings and fears are drawn on repeatedly. Indeed, in the hands of Aleister Crowley magical rites became synonymous with prolonged sexual activities of all types, from sodomy to bestiality.

If we reconsider D'Onston's explanation of 1 December we see that it stresses the ritualistic nature of the murders, with the murder-sites marking a cross. Yet in his Scotland Yard statement of 28 December, when he involved 'Dr Davies', the sexual element alone is stressed. At first sight this may seem contradictory, but in fact we are being shown two halves of the same story. This is confirmed beyond doubt by D'Onston's explanation to Cremers, when he seized her from behind and terrified her. He first stated that the doctor's drives were sexual, then he went on to include the ritualistic element, saying:

> He [the doctor] told me that he always selected the place where he intended to murder the women… It was for a very special reason, Vittoria, which you would not understand. He took the Whitechapel Road as a sort of base for his operations, and made several journeys before deciding on the spots best suited to fit in with his scheme of things. Then, having got his victims to these particular places, he manoeuvred to get behind them.

In playing his cruel game of words with Cremers, D'Onston was quite emphatic about the sexual aspects of the murders; so much so that Cremers guessed D'Onston was talking about himself. But even so, he was deliberately evasive about the rituals involved in them.

Unlike Cremers, we have read all of D'Onston's writings, so with hindsight we know that the 'very special reason' mentioned by D'Onston is identical with the ritualistic profaning of the cross detailed in his December piece. His four prime victims were chosen to mark the points of a giant cross thrown across Whitechapel. Let no one balk at the idea of an imaginary cross; millions of Christians create them every day.

CHAPTER THIRTY

This Man Dodged the Noose

We are now in a position to bring together all that we know about D'Onston and show that his actions and words condemn him utterly. This man is no casual observer at the fringes of the mystery. This man is at the *very heart* of the mystery.

That he was callous, cold blooded, unmoved by human suffering has been proved beyond doubt. Not a single line written by him speaks of love for humanity. Evil and hate and the macabre were always present in his works, for that was the man.

We know for certain that he slaughtered as a soldier while still impressionable. His licence to slash through flesh and bone, to disembowel, to behead with a sabre stroke, gave him a taste for killing that festered within him. His medical butchery provided practical lessons in anatomy, made him indifferent towards suffering and developed his fast, crude knifework.

His complex, bitter-sweet involvement with a prostitute left him with a raw hatred of all other prostitutes; while his fanatical obsession with Black Magic interlocked with his sexual passions and created perverted drives. So perverted that when they peaked, they led to his carefully planned serial sexual murders. Such careful, even meticulous, planning is one of the essential features of most sexual serial murderers. But what of the other essential features?

Comparing D'Onston with modern serial killers is both revealing and chilling. Here was a fastidious man bathing every day, brushing his clothes to the point of wear; and yet he preserved those huge black ties in a stained and encrusted condition. These two attitudes don't make sense. They become understandable *only* when we realize that the keeping of fetishistic mementos of killings is one of the *hallmarks* of sexual serial killers. And remember that he spoke of the ties ages before Cremers found that they still existed. Joel Norris has drawn attention to both aspects of such compulsive behaviour, saying:

Serial killers and potential serial killers have deeply compulsive personalities, and the compulsivity is manifested in more than one or two ways at a time. Several of the killers researched…had compulsivity concerning their physical appearance. Bobby Joe Long took several showers a day, sometimes as many as six, during most of his adult life even before the motorcycle accident… Carlton Gray was also a compulsive showerer. Leonard Lake also had a compulsivity about being neat and clean around the home, according to his ex-wife Cricket Balazs, who reported that the two often argued about her cleanliness. As part of his murder ritual, he forced his victims to take showers prior to their rape and eventual murder.

Many serial killers are also compulsive record-keepers. They maintain scrapbooks and organized memorabilia concerning the killings as well as preserving parts of their victims' bodies or clothing. This pattern is so common among the killers that some homicide detectives feel that the discovery of souvenirs is a high-priority piece of evidence during the investigation. Among the items of memorabilia catalogued by the serial killers in our study were scrapbooks with press clippings of the murders, press clippings of other or similar serial killings, books on psychology and deviant behaviour, books on people who suffered from multiple personalities and manifested violent criminal behaviour, biographies of Hitler and other mass murderers, personal items or body parts of the victims. These are especially indicative of the serial murderer syndrome because the taking of a victim's body part is associated with the ritualistic fantasy and it becomes a totem. Among the items catalogued were teeth, fingers, toes, nipples, breasts and penises. Clothing and underwear were also collected as were snippets of hair, barrettes, and articles of decoration that the victims wore.

In some cases, killers have preserved whole sections of their victim's bodies, such as legs, trunks, and torsos. Edmund Kemper, for example, murdered his mother and kept her head… Ed Gein kept his mother's cadaver, which he had amateurishly embalmed on the property for many years… He also made lampshades out of the skins of his victims and wove bracelets out of their hair.

Did D'Onston preserve any of the body parts he took away with him? This would have been quite in keeping with his personality. Those preserved ties, though, were tangible enough and significant enough. They count as the 'high priority' type of evidence that Joel Norris draws attention to.

D'Onston's actions in courting the attention of the police are also mirrored in many modern cases. Edmund Kemper, for one, hung out at a bar near his local Court House and made friends with the policemen using it. By talking to the officers about the unsolved murders (*his* murders), he came to be looked on as a friendly nuisance. 'It was deliberate,' said Kemper. 'Friendly nuisances are dismissed.' How right he was!

FBI profiler Robert Ressler has summed up this type of post-crime behaviour as something, '…which in some cases can be quite important, as some offenders attempt to inject themselves into the investigation of the murder, or otherwise keep in touch with the crime in order to continue the fantasy that started it'.

On the same theme, Patricia Cornwell has this to add:

> This type of killer is frequently fascinated by police work and may even emulate cops…classic postoffense behavior is to become involved in the investigation. He wants to help the police, to offer insights and suggestions, and assist rescue teams in their search for a body he dumped in the woods somewhere. He's the kind of guy who wouldn't think twice about hanging about at the Fraternal Order of Police lounge bar clacking beer mugs with the off-duty cops.

This brings strongly to mind D'Onston's appeal to Stead asking for funds to 'hunt the Ripper'; his letter of 'help' to the City Police sent from his hospital ward; and his 'Dr Davies' statement to Inspector Roots of the Yard, a police officer he'd known for almost twenty years. This is exactly the type of behaviour logged by the FBI.

Even occult trappings are linked with some of the modern serial killers profiled by the FBI. Few of these moderns show the same intense involvement that we find in D'Onston, but the raw basics are there.

Richard Ramirez, feared as the 'The Night Stalker', and murderer of thirteen people, left a satanic pentagram sketch at the scene of several of his crimes. The still-unknown killer who used the name 'Zodiac', signed some of his taunting letters with a circle overlaid with a cross, an astrological symbol, tied in with his killings.

But D'Onston was a creature of a different time and culture, so we should not look for exact correspondences and we should remember that profiling remains an art and not a science. Even so, everything learned from the FBI studies, points to this man, and this man only. Indeed, everything we have considered so far unites D'Onston's name with these murders; nothing diverges. And everything we know about him fits in perfectly with my master profile. A profile drawn up long before D'Onston was ever considered seriously.

When we look back at his youth in Hull we see the beginning of a pattern. His involvement with the sordid world of the dockside prostitutes showed him their weaknesses. In later years, this gave him an edge. He could lull the Whitechapel drabs into a false sense of security with a few chosen words.

Apart from that, there was nothing in his bearing or manner to raise the slightest sense of alarm. On the contrary, we know for certain that he was a quiet-moving, quiet-spoken man, of unassuming appearance.

But there was a hidden side. Behind that quiet facade lurked 'the quickness of eye and foot of an old swordsman', a fighter with an iron-willed command of his emotions, and a man with a military sense of order.

Of his capacity to scheme and organize, there are no doubts. He 'possessed a cool, logical brain and iron nerve'. With the geography of Whitechapel etched into his memory, he planned all his moves with military precision.

Few people have ever pictured the Ripper in this way. The vacant or slobbering madman has dominated thoughts for far too long. Yet, over twenty-eight years ago, long before the Scotland Yard material on D'Onston came to light, the American author, Tom Cullen gave this surprisingly accurate picture of the Ripper:

> ...he undoubtedly was quiet-spoken, with nothing in his looks or manner to attract attention, let alone to raise alarm... Here was someone who knew how to approach prostitutes without arousing their suspicion, who could talk their language, catch them off guard. And it should be remembered that the whores who worked in Whitechapel were in a state bordering on hysteria... He had studied the terrain as a general might study a situation map.

Without knowing it, Cullen has described D'Onston incisively.

Until recently, the full facts of D'Onston's life remained elusive. Now the essential records have given up their secrets, the case against D'Onston is so compelling that we can say with certainty that he was the killer.

If we take the many-stranded case against him step-by-step, then concentrate on the periods just before and after the murders, we can see that his every move, his every statement written or spoken brands him as *the insider*.

When we summarize his life we can see that the seeds of destruction were sown at an early stage.

In his teens, the magical teachings provided by Lord Lytton gave him warped dreams of glory.

The brutal conflict in Italy gave his cruel streak a free rein.

Back home, the end of his sole love affair killed all tenderness within him.

The death of prostitute Ada-Louise fuelled his hatred of the harlotry that had doomed his lover's life.

His family cut him off from their money and influence. In revenge he married his mother's maid and confirmed himself as an outcast.

His megalomania grew. His obsession with magic convinced him that he could elevate his status and astonish the world.

Yet greatness eluded him. His thoughts became more compulsive and corrosive. Even the extremes of Black Magic became inviting. Only his wife stood in the way, but not for long.

In 1887, his wife 'vanished' without trace. Had he murdered her? He implied that he had. So was it *her* death that finally triggered off the spate of other deaths in Whitechapel?

With his wife eliminated, he posed as single, and feigning illness returned to Whitechapel. There in his ideal hospital retreat, he lay within easy reach of each planned murder-site. And then the murders began.

D'Onston needed no nickname, he killed anonymously. While the world was convinced and horrified by the 'Jack the Ripper' letter and postcard, he completely ignored them. They were not from his pen. They were nothing but empty hoaxes.

When he did write, it was simply to inject himself into the inquiry. This tactic began even before the last murder was staged. Letters to Stead and the City Police began the charade. Then followed his infamous Calvary Cross article of December.

Of all the journalists he was the only one to *insist* that the notorious writing on the wall had used the word 'Juwes' and had used an eccentric grammar. 'This points to a Frenchman', D'Onston teased.

But D'Onston always knew more than the other involved journalists. He even turned his back on Whitechapel, and left at the very time when all the other newsmen remained, certain that the killer would strike again. But he knew better and his colleagues waited in vain.

He was adamant that the killings were the *sexually* inspired deeds of a sophisticated man, never the work of a madman. At that time, only the Ripper himself could affirm that with such certainty.

He said that there would be no more Ripper murders; and there were none. Only the killer himself could speak with such authority.

With the same authority he told Cremers that the murders were five in number, and five only. In 1890 no one except the killer knew that; and for many years to come, right up until the 1960s, few people would even guess that the number was so low.

After confessing his guilt to Mabel Collins, he silenced her successfully with potent Satanic threats. He tongue-tied the only person able to denounce him.

At Scotland Yard he toyed with the police. Having drawn attention to himself, he deflected suspicion by issuing statements that looked wildly extravagant. He was easy to dismiss.

But in the long run, he escaped the police simply because they were blind to the true nature of his killer-impulses. Yet others did see through to the terrifying evil within him. We have their testimony.

Though D'Onston dodged the noose he failed to silence the voice of condemnation within himself. Remember his words: '...you cannot have...a personal Deity without an equally personal evil principle'? Now these words came home to him in a poignant way. He had embraced the evil principle, but like so many other transgressors he grew to want a form of absolution. Like Saul on the road to Damascus he experienced the anguish and relief of religious conversion.

He was not the first killer to be moved in this way. Prison records are full of accounts of such 'brands plucked from the burning'. In his case he would have been well aware of the tremendous promises made by the clerics who surrounded him. Promises that offered redemption even to the lowest of all. Did he heed these famous words of Dr Spurgeon?

> There is no sort of a man, there is no abortion of mankind, no demon in human shape, that Christ's blood cannot wash. Hell may have sought to make a paragon of iniquity, it may have striven to put sin and sin together, till it has made a monster abhorred even of mankind; but the blood of Christ can transform that monster... *No* case can exceed its virtue, be it ever so black or vile.

Once converted, this man, whose writings had never echoed a single Christian sentiment, now devoted himself to the strangest of all tasks.

For years he toiled away at a slim volume of atonement. It was a scholarly study of the Holy Gospels as they existed in the second century. Increasingly troubled by ill-health, he pored over hundreds of ancient and modern texts in many tongues and in 1904 finally completed his only book: *The Patristic Gospels*. It was published by Grant Richards, and in its foreword D'Onston wrote this of his years of work: '...most of this time has been one long fight against pain and paralysis; and nothing but the undeniable aid of the Holy Spirit could have enabled them to have been completed single-handed, and without assistance whatever from anyone.'

His book was hardly a best-seller, but it was never meant to be more than a convert's penance, and soon after it appeared, D'Onston became a man of mystery once more. He simply *vanished* without trace. Despite repeated searches no death certificate can be found within the British Isles or anywhere else. No memoirs or letters tell us how he survived, how long he lived, or how he met his end.

The last person known to have had contact with him was his publisher, Grant Richards, who remembered him well as:

> A weird uncanny creature who would come into the office and sit in silence without uttering a word until I could see him. When he was shown in he would scarcely open his mouth beyond asking for an advance of payment on his book. I felt sure D'Onston was not his real name. He was a quiet, calculating sort of fellow, nerveless and with a calm that nothing would disturb, I should imagine.

And that was almost everything that his publisher had to say, except for one passing thought: at one time D'Onston had spoken of moving to Paris. Paris; the place of his student days; the venue of his fateful meeting with Lord Lytton's son. The city that had a special allure unmatched in all Europe.

Does Paris, then, hold the secret of D'Onston's last days? Did he find a retreat there, teaching English from the comfort of an armchair? To these questions there are still no answers, so my original conclusion still stands:

'We may not know how and when D'Onston died, but this much is certain: the Ripper died the moment D'Onston was born again.'

Bogus Claims, Lamentable Errors

No serious study of the D'Onston saga can avoid dealing with the handful of writings which distort the story – either through ignorance, muddle or sheer lack of integrity. First of these spurious accounts is a newspaper story which ran in the *East Anglian Daily Times* on 30 November 1929:

JACK THE RIPPER: ANOTHER VERSION OF THE MYSTERY
BY PIERRE GIROUARD (LATE PARIS POLICE)

The 'Jack the Ripper' mysteries at present occupying the attention of the German police have naturally revived interest in other crimes of this character.

A maniac with similar tendencies to that apparently possessed by this German 'Jack the Ripper' might arise in any country. It so happened that, a few years ago, when I was on a visit, a non-professional visit to London, I met the Baroness K—, a very clever and well-educated woman who bears a well-known Continental title.

We talked of many things and gradually the conversation led to superstition, sorcery, theosophy and gradually up to the question of the ancient wisdom, Black and White Magic.

I give here the story she told me.

At the time of the Ripper outrages, there lived a doctor in the Harrow Road. He had been disbarred from practice because of some malfeasance or other, but he earned a good livelihood by selling perfumes, rare perfumes, and in giving lectures on Occultism and allied subjects to a number of rich women who were 'dabbling in the Occult', as the expression ran in those days.

He was undoubtedly rather insane but brilliantly clever. One day, the Baroness asked him if he had ever been married and he was strangely aroused; stalked up and down his consulting-room and then made the motion of cutting his throat, emitting a strange gurgle at the same time.

There was a room in his house where no one was allowed, but the Baroness, young and inquisitive, managed to get herself a key made and when the doctor was out one afternoon, opened the door of the forbidden room with the purchased complicity of one of the servants.

She opened the drawers of the wardrobe and, to her horror, discovered a number of ties of the so-called 'Latin Quarter' variety, all maculated with blood.

She shrank back, appalled; locked the door hastily and left the house.

She reported her discovery to the society of which she was a member, or rather to the chiefs of this society whose address you will not find in any telephone directory, and which has been disbanded since, but whose members probably belong to other organizations.

They took steps to deal with the doctor, for they understood just how guilty he was.

He was sent away to the United States, where it is possible that he is still living in a nursing home, though George Dougherty, formerly of Pinkerton's agency, and later of New York Municipal Police, stated that the man finished up in a New York hospital not so long ago and confessed his guilt.

The wretched murderer had become obsessed with a dangerous form of madness. He wished to perpetrate certain heathen rituals, and in order to do this, he had to make what amounted to a human sacrifice.

His unfortunate victims were all slain in the same fashion.

Now, after the war, a Jew of the East End of London was accused and found guilty of slaying his own daughter in the foul manner of Jack the Ripper.

He was found guilty and duly hanged, and this is one of the rare occasions that the Jewish community in England did not ask for a commutation of the sentence.

Jack the Ripper: Dr. H… was a victim of studies which should not be permitted.

Personally, I think that the Baroness's tale is perfectly true. The CID story is that the murderer committed suicide and that his body was found in the Thames, but that may have been put out simply to allay public alarm.

The police cannot always make public what they know and what they do not know.

If Scotland Yard had been given a little more rope in the time of the outrages, I have no doubt that they would have narrowed down their investigations and ultimately caught the guilty party.

The Dusseldorf murders present rather different phases to the Ripper crimes, yet they may be inspired by the same maniacal motives.

Girouard's article is a classic example of misremembered details mixed in with unrelated stories. It is a dire warning that policemen can have memories that are just as bad as those owned by the worst scatterbrains. Compare this concoction with Cremers' memoirs and a number of the absurdities become obvious. What may not be obvious, though, is that the references to the man in the New York hospital is in fact a tale about someone completely unconnected with D'Onston and his circle. It was told about a Norwegian seaman called Fogelma; a deluded man who had convinced himself that he was the Ripper and confessed 'his crimes' before dying. The absurdities about the 'secret society' derive from the fact that at one time Cremers had worked for Anthony Comstock's Society for the Suppression of Vice in New York. This society employed secret agents who conducted surveillance operations; and other underground agents who specialized in entrapment. In the fight against drugs, prostitution and 'pornography', such methods were considered justified.

Since Girouard has intermixed the Fogelma story with Cremers' reminiscences, I include it at this point. In one form or another it was circulating from 1902 onwards then it was resurrected as a response to William Le Queux's 'Russian Ripper' fabrication. Girouard probably read the story at that time (1923) and talked to Cremers about it. In a few years he had hopelessly dovetailed these disparate accounts together, as his column of 1929 proves. In Britain Fogelma featured in the following story from *Empire News* of 23 October, 1923:

NEW STORY OF 'JACK THE RIPPER'
RASPUTIN DOCUMENT CHALLENGED
SPECIAL TO 'EMPIRE NEWS'

In his book, 'Things I Know', published this week – see page eight – Mr. William Le Queux claims to have revealed the actual identity of Jack the Ripper. He cites a Rasputin manuscript to the effect that the amazing criminal who terrorized London was a mad Russian doctor sent here by the Secret Police to annoy and baffle Scotland Yard.

He gives the name of this doctor as Alexander Pedachenko, who, when in London, lived in Westmorland-road, Walworth. The 'revelation' has opened up controversy, and it can be said that the evidence in favour of the Russian doctor theory is not convincingly strong. The theory is directly challenged by an *Empire News* student of criminology, who writes:

'Every head of police knows that Jack the Ripper died in Morris Plains Lunatic Asylum in 1902.

'He was sent there from Jersey City in 1899, and was, for a time, employed in the infirmary of the institution. He was not a "permanent"; he had fits of insanity, and I, who knew him as a patient, gave information to the Mulberry-street authorities concerning the patient's identity.

'He was not "wanted" in the United States, so the Detective Department of New York took no steps in the matter. A letter, giving the facts of the case, was sent to Scotland Yard, and as nothing further was heard of the matter it was allowed to lapse.

'The man was not a Russian. He was a native of Norway and had no knowledge of surgery. He was just a simple sailor suffering from an incurable and terrible disease.

'During the three months before his death two women called to see him. One was known to the patient as Olga Storsjan, and the other – who said she was his sister – gave her name as Helen Fogelma.

'As Fogelma the patient was entered in our books. He was subject to fits of terrible depression, and before his death became a fearful coward.

'He had all the weird superstition of his race, and on one occasion I heard him scream out in the night, calling upon God to have mercy upon his soul.

'But during the intervals when his brain worked he muttered of scenes and incidents that connected him clearly with the atrocious crimes of 1888.

'His sister, to whom I mentioned these muttered facts, became fearful for his life, but when I assured her that, being now certified as a lunatic, he was immune from the death penalty, she told me that he had done some terrible things in London.

'She showed me cutting(s) from the Press of New York and from the London papers. These she had found in the trunk of her brother, who after he landed in New York lived with her at 324, East 39th-street.

'Many of the passages were underscored, and marginal notes, in sarcastic vein, gave an insight into the working of the madman's brain.

'His sister told me that in his native town of Arendal he was known as a good-living youngster. His passion was for the sea, and he came to London with no idea of staying there.

'Then, for a year or so, she lost sight of her brother, and heard no more of him until in 1898 he came to her and the other girl, both of whom had come to New York to seek a living.

'When he appeared in their flat at the above address, the girls did not know him. He was worn to a skeleton, and in rags. They kept him for some months, and all the time he had to spare he would read over and over again the cuttings relating to the Ripper crimes.

'Olga Storsjan was the old-time sweetheart of this awful wreck of a man, and soon after his coming to their flat she decided to leave it. She went to Jersey City, but the man followed her, and it was upon her information to the police that he was arrested and committed to the asylum.

'Before he died this man sent for the Rev. J. Miosen, the pastor of a Nestorien church in New York. To him the dying man told enough to connect him with the crimes committed in London.

'Three letters found in his tin trunk were copied, and one of these is in answer to a letter to one Carol Mackonvitch. In it he makes mention of a great necessity to leave England, and the money appears to have been supplied by the man Carol.

'Against this theory, Sir Melville Macnaghten, Chief of the CID at the time, says in his memoirs:-

'"I incline to the belief that the individual who held up London in terror resided with his own people; that he absented himself at certain times, and that he committed suicide on or about November 10, 1888."

'And in favour of the Russian doctor theory, Sir Robert Anderson, who was Commissioner of the Police at the time, always maintained the view that the murders were the work of a medical man.'

With our third example we meet up with sheer mendacity. This is not too surprising when you learn that this particular essay is by Aleister Crowley, whose concern for the truth was minimal. The piece is of extra interest since its opening passages have been so misread, that Blavatsky herself has been listed as a Ripper suspect. But the complete text shows that Crowley is just introducing the two characters involved with her who became enmeshed with the Ripper. The only thing worth noting about Blavatsky in this context is that at one time she had the temerity to sign her letters 'Jack'! Make of that what you will. Crowley's essay reads:

JACK THE RIPPER

To acquire a friendly feeling for a system, to render it rapidly familiar, it is prudent to introduce the Star to which the persons of the drama are attached. It is hardly one's first, or even one's hundredth guess, that the Victorian worthy in the case of Jack the Ripper was no less a person than Helena Petrovna Blavatsky. She has, however, never been unveiled to the unthinking multitude; very few, even of those who have followed her and studied her intently for years, have the key to that 'Closed Palace of the King'.

If the reader happens to have passed his life in the study of what is nauseatingly known as 'occult science', he would, if he were sufficiently intelligent, grasp one fact firmly: that is, that the persons sufficiently eminent in this matter who have become known as teachers, are bound to have possessed in overflowing measure the sense of irony and bitter humour. This greatest treasure in their characters is their only guarantee against going mad, and the way they exercise it is notably by writing with their tongues in their cheeks, or making fools of their followers. H.P.B. is known by the profane and vulgar as an old lady who played tricks and was exposed; but her motives were not what such persons supposed. These tricks were a touchstone for her followers; if they were so little understanding of the true nature of her Work that any incidents of this kind affected in the smallest degree their judgement, then the sooner she was rid of them the better.

The truth of H.P.B., as in the case of any artist, is to be known by a study of her best work; in this case a small volume called *The Voice of the Silence*.

One of the closest followers of H.P.B., and in the sphere of literature unquestionably the most distinguished, with the possible exception of J.W. Brodie-Innes, was a woman named Mabel Collins. Her novel, *The Blossom and the Fruit*, is probably the best existing account of the theosophic theories presented in dramatic form. One of the great virtues acclaimed and defended by this lady was that of chastity. She did not go quite as far as the girl made famous by Mr. Harry Price upon the Brocken a few years ago, whose terror of losing the jewel of her maidenhood was such that she thought it unsafe to go to bed without the protection of a man; but Mabel Collins had considerable experience of this form of chastity *à deux*; at the same time, reflecting that one of the points of H.P.B.'s mission was to proclaim the Age of the Woman, she occasionally chose a female for her bed-fellow.

Some few years before Whitechapel achieved its peculiar notoriety, the white flame of passion which had consumed the fair Mabel and her lover, who passed by the name of Captain Donston, had died down; in fact he had become rather more than less of a nuisance; and she was doing everything in her power to get rid of him. Naturally eager to assist in this manoeuvre was her new mistress, a lady passing under the name of Baroness Cremers, whose appearance and character are very fully and accurately described in a novel called *Moonchild*:

'An American woman of the name of Cremers. Her squat stubborn figure was clad in rusty-black clothes, a man's except for the shirt; it was surmounted by a head of unusual size, and still more unusual shape, for the back of the skull was entirely flat and the left frontal lobe much more developed than the right; one could have thought that it had been deliberately knocked out of shape, since nature, fond, as it may be, of freaks, rarely pushes asymmetry to such a point.

'There would have been more than idle speculation in such a theory; for she was the child of hate, and her mother had in vain attempted every violence against her before her birth.

'The face was wrinkled parchment, yellow and hard; it was framed in short, thick hair, dirty white in colour; and her expression denoted that the utmost cunning and capacity were at the command of her rapacious instincts.

'But her poverty was no indication that they had served her and those primitive qualities had in fact been swallowed up in the results of their disappointment. For in her eye raved bitter hate of all things, born of the selfish envy which regarded the happiness of any other person as an outrage and affront upon her. Every thought in her mind was a curse – against God, against man, against love, or beauty, against life itself. She was a combination of the witch-burner with the witch; an incarnation of the spirit of Puritanism, from its sourness to its sexual degeneracy and perversion.'

A prolonged contemplation of the above portrait may possibly fertilize the seed of doubt in some minds as to whether this woman was in every respect an ideal companion on one's passage through this vale of crocodile tears; but tastes differ, and she certainly mastered exquisite Mabel Collins, turned her against her teacher, persuaded her to embark on the most contemptible campaign of treacheries. For, recognizing in H.P.B. one of the messengers sent from time to time by the Masters to take a hand at the carpenter's bench where humanity is slowly sharpened, she thought that to destroy her would be as acceptable to the powers of darkness as could be imagined.

Of Donston less is known; it is believed that he was a cavalry officer, of the Household Cavalry at that, but under another name. Cremers tried to persuade people that he had been caught cheating at cards, but there is no reason to suppose that any disgrace attached to his leaving the Service. He was by all accounts a sincere sympathizer with the sufferings of our maudite race; his profession was obviously of no particular use to him, holding those sentiments, and apparently he drifted first into studies medical, and (later) theological. He was a man of extremely aristocratic appearance and demeanour; his manners were polished and his whole behaviour quiet, gentle and composed; he gave the impression of understanding any possible situation and of ability to master it, but he possessed that indifference to meddling in human affairs which often tempers the activity of people who are conscious of their superiority.

These three people were still living together in Mabel Collins' house in London; but as previously hinted, they were trying to get rid of him. This, however, was not an altogether easy task. The reputation of the novelist was a very delicate flower, and in the early days of her beguine for Donston she had written him many scores of letters whose contents would hardly have appeared altogether congruous with the instructive and elevating phrases of *The Blossom and the Fruit*.

Now, although Donston was so charming and pleasant a personality, although his graciousness was so notable, yet behind the superficial gentleness it was easy to recognize an iron will. His principal motif was righteousness; if he thought anything his duty, he allowed nothing else to stand in the way of performing it, and for one reason or another he thought it right to maintain his influence over Mabel Collins. One theory suggests that he was loyal to H.P.B., and thought it essential to fight against the influence of Cremers. This, at any rate, is what she thought, and it made her all the more anxious to get rid of him; judging everybody by herself, she was quite sure he would not hesitate to use the love-letters in case of definite breach; so, to carry out her scheme, the first procedure must obviously be to obtain possession to the compromising packet and destroy it.

The question immediately arose – where is it? Donston, with most men of his class, was contemptuously careless of interference with his private affairs; he left everything unlocked; but there was, however, a single exception to this rule. One of the relics of his career in the cavalry was a tin uniform case, and this he kept under his bed very firmly secured to the brass framework. This, of all his receptacles, was the only one which was always kept locked. From this, Cremers deduced that as likely as not the documents of which she was in search were in the trunk, and she determined to investigate at leisure.

In those days, transport in London was almost slower than today; from Bayswater or Bloomsbury – memory is not quite sure as to where they lived – to the Borough was certainly more than a Sabbath day's journey; the only evidence of speed in the whole city was the telegraph. Accordingly Cremers arranged one day for a telegram to be despatched to Donston, informing him that some friend or near relative had met with a street accident, had been taken to Guy's Hospital and wanted to see him. Donston immediately started off on this fictitious errand. As he left the house, Mabel laughingly warned him not to get lost and run into Jack the Ripper.

While he is changing buses, it may be proper to explain that these events coincided with the Whitechapel murders. On the day of his journey, two or three of them had already been committed – in any case sufficient to start talk and present the murderer with his nickname. All London was discussing the numerous problems connected with the murders; in particular it seemed to everyone extraordinary that a man for whom the police were looking everywhere could altogether escape notice in view of the nature of the crime. It is hardly necessary to go into the cannibalistic details, but it is quite obvious that a person who is devouring considerable chunks of raw flesh, cut from a living body, can hardly do so without copious evidence on his chest.

One evening, Donston had just come in from the theatre – in those days everyone dressed whether they liked it or not – and he found the women discussing this point. He gave a slight laugh, went into the passage, and returned in the opera cloak which he had been wearing to the theatre. He turned up the collar and pulled the cape across his shirtfront, made a slight gesture as if to say: 'You see how simple it is'; and when a social difficulty presented itself, he remarked lightly: 'Of course you cannot have imagined that the man could be a gentleman', adding: 'There are plenty going about the East End in evening dress, what with opium smoking and one thing and another.'

After the last of the murders, an article appeared in the newspaper of W. T. Stead, the *Pall Mall Gazette*, by Tau Tria Delta, who offered a solution for the motive of the murders. It stated that in one of the grimoires of the Middle Ages, an account was given of a process by which a sorcerer could attain 'the supreme black magical power' by following out a course of action identical with that of Jack the Ripper; certain lesser powers were granted to him spontaneously during the course of the proceedings. After the third murder, if memory serves, the assassin obtained on the spot the gift of invisibility, because in the third or fourth murder, a constable on duty saw a man and a woman go into a cul-de-sac. At the end there were the great gates of a factory, but at the sides no doorways or even windows. The constable, becoming suspicious, watched the entry to the gateway, and hearing screams, rushed in. He found the woman, mutilated, but still living; as he ran up, he flashed his bulls-eye in every direction; and was absolutely certain that no other person was present. And there was no cover under the archway for so much as a rat.

The number of murders involved in the ceremonies was five, whereas the Whitechapel murders so-called, were seven in number; but two of these were spurious, like the alien corpse in *Arsenic and Old Lace*. These murders are completely to be distinguished from the five genuine ones, by obvious divergence on technical points.

The place of each murder is important, for it is essential to describe what is called the averse pentagram, that is to say, a star of five points with a single point in the direction of the South Pole. So much for the theory of Tau Tria Delta.

It is not quite clear as to whether this pseudonym concealed the identity of Donston himself. The investigation has been taken up by Bernard O'Donnell, the crime expert of the *Empire News*; and he has discovered many interesting details. In the course of conversation with Aleister Crowley this matter came up, and the magician was very impressed with O'Donnell's argument. He suggested an astrological investigation. Was there anything significant about the times of the murders? O'Donnell's investigations had led him to the conclusion that the murderer had attached the greatest importance to accuracy in the time. O'Donnell, accordingly, furnished Crowley with the necessary data and figures of the heavens were set up.

A brief digression about astrological theory: the classical tradition is that the malefic planets are Saturn and Mars, and although any of the planets may in certain circumstances bring about misfortune, it is to these two that the astrologer looks first of all for indications of things going wrong.

Some years before this conversation, however, Crowley had made extensive statistical enquiries into astrology. There is a small book called *A Thousand and One Horoscopes* which includes a considerable number of nativities, not only of murderers, but of persons murdered. Crowley thought this an excellent opportunity to trace the evil influence of the planets, looking naturally first of all to Saturn, the great misfortune, then to Mars, the lesser misfortune; but also to Uranus, a planet not known to the ancients, but generally considered of a highly explosive tendency. The result of Crowley's investigations was staggering; there was one constant element in all cases of murder, both of the assassin and the murdered. Saturn, Mars, and Herschel were indeed rightly suspected of doing dirty work at the cross-roads, but the one constant factor was a planet which had until that moment been considered, if not actively beneficent, at least perfectly indifferent and harmless – the planet Mercury. Crowley went into this matter very thoroughly and presently it dawned on his rather slow intelligence that after all this was only to be expected; the quality of murder is not primarily malice, greed, or wrath; the one essential condition without which deliberate murder can hardly ever take place, is just this cold-bloodedness, this failure to attribute the supreme value to human life. Armed with these discoveries the horoscopes of the Whitechapel murders shone crystal clear to him. In every case, either Saturn or Mercury were precisely to the Eastern horizon at the moment of the murder (by precisely, one means within a matter of minutes).

Mercury is, of course, the God of Magic, and his averse distorted image the Ape of Thoth, responsible for such evil trickery as is the heart of black magic, while Saturn is not only the cold heartlessness of age, but the magical equivalent of Satan. He is the old god who was worshipped in the Witches' Sabbath.

Naturally, to his devotees, Saturn is not to be associated with misfortune 'redeunt saturnia regna'; Saturn has all the fond wisdom of the grandfather.

To return from this long explanatory digression, it was necessary in order to give the fair Cremers time to extricate the uniform case from its complex ropes, the knots being carefully memorised, and to pick the locks.

During this process her mind had been far from at ease; first of all, there seemed to be no weight. Surely a trunk so carefully treasured could not be empty; but if there were a packet of letters more or less loose, there should have been some response to the process of shaking. Her curiosity rose to fever pitch; at last the lock yielded to her persuasive touch; she lifted the lid. The trunk was empty, but its contents, although few, were striking.

Five white dress ties soaked in blood.

This fantasy by Crowley resulted from two events. In 1925 Bernard O'Donnell acted as 'ghost-writer' for a series of newspaper articles based on the autobiographical memories of Betty May, a former model for the sculptor Epstein. Betty May had married a young Oxford undergraduate, Raoul Loveday, but their union was doomed. Loveday fell under the influence of Aleister Crowley and went to live at his 'Abbey of Thelema' at Cefalu in Sicily; there he became 'High Priest'. The infantile humbuggery ended for Raoul after a ceremonial slaughter of a cat and the drinking of its blood. He developed acute enteritis on 13 February 1923 and died three days later.

Betty May was determined to expose Crowley and on her return to Britain gave interviews to the *Sunday Express*, stressing the sinister side of Crowley's rituals. Betty May soon discovered that the public found a vicarious pleasure in reading about evil goings-on. She then decided to make her stories as lurid as possible, even if it meant inventing whole episodes. One of the episodes invented by her involved a chest containing ties once belonging to Jack the Ripper, and this was included in the material given to O'Donnell for 'ghosting'. But there was no such chest at Cefalu; her story was based on nothing more than the account given to Crowley by Vittoria Cremers. After the articles ran in the *World's Pictorial News* (1925) they were published in book form as *Tiger Woman* in 1929. On reading the book Crowley scrawled his cynical comment in the margins of his copy. Against the chest of ties episode he wrote: 'Victoria (*sic*) Cremers' story!!!'

Later on, when O'Donnell asked about these ties, Crowley amused himself by pretending that he had known D'Onston and had been given these mementos of the murders. But in fact Crowley never knew D'Onston and had even misremembered Cremers' story. The five large, black, bohemian-style ties that she had seen, became five white bow-ties in his essay. Cremers herself confirmed to O'Donnell that Crowley had never at any time mentioned that he had known D'Onston; all his talk about the man was based on his fuddled recollections of Cremers' anecdotes, and nothing more.

This, then, is Betty May's fiction, as it appeared in book form:

...one day I was going through one of the rooms in the abbey when I nearly fell over a small chest that was lying in the middle of it. I opened it and saw inside a number of men's ties. I pulled some of them out, and then dropped them, for they were stiff and stained with something. For the moment I thought it must be blood. Later I found the Mystic and asked him about the ties. He was in one of his kindly moods. 'Sit down,' he said, 'and I will tell you about them.' He then went on to say that these were the relics of one of the most mysterious series of murders that the world had ever known. They had belonged to Jack the Ripper! 'Jack the Ripper was before your time,' he went on. 'But I knew him. I knew him personally, and know where he is today. He gave me those ties. Jack the Ripper was a magician. He was one of the cleverest ever known and his crimes were the outcome of his magical studies. The crimes were always of the same nature, and they were obviously carried out by a surgeon of extreme skill.

'Jack the Ripper was a well-known surgeon of his day. Whenever he was going to commit a new crime he put on a new tie. Those are his ties, every one of which was steeped in the blood of his victims. Many theories have been advanced to explain how he managed to escape discovery. But Jack the Ripper was not only a consummate artist in the perpetration of his crimes. He had attained the highest powers of magic and could make himself invisible. The ties that you found were those he gave to me, the only relics of the most amazing murders in the history of the world.'

It only remains to add that when Betty May acted as a defence witness in a libel action brought by Crowley, she cut a sorry figure. In court she admitted that whole sections of *Tiger Woman* were fabricated. She even acknowledged that accounts in her book differed from accounts printed in the *Sunday Express* and from the evidence given in court; yet all three differing stories related to one and the same set of incidents.

Finally, there exists one further curious item of note, in the form of a letter written on 24 September 1907, by Ernest Crawford of 2 Rosehill Terrace, Larkhall, Bath. It was sent to Robert George Sims, the journalist who took a keen interest in the Ripper case but is best remembered as the author of 'Christmas Day in the Workhouse'. It is obviously based on two of D'Onston's ideas, since the first part mirrors his *Pall Mall* article, while the second echoes his statements to Marsh, to Cremers and to Scotland Yard. But the sudden introduction of Jesuits into the arena is strange indeed. It looks as if someone with an anti-Jesuit fixation had decided to adapt D'Onston's ideas for his own ends. And who is the mysterious 'Mr S' of the letter? Most of the details seem to fit Stead, especially since he developed a fierce antagonism towards the Jesuits. But how on earth could anyone describe him as '…leaping into fame as an inventor'? An enigma, for certain… This letter reads:

> an acquaintance of mine, a man well known in reform movements and as an editor of magazines and Journals who is now leaping into fame as an inventor. Mr S as I will call him, told me that he believed that the outrages were instigated by the Jesuits who had reasons for getting foreign detectives into the London service (you remember that the importation of foreign detectives was talked of at the time), the miscreant never passed through the cordon of police because in the centre of the district was a Jesuit college in which he took refuge after his deeds. The Jesuits, according to Mr S left the sign of the cross on all their work and sure enough lines drawn from the points on your map make a fairly regular cross. I am afraid Mr S's theory must be regarded as a wild speculation but it is curious nevertheless. I am not aware that there is any Jesuit religious house in that particular locality. Another theory by the same gentleman is more plausible; you remember that the cut in the throat of the victims gave the investigators the idea that the murderer was left handed. Mr S thought that the Ripper had induced the women to allow connection from behind, a very convenient position for concealing his purpose and using the knife effectively. I see you make no mention of the Ripper letters which caused so much sensation at the time. I do not think that they had any connection with the crimes and probably you are of the same opinion.
>
> You are welcome to use any matter in this letter; I have only marked the envelope private to save it from being opened by a lady clerk or amanuensis.

For the sake of completeness I include the following poem from the *Star* of Friday 5 October 1888, together with an English translation made specially for this book. It is unusual since it appears in French, without any attempt at translation; it appears without any comment whatsoever; and the author is unnamed. Could this be one of D'Onston's taunts? At one time, he pretended that the Ripper was a Frenchman; and his preferred name had a French ancestry. We also know that he himself thought and spoke in French fluently, so the possibility of a macabre, hypocritical taunt is by no means absurd. No great store is set on this, however, but the event could not be passed over, because as D'Onston has written: '…in endeavouring to sift a mystery like this one cannot afford to throw aside *any* theory, however extravagant, without careful examination, because the truth might, after all, lie in the most unlikely one.'

La Fille

(And at that hour she, who had perhaps a happy and innocent girlhood, and was once a wife, had to turn out, and seek through the sale of her body the price of a bed. A few hours afterwards she was found a corpse. – The *Star*, 27 Sept 1888.)

Ne jetez pas l'insulte à cette pauvre fille;
Tant de pleurs sont mêlés à son destin affreux!
Si son ocil est ardent, c'est de fièvre qu'il brille,
Et son sourire n'est qu'un rictus douloureux.

Vous qui ne savez point le drame de sa vie,
Ni quels sentiers glissants l'ont conduit sie bas;
Vous qui dès son berceau ne l'avez point suivie
Et n'avez point connu les pièges sous ses pas;

Ne jetez pas l'insulte à la fille honnie!
Car souvent sur ces fronts, même les plus osés
Vous pourriez découvrier de traces d'àgonie
Dans les morne sillons que l'orgie a creusés.

Une mère a manqué peut-être à son enfance;
L'ange gardien n'a pu vieller sur son berceau,
Et quelque lâche amant, la trouvant sans défense,
Après s'être assouvi, l'a jetée au ruisseau.

Il en est tant, hélas! comme la Madeleine,
Qui sentent de dègoût leur front s'appesantir,
Et dont l'âme troublée est anxieuse et pleine
De ce vague tourment qui meme au repentir!

Oh! ne l'accablez pas, vertueux de ce monde!
Car son affreux destin, souvent immérité,
Ne doit vous inspirer qu'une pitié profonde
Et que ce sentiment divin: La Charité!

The English translation reads as follows:

> Don't hurl insults at this poor girl;
> So many tears have combined with her awful destiny!
> If her eye is inviting, it is the fever which burns,
> And her smile is nothing more than a painful grimace.
>
> You cannot know the drama of her life,
> Or the slippery paths which have led her astray:
> You have not followed her from her cradle
> And cannot know the traps under her feet.
>
> Do not insult this scorned woman!
> Since even when she is most wanton
> You can still discover the traces of agony
> In the dull furrows this immoral life has created.
>
> Perhaps her mother neglected her as a child;
> Her guardian angel couldn't watch over her cradle,
> And some cowardly lover, finding her defenceless,
> After satisfying himself, threw her in the gutter.
>
> Alas, there are so many like Mary Magdalen,
> Who feel themselves weighed down with disgust,
> And whose troubled soul is anxious and full
> Of this vague torment which leads to repentance!
>
> Oh, do not be overcome, all you virtuous!
> Since her awful destiny, often undeserved,
> Should only inspire you with a profound pity
> And that divine sentiment: Charity!

Behind the Symbols

We now know D'Onston to be a character who was ice cold, devious, arrogant and taunting. One of the most rewarding forms of taunting involves the shrouding of a *simple* message in a baffling and complex form. Tautriadelta was such a message. It has set brains sizzling. It has led to determined searches through dictionaries and occult tomes and it has prompted bizarre solutions. D'Onston said this of Tautriadelta:

> A strange signature indeed but one that means a devil of a lot. There are lots of people who would be interested to know why I use that signature. In fact, the knowledge would create quite a sensation, but they will never find out – never.

Yet D'Onston wasn't a public figure – a man of prominence, but a shabby, unmemorable nonentity. So what secret could he possibly cherish that would *ever* create a sensation?

The answer is obvious. He knew the true identity of Jack the Ripper. All his charges against Dr Davies were fabricated. The real killer-doctor from the London Hospital was D'Onston himself. It is no accident that Tautriadelta was only used by him *after* the Whitechapel murders had ended; before then it would have lacked real meaning. What then is the precise meaning?

Tautriadelta – equals 'cross-three-triangles'. The triangles are the enticing female genitals, a snare and distraction for a man with great deeds to perform. But the genitals were also revered by all occultists as the repository of vital and magical essences.

In Black Magic this was taken one step further; the female sex organs were viewed as a source of potent substances for use in ultra-powerful rituals. And the donor of these substances need not be alive. Warped ideas like these provide the excuse or the rationalization for wildly perverted sex drives; perverted even to the point of murder.

In the light of this knowledge, now look at the clues D'Onston gives in his writings: the cross has to be profaned; a preparation made from a certain portion of the body of a harlot (the uterus) has to be utilized; the sacrifice of human victims is necessary; the sites of the murders form a perfect cross. Yet if you mark the sites of the murders on an ordnance survey map of the period (not the usually inaccurate sketch-maps) you will find that the first four murders *alone* provide the aimed-for cross. But the Berner Street victim escaped mutilation, thus only three of the four crucially positioned women were ritually slashed across their deltas. 'I reveal in my signature,' D'Onston is saying, 'the things I did to profane the cross.'

As for Kelly she was the high point of a long-drawn-out surfeit of twist-ed passions and unknown monstrous and pathetic rituals. But she was not one of the ladies of the cross; she was an extra.

Like all magical labels and symbols Tautriadelta probably contains other meanings, indeed one of the aims of the occultists is to make their mes-sages as complex as possible. Having said that, it is certain that the sexual aspect takes precedence in D'Onston's chosen name. As a devotee of Alexan-drian mysteries he would cherish all the lore drawn from ancient Egypt, and among that lore was the association of the Nile Delta with the female genitals, and indeed with sexual mutilation. The famous inscription at Sais reads: 'I Isis am all that has been, that is or shall be; no mortal Man hath ever me unveiled.' But this message is so laid out that to the eye it suggests both the shape of the Delta and the lower portion of the body of a female. This is deliberate. Isis and her Delta play powerful roles in Egyptian Magic. Her very amulet, the *thet* is so shaped that its sexual aspects become self-evi-dent to the knowledgeable.

The great Egyptologist, Sir Ernest Budge had no doubts about this when he described her amulet in these words:

> The form of *thet* as it appears in the Papyrus of Ani suggests that it rep-resents the vagina and uterus, as seen when cut out of the body and laid upon some flat surface, the flaps at the sides being the thick ligatures by which the uterus is attached to the pelvis, which have dropped from their normal position after death. I have submitted this view to a medical authority, Dr W. L. Nash, and he agrees with me that this amulet does represent the genital organs of Isis.

Tautriadelta is an amalgam of all the ideas which involve the Whitechapel rituals and the ancient teachings that lay behind them.

Magical Imaginings

Arthur Diosy was a famous author, lecturer, linguist and criminologist; and one of the many eminent writers engaged by various newspapers to make on-the-spot investigations into the Ripper crimes. Diosy spent some time in the Whitechapel area on behalf of the *Star* and later became convinced that there was a Black Magic dimension to the killings. His proofs were hardly convincing, but some of his ideas have become confused with the explanations given by D'Onston, so they need to be noticed, if only to be dismissed. It is also worth remembering that the first public mention of Diosy's ideas was prompted by D'Onston's article of 1 December 1888.

Ingleby Oddie in his autobiography *Inquest* gives details of Diosy's investigations:

> Arthur Diosy a member of *Our Society*, thought the murders were the work of some practitioner of Black Magic. According to him, amongst the quests of these people in the East is the *elixir vitae*, one of the ingredients of which must come from a recently killed woman. Diosy got quite excited when he heard of the bright farthings and burnt matches which he said might have formed the 'flaming points' of a magical figure called the 'pentacle', at each angle of which such points were found, and according to ritual certain 'flaming' articles had to be thus disposed. Diosy said later that he had paid a visit to Scotland Yard to place his theories before the authorities, but had been received without enthusiasm as one can well understand.

When investigating D'Onston, Bernard O'Donnell heard something similar from the late Sir Max Pemberton, a friend of Diosy's in 1888. As O'Donnell recalled, 'Diosy and Max Pemberton later became founder members of *Our Society*, a dining club which met regularly to discuss crime in general and murder in particular.'

H. B. Irving, a well-known criminologist in his day, and son of the great Sir Henry Irving, was the originator of the club. Other members included Conan Doyle, A. E. W. Mason, Fletcher Robinson, editor of *Vanity Fair*, G. R. Sims of the *Referee*, Professor Churton Collins, Arthur Lambton, Arthur Diosy and Ingleby Oddie the famous London coroner. In later years *Our Society* numbered Sir Edward Marshall Hall and Sir Bernard Spilsbury among its members.

'Diosy was a great student of the occult,' Max Pemberton told me as we chatted together at his home in London, 'and he built up an immense train of evidence to prove that Jack the Ripper was a Black Magician. On one occasion he described how the grimy stubs of five candles had been found at the scene of one of the Ripper crimes set out in the form of a pentagram. On another occasion, he told me that five matchsticks were found stuck in the cracks between the cobblestones where another victim was found dead. It is so long ago that I do not remember many details, but I know that Diosy was so impressed that he went to Scotland Yard with his information. As a result of his visit Yard men visited the shop of a bookseller who was an agent for selling certain works on Black Magic, and a list of the customers who regularly purchased these books was obtained and made the subject of enquiries.'

Abberline's Answer

Was Jack the Ripper executed in 1903? Was he hanged after poisoning at least three women? Did he call himself George Chapman, to hide his criminal past and his real identity as Severin Klosowski? These questions were first raised seriously by Hargrave Adam in 1903, but were alleged to represent ideas that first germinated in 1888.

In his book, *The Trial of George Chapman*, Adam devoted nine pages to the proposition that Chapman could have been the Whitechapel killer. He made it clear that the reasoning was not evolved by him, but was the direct result of a conviction held by ex-Inspector Fred Abberline.

Unfortunately, in dealing with the issues, Adam was lax and confusing. As a consequence his words have misled many readers. Near the end of his summary he wrote:

> Chief Inspector Abberline, who had charge of the investigations into the East End murders, thought that Chapman and Jack-the-Ripper were one and the same person. He closely questioned the Polish woman, Lucy Baderski, about Chapman's nightly habits at the time of the murders. She said that he was often out until three or four in the morning, but she could throw little light on these absences. Both Inspector Abberline and Inspector Godley spent years in investigating the 'Ripper' murders. Abberline never wavered in his firm conviction that Chapman and Jack-the-Ripper were one and the same person. When Godley arrested Chapman, Abberline said to his confrere, 'You've got Jack-the-Ripper at last!'.

Now those words in particular have been misunderstood by many readers. They give the false impression that Abberline suspected Chapman at the time of the murders. They can be misunderstood as stating that Lucy Baderski was questioned back in the vital months. The truth is very different. Abberline only came to his strange conclusion after Chapman had been arrested and charged in October 1902; at that time he had been out of the police force for ten years. Adam himself, in opening his account, actually makes it plain that the theory had arrived late in the day, when he wrote:

> After the investigations had been completed and the case against Chapman was fully established, the police authorities entertained a strong idea that some sinister connection existed between the Borough poisoner and the mysterious murderer of Whitechapel, popularly known as Jack-the-Ripper.

At this point we have to remind ourselves that Adam is not speaking from first-hand knowledge. Everything he has to say about Chapman and the Ripper was gleaned second-hand from ex-Chief Inspector Godley, some twenty-seven years after Abberline made his remarkable connection. The 'police authorities' referred to would simply be the inexperienced officers who listened to Abberline, and, out of respect for his record, took him seriously. If Godley agreed with his former superior he certainly failed to add anything of his own that would buck up Abberline's identification.

What was there, then, about the Chapman hearings that led Abberline to make his extraordinary identification? The answers lie in one name and address. The address was that of Chapman's place of work in 1888. And where was that? Well, most of the witnesses at the hearings weren't quite sure. 'A barber's shop under a public house,' said Stanislaus Baderski. 'The barber's shop underneath the public house in High Street, Whitechapel...' said George Schumann. By contrast, with such vagueness one witness seemed spot-on. A commercial traveller in hairdressers' materials testified that Chapman worked, '...in a shop under the White Hart public-house, 89 High Street, Whitechapel, in 1888.' That traveller's name was Wolff Levisohn. Levisohn also stated that when he first met Chapman he was using the name Ludwig Zagowski. Zagowski had asked Levisohn to supply a certain medicine (not named in court) but Levisohn refused, saying that the did not want to get twelve years. (The mention of a jail sentence makes it certain that Zagowski/Chapman had asked for a listed poison.)

But the White Hart (and its dive barber's shop) enjoyed a dual address. It was also known as the White Hart, George Yard, since its rear doors opened onto George Yard. A contemporary drawing shows the main entrance to George Yard as a low archway cut through Whitechapel High Street. To the right is a carpet shop; to the left is the White Hart. A bizarre inscription is placed above the arch which reads: 'SIR GEORGE'S RESIDENCES. BOARD AND LODGING FOR RESPECTABLE GIRLS.'

Wolff Levisohn pinpointed Chapman's White Hart address at the Police Court Proceedings held on 7 January, 1903. On reading the account of the proceedings Abberline would have seen this address as significant and evidential. This would have misled him into believing that it tied Chapman to the murders by imperfectly recalling a number of 'White Hart – Ripper' connections. The events that churned around in his head all led to George Yard and its pub, but that was all they had in common. They were not connected one to the other. And they were in no way connected to Chapman. However, blurred memories would allow them to be forced into a suggestive pattern.

The events surrounding the address began with the murder of Martha Tabram on 7 August 1888. Her body was found on the first-floor landing of George Yard Buildings. Thirty-nine stab wounds were logged by the police surgeon. At the time it was seen as an isolated killing, but after the Buck's Row murder it was taken to be an earlier atrocity by the Ripper.

The address featured again on 11 November 1888, just two days after the Kelly murder, when public terror was at its peak. *The Times* says, 'Shortly after 10 o'clock last night as a woman named Humphreys was passing George-yard, Whitechapel, she met in the darkness and almost on the identical spot where Martha Tabram was murdered, a powerful-looking man wearing large spectacles.' This man so terrified the woman that she raised the cry of 'Murder!' Her shouts led to a hue-and-cry and the man was seized and hustled off to Leman Street Police Station. Other papers followed with more detailed and lurid accounts of the arrest of this man, who has entered Ripperologist lore as 'Black Face/White Eyes'. He was just a stupid doctor engrossed in his self-imposed role as an amateur detective, but at the time of his arrest the rumour spread that the Ripper had been caught at last. As a result this incident gained a great deal of publicity and the George Yard vicinity became more closely tied to Ripper fears. George Yard featured once more after the murder of Alice McKenzie. On 18 July 1889 the *New York Herald* (London Edition) carried an interview with a barman at the White Hart. The barman said:

…A queer thing happened yesterday that may have some connection with the murder. About noon two fellows drove up in a cab and came in for drinks… They got talking to three girls who were in here, and one of them said, 'What has become of Jack the Ripper? He has been keeping it dark lately. It is about time he showed himself again, isn't it?' I thought little of the remark until I heard of the murder a few hours later.

On 13 February, 1891, Frances Coles was knifed to death. Her last drinks were taken in the White Hart. Her drinking companion, Ellen Callaran told *The Times* (14 February):

Last night we were walking up Commercial-street about half-past 12, having come out of the White Hart, George-yard, when we met a man dressed in a sailor suit... He accosted me, but I did not like his looks. He caught hold of me, tore my jacket, and struck me in the face, giving me a black eye. He made an offer to Frances, and I left, after advising her not to go with him...this morning...someone told me that a woman had been murdered near Leman-street. I said at once, 'I believe that's Frances.'

So much for the address, but the crucial name that emerged from the Police Court Proceedings in 1903, was not one of the aliases used by Chapman, but it was the name of a Polish Jew. A Jew, who like Chapman, had once been a Feldscher. And it was a name first brought to Abberline's attention in November 1888, in the week following Kelly's murder. The *Illustrated Police News* (24 November) tells us that this Polish Jew visited Whitechapel as part of his job as a traveller. At half-past eleven, on his way home, he was accosted by Mary Ann Johnson, a known prostitute, who cried out, 'You are Jack the Ripper!'. At this, another woman took up the cry and an excited crowd gathered. The traveller '...fearing that the consequences might be very unpleasant for himself...took refuge in the Commercial-street Police-station, and then the police took the women into custody.'

This Jew, attacked as 'Jack the Ripper' in 1888, was none other than Wolff Levisohn, the very man who, fifteen years later was heard at Chapman's trial. The very man who linked Chapman with George Yard, and all its dramatic overtones.

It is certain that the Levisohn connection was enough to start trains of thought running through Abberline's head. But the chances are that he was quite blind to the way his mind was engineering faulty connections. Once made, these connections begot certainties, a seemingly coherent theory emerged, and yet again another myth was entered into the Ripper files.

In Adam's account, this myth is added to by the claim that though the last Ripper murder in London was in July 1889, after Chapman's move to Jersey City (May 1890), Ripper-style killings then commenced in the 'locality of Jersey City'. These murders, according to Adam, ended at the beginning of 1892. And in May 1892 Chapman left America and returned to London.

These alleged Jersey City murders have puzzled researchers for years, since no one has ever unearthed anything remotely related to a Ripper murder. So how did the strange idea arise? I can now supply the definitive answer. The idea is based on the garbled memory of a sensational item printed in the *National Police Gazette*, published in New York. On 16 February, 1889, it ran a story headlined 'ANOTHER VICTIM OF JACK THE RIPPER'. The text read:

> Camden, New Jersey, was plunged into a fever of excitement on Saturday over what is likely to prove a murder, the horrible details of which in many respects resemble the terrible Whitechapel murders in London. Miss Annie Eisenhart, head nurse of the Cooper Hospital, in Camden, was the victim of an outrage. About two in the morning she was attacked by an unknown man, her hair was cut from her head, her scalp slashed terribly with a knife, her bosom mutilated, and her body and limbs kicked and bruised until they were discoloured and broken. After attempting other more dastardly outrages the assassin fled in alarm, making his escape through a window with the aid of a rope made from knotted towels.

The report was illustrated (in the centre of the paper) by a drawing also captioned: 'ANOTHER VICTIM OF JACK THE RIPPER'. It is understandable that most readers would have drawn false conclusions from this piece, and imagined that the Ripper had shifted from England to the USA. Even so, this story does nothing to incriminate Chapman. At the time of the attack he was still living in London.

Despite Abberline's muddles, one thing of importance does emerge from his statements. He never, at any point in his career, encountered any information that convinced him that the Ripper was either dead or in a place of safe keeping. Indeed, like many other police officers, including Munro, he even entertained the idea that the Ripper went on killing after 9 November 1888. His questioning of Lucy Baderski shows that. From the hearings, he knew that Lucy had not joined up with Chapman until 1889, yet he still questioned her about Chapman's 'nightly habits at the time of the murders'. His actions reinforce the statement he made to *Pall Mall Gazette* in March 1903. He rejected the view, advanced by George Sims, that the Ripper had committed suicide: 'Yes, I know all about that story. But what does it amount to? Simply this. Soon after the last murder in Whitechapel the body of a young doctor was found in the Thames, but there is absolutely nothing beyond the fact that he was found at the time to incriminate him.'

Sims, of course, was merely echoing the views voiced by Major Arthur Griffiths in his *Mysteries of Police and Crime*. In turn Griffiths was echoing Macnaghten. They were all, in fact, talking of Druitt, and all were wrong in classing him as a doctor. That Druitt's details were erroneous simply emphasizes the lack of exactitude in many of the police dealings in the Ripper case. The plentiful shortcomings make it certain that no single suspect in the police 'short-list' can be taken seriously; Abberline, for one, did not take them seriously. Druitt and Kosminski were for him simply time-wasting outsiders. No matter how muddled he was in 1902, back in 1888, and until he retired in February 1892, he remained adamant in his belief that the Ripper was still alive and undiscovered.

Foundation Hoax

Throughout the world countless books and articles are tainted by their continual harping on one theme: that the Ripper murders have a Royal dimension. My first book on the murders, *The Bloody Truth*, showed beyond doubt that the Royal involvement is the result of fantasies, hoaxes and deliberate lies. I also demonstrated that this Royal aspect has no roots in the last century, indeed this whole phase of distortion only begins in the 1960s. There is, though, a massive hoax of the last century which was later used to to create a fantasy tapestry bearing Royal images. Since these particular grotesqueries die hard, it is timely to reprint this master hoax which first appeared in print on 28 April 1895, as a feature in the *Sunday Times-Herald* of Chicago:

The Capture of Jack the Ripper

The story recently told by Dr. Howard, a well-known London physician, to William Greer Harrison, of the Bohemian Club in San Francisco, in regard to the fate of Jack the Ripper, and which is at last given to the world, unseals the lips of a gentleman of this city, who is thus enabled to give the *Times-Herald* a full and exhaustive account of that exhaustive research by London detectives, which at the conclusion of years of unremitting labor, has resulted in fixing the identity of the famous Whitechapel murderer beyond the shadow of a doubt.

The Dr. Howard referred to was one of a dozen London physicians who sat as a court of medical inquiry or as a commission in lunacy upon their brother physician, for at last it was definitely proved that the dreaded 'Jack the Ripper' was no less a person than a physician of high standing, and in fact was a man enjoying the patronage of the best society in the west end of London. When it was absolutely proved beyond peradventure that the physician in question was the murderer, and his insanity fully established by a commission *de lunatico inquirendo*, all parties having knowledge of the facts were sworn to secrecy. Up to the time of Dr. Howard's disclosure this oath had been rigidly adhered to.

A London clubman, now in Chicago, who is acquainted with Dr. Howard, is of the opinion that, being in a foreign country and perhaps under the influence of wine, Dr. Howard has permitted his tongue to wag too freely. Coupled with this conjecture he said yesterday to a reporter of the *Times-Herald*:

'I notice that Dr. Howard has not revealed the name of the physician who committed the murders. For this he has reason to be thankful, as such an act would have resulted in the total destruction of his London practice. As it is, he will doubtless be privately reprimanded by the Royal College of Physicians and Surgeons, as an oath administered under such circumstances is considered of the most sacred and binding nature.'

The story of Dr. Howard is substantially correct, as far as it goes. When 'Jack the Ripper' was finally run to earth it was discovered that he was a physician in good standing, with an extensive practice. He had been ever since he was a student at Guy's Hospital, an ardent and enthusiastic vivisectionist.

Through some extraordinary natural contradiction, instead of the sight of pain softening him, as is the case with most devotees of scientific experiments, it had an opposite effect. This so grew upon him that he experienced the keenest delight in inflicting tortures upon defenceless animals. One of his favourite pastimes was to remove the eyelids from a rabbit and expose it for hours, in a fixed position, to a blinding sun. He would take a seat near it, totally forgetful of meals, of the passage of time and of everything except the exquisite sensations he experienced in watching the agonized contortions of his victim.

This passion for inflicting pain so grew upon the man, who was afterwards to rank as a disciple of cruelty with Nero or Ghengis Kahn, that as he approached manhood and his softer nature impelled him to seek a wife he could hardly restrain himself from an indulgence in his barbaric pursuits long enough to woo and win her. He had scarcely been married a month before his wife discovered that he had a mania for inflicting pain. In testifying before the commission she gave the following extraordinary evidence:

'One night we were sitting in the drawing room. It was quite late. I arose to go to bed. When I arrived upstairs I remembered that I had left my watch upon the drawing room mantelpiece. I descended the stairs.

As I approached the drawing room I heard the sounds of a cat mewing piteously. Looking through the door, which happened to be open, I was horrified to see my husband holding a cat over the flame of the moderator lamp. I was too frightened to do anything but retreat upstairs. When my husband came to bed along toward daylight I felt that I was occupying the same couch with a monster. I discovered later that he had spent almost the whole night in burning the cat to death.

'The next day he was as kind and loving as possible. I discovered later that he was subject to an unconquerable mania for inflicting pain. It was quite possible for me, as I studied him closely, to tell when these moods were coming on. On such occasions some apparently trivial act would put me on my guard. He was apt at such times to begin by catching a fly and twirling it impaled upon a pin. He was a strange contradiction. When our little boy, only four years old, imitated him once in this respect the father was actually shocked and was so indignant that he gave the child a sound whipping. As the boy screamed with the pain of the punishment the ferocious side of my husband's nature asserted itself. He would in all probability have beaten the child to death if I had not interfered. In his normal moods he was an excellent husband and father and one of the gentlest and most tractable of men. I have frequently heard him express sincere sympathy with persons in misfortune.'

The circumstances which led to the detection of this inhuman monster with a dual nature are extraordinary and altogether unparalleled in the history of crime. As the fact of the arrest and imprisonment of Jack the Ripper has now been divulged by Dr. Howard, it is only right that proper credit should be given to the man who put the London police upon his track. He himself has sacredly observed his promise – he refused to take any oath on the ground of religious scruples – not to divulge the identity of the Ripper.

Robert James Lees, the gentleman to whom the unfortunates of the east end of London owe their present immunity from the attacks of a monster who for long years made every one of them venture out at night literally with her life in her hands, is the person entitled to the credit of tracking Jack-the-Ripper. Mr. Lees is at present the proprietor of a novel institution for the higher education of the workingmen at Peckham, a suburb of London. Over 1,800 workmen attend his classes and he has invested a large fund of money in the enterprise which is now on a paying basis. Mr. Lees is recognized today as one of the most advanced labor leaders in England and is an intimate friend of

Keir Hardy, the leader of the independent labor party. He at present resides at 26 The Gardens, Peckham Rye, London, S.E.

In his early years Mr. Lees developed an extraordinary clairvoyant power, which enabled him to discern, as with the eyes of a seer, things hidden from the comprehension of ordinary men born without this singular gift. At the age of 19 he was summoned before the queen at Birmingham, where he gave evidence of his powers as a clairvoyant which excited her majesty's utmost astonishment. Having considerable means of his own, however, he devoted himself to literary pursuits, became a profound theologian and ultimately took up the study of spiritualism and theosophy. He is at present the recognized leader of the Christian Spiritualists in Great Britain.

At the time of the first three murders by the ripper, Mr. Lees was in the height of his clairvoyant powers. One day he was writing in his study when he became convinced that the ripper was about to commit another murder. He tried in vain to dispel the feeling. As he sat at his table the whole scene arose before him. He seemed to see two persons, a man and a woman, walking down the length of a mean street. He followed them in his mind's eye and saw them enter a narrow court. He looked and read the name of the court. There was a gin palace near this court, ablaze with light. Looking through the windows he saw that the hands of the clock in the bar pointed to 12.40, the hour at which the public houses are closed for the night in London.

As he looked he saw the man and woman enter a dark corner of the court. The woman was half drunk. The man was perfectly sober. He was dressed in a dark suit of Scotch tweed, carried a light overcoat on his arm and his hard blue eyes glittered in the rays of the lamplight which dimly illuminated the dingy retreat the pair had chosen.

The woman leaned against the wall and the man put one hand over her mouth. She struggled in a feeble manner, as if too much overcome by liquor to make any effectual resistance. The man then drew a knife from his inside vest pocket and cut the woman's throat. The blood streamed out from the wound, some of it spurting over his shirt-front. He held his hand over the woman's mouth until she fell to the ground. Then divesting the lower limbs of his victim of their apparel, the butcher inflicted sundry gashes upon her with his long knife. These were delivered in a scientific manner, and resulted in the ripper's laying certain organs beside the body of his victim. He then deliberately wiped his knife on the clothes of the woman, sheathed it, and, putting on his light overcoat, deliberately buttoned it up so as

to hide the bloodstains on his shirt-front, after which he walked calmly away from the scene of the murder.

Such was the extraordinary clairvoyant vision presented to the second sight of Mr. Lees. So impressed was he by what he had thus
miraculously witnessed, that he at once went to Scotland Yard and
detailed the whole matter to the detectives. As they regarded him as
nothing short of a lunatic, and had been for some months visited by all
sorts and conditions of cranks with Jack-the-Ripper theories, he naturally received little attention.

By way of humouring one whom they considered a harmless lunatic,
the sergeant on duty took down the name of the place where Mr. Lees
said the crime would be committed and also noted that the hands of
the clock in the mythical public-house had pointed to 12.40 at the
moment when the ripper and his victim had entered the court.

At 12.20 on the following night a woman entered the public-house
facing on the court in question. She was quite under the influence of
liquor, and the barkeeper refused to serve her. She left the place swear-
ing and using vile language. She was seen by another witness to enter
the court again at 12.30 in company with a man dressed in a dark
suit and carrying a light overcoat upon his arm. Witness thought the
man was an American because he wore a soft felt hat, and added that
'he looked like a gentleman'.

This was evidence given before the deputy coroner, who held an
inquest on the body of a woman who had been found in the very spot
described by Mr. Lees, 'with her throat cut from ear to ear, and otherwise indecently and horribly mutilated' – to quote the coroner's
records. Mr. Lees himself was indescribably shocked when he learned
of the murder next day. Taking with him a trusted manservant he visited the scene of the outrage. To use his own language – 'I felt almost
as if I was an accessory before the fact. It made such an impression
upon me that my whole nervous system was seriously shaken. I could
not sleep at night and under the advice of a physician I removed with
my family to the continent.'

During his visit abroad Mr. Lees was no longer troubled by these
strange hallucinations, notwithstanding the fact that while he was
absent the 'ripper' had added to his list of crimes no less than four
additional atrocious murders. It then became necessary for Mr. Lees to
return to London.

One day, while riding in an omnibus from Shepherd's Bush in company with his wife, he experienced a renewal of the strange sensations

which had preceded his former clairvoyant condition. The omnibus ascended Notting Hill. It stopped at the top, and a man entered the interior of the vehicle. Mr. Lees at once experienced a singular sensation. Looking up he perceived that the new passenger was a man of medium size. He noticed that he was dressed in a dark suit of Scotch tweed, over which he wore a light overcoat. He had a soft felt hat on his head.

Over a year had elapsed since Mr. Lees' clairvoyant vision, but the picture of the murderer had been indelibly impressed upon his mind.

Leaning over to his wife he remarked earnestly, 'That is Jack the Ripper!' His wife laughed at this, and told him not to be foolish. 'I am not mistaken,' replied Mr. Lees, 'I feel it.'

The omnibus traversed the entire length of the Edgware road, turning into Oxford street at the Marble Arch. At this point the man in the light overcoat got out.

Mr. Lees determined to follow him. Bidding his wife continue on her journey in the direction of her home, he followed the man down Park lane. About halfway down the thoroughfare he met a constable, to whom he pointed out the man in the light overcoat informing him that he was the dreaded 'ripper' and asking that he be arrested. The constable laughed at him, and threatened to 'run him in'.

It seems that the 'ripper' must have entertained some apprehension that he was in danger, for on reaching Apsley House he jumped into a cab and was driven rapidly down Piccadilly. A minute later Mr. Lees met a police sergeant, to whom he confided his suspicions.

'Show me the constable who refused to arrest him!' exclaimed the sergeant. 'Why it was only this morning that we received news at the Bow Street station that the "ripper" was coming in this direction.'

That night Mr.Lees again received premonitions that the 'ripper' was about to commit another murder. The scene of this outrage was not so distinct as on the former occasion, but the face of the murdered woman was clearly defined. Mr. Lees noted with great particularity the aspect of the 'ripper's' victim. A peculiarity of the mutilations, which were somewhat similar to the first, was that one ear was completely severed from the face and the other remained hanging by a mere shred of flesh.

As soon as he recovered from his trance and the consequent shock he experienced in witnessing this dreamlike tragedy, Mr. Lees hastened to Scotland Yard, where he insisted on having an immediate audience with the head inspector of police. That functionary listened with a smile of incredulity to the first portion of his visitor's story, which died away at once, however, upon his reaching that portion of his narrative, which spoke of the victim's ears being severed from her head.

With a trembling hand and a face which plainly betokened the effect of Mr. Lees' communication, the officer drew a postal card forth from his desk and laid it before his visitor.

It was an ordinary postal card, written in red ink. In addition it bore the marks of two bloody fingers, which had been impressed upon it by the writer, and which remained as a kind of bloody sign manual upon its calendered surface.

This postal card read as follows:

'Tomorrow night I shall again take my revenge, claiming, from a class of women who have made themselves most obnoxious to me, my ninth victim.

JACK THE RIPPER

PS To prove that I am really 'Jack the Ripper' I will cut off the ears of this ninth victim.'

Dr. Lees was no sooner confronted with this awful confirmation of his second vision than he fainted dead away and remained as one absolutely insensible to what was going on around him.

It must be recollected that at this time the entire British metropolis, comprising within a radius of twenty miles of Charing Cross, a population of nearly 7,000,000 souls, was completely terrorized by this awful series of murders, which shocked indeed the whole of christendom by their unparalleled barbarity, the frequency of their occurrence and the apparent complete immunity enjoyed by their inhuman perpetrator.

The inspector himself, who was a religious man, looked upon the extraordinary coincidence of the receipt of the postcard – with the contents of which he alone was familiar – and the story of Mr. Lees, as a warning sent from heaven, and as a divine intimation that he must leave no stone unturned to bring this monster to justice. All that day he concentrated his entire energies upon the problem of how best to cover the intricate territory known as 'the Whitechapel district'. He had at his command a force of nearly 15,000 constables. By dusk of next day no less than 3,000 of these in citizens' clothes, in addition to 1,500 detectives, disguised as mechanics and dock laborers, were patrolling the courts and alleys of Whitechapel.

Notwithstanding these precautions 'Jack the Ripper' penetrated the cordon, slew his victim and made his escape. The inspector, when told that this victim had been discovered with one ear completely severed from her body and the other hanging from her head by a mere shred of flesh, turned deathly pale and it was some time before he recovered his usual self-possession.

Mr. Lees was so affected by this last tragedy that he at once removed to the continent. While he was thus abroad, the 'Ripper' completed his sixteenth murder, and had coolly informed the Scotland Yard authorities that he 'intended to kill twenty and then cease'.

Shortly after this Mr. Lees returned to England where he made the acquaintance of Roland B. Shaw, a mining stockbroker of New York, and Fred C. Beckwith, of Broadhead, Wis. who was then the financial promoter of an American syndicate in London.

These three gentlemen were dining one day in the Criterion when Mr. Lees turned to his two companions suddenly and exclaimed: 'Great God! "Jack the Ripper" has committed another murder.'

Mr. Shaw looked at his watch and found it was eleven minutes to eight. At ten minutes past eight a policeman discovered the body of a woman in Crown court in the Whitechapel district, with her throat cut from ear to ear and her body bearing all the marks of the ripper's handiwork.

Mr. Lees and his companions at once went to Scotland Yard. The news of the murder had not yet reached the inspector, but while Mr. Lees was relating his story a telegram arrived giving full details of the outrage.

The inspector, taking with him two men in plain clothes, at once drove to Crown court, in company with Mr. Lees and the two Americans. As they entered the court Mr. Lees exclaimed:

'Look in the angle of the wall. There is something written there.' The inspector ran forward, and not having a dark lantern with him struck a match. As the tiny flame flared up, the words: 'Seventeen, Jack the Ripper', done in chalk upon the wall, were distinctly visible.

The inspector by this time was in a condition closely bordering on insanity. It must be borne in mind that this madman had for years baffled all the resources of the greatest police force in the world – that, rendered desperate at last, the British authorities had summoned to their assistance the most experienced detectives in France, Germany, Holland, Italy, Spain and America; that they had lavished immense sums in an endeavour to trace the fiend; that there was then pending an aggregate reward of £30,000, together with a life pension of £1,500 per annum, all to go to the man who should first deliver to justice the terrible 'Ripper'.

As before stated, the inspector seemed to recognize in Mr. Lees an instrument of providence, and he determined then and there to avail himself of his marvellous though altogether incomprehensible powers.

After an earnest appeal from the inspector, Mr. Lees consented to try and track the 'Ripper' – much in the same way as the bloodhound pursues a criminal. There seemed to be some magnetic wave connecting an impalpable sense he possessed with the fugitive. All that night Mr. Lees submitted himself to his strange magnetic influence and traversed swiftly the streets of London. The inspector and his aids followed a few feet behind him. At last, at 4 o'clock in the morning, with pale face and bloodshot eyes, the human bloodhound halted at the gates of a west end mansion, gasping, with cracked and swollen lips, as he pointed to an upper chamber where a faint light yet gleamed.

'There is the murderer – the man you are looking for.'

'It is impossible.' returned the inspector, 'That is the residence of one of the most celebrated physicians in the west end.'

The most extraordinary part of this well-nigh incredible narrative is now to come. The inspector had been so strongly impressed with the clairvoyant powers of Mr. Lees that he determined to put them to the crowning proof.

'If you will describe to me,' he said, 'the interior of the doctor's hall I will arrest him, but I shall do so at the risk of losing my position, which I have won by over twenty years' faithful service.'

'The hall has a high porter's chair of black oak on the right hand, as you enter it, a stained glass window at the extreme end, and a large mastiff is at this moment asleep at the foot of the stairs,' replied Mr. Lees, without any hesitation.

They waited then till 7 o'clock, the hour at which the servants begin to stir in a fashionable London residence. They then entered the house and learned that the doctor was still in bed. They requested to be allowed to see his wife. The servant left them standing in the hall, and Mr. Lees called the inspector's attention to the fact that there was no mastiff visible as he had described, though his description of the hall in all other respects tallied exactly. Upon questioning the servant as to the whereabouts of the dog she informed Mr. Lees that it generally slept at the foot of the stairs, and that she let it out into the back garden every morning.

When the inspector heard this he exclaimed: 'Great heavens!' adding in an undertone to his companion: 'It is the hand of God.'

In the course of half an hour's searching examination the doctor's wife, who was a beautiful woman, confessed that she did not believe her husband was of sound mind. There had been moments when he had threatened herself and her children. At such times she had been accustomed to lock herself up. She had noted with heart-breaking dread that whenever a Whitechapel murder occurred her husband was absent from home.

An hour later the inspector had completed his arrangements for the examination of the doctor, and had summoned to his aid two of the greatest experts on insanity in the metropolis. When accused, the doctor admitted that his mind had been unbalanced for some years and that of late there had been intervals of time during which he had no recollection of what he had been doing. When told that they believed he had been guilty of the Whitechapel murders during those intervals, he expressed the greatest repugnance and horror of such deeds, speaking as if the murderer was quite a different person to himself, and expressing great willingness to bring him to justice. He told the physicians that he had on one or two occasions found himself sitting in his rooms as if suddenly aroused from a long stupor, and in one instance he had found blood upon his shirt front, which he attributed to nosebleed. On another occasion his face had been all scratched up.

On hearing this the inspector caused a thorough search of the house to be made, when ample proofs were found that the doctor was the murderer. Among others the detectives brought to light the famous Scotch tweed suit and the soft felt hat, together with the light overcoat. When convinced of his guilt, the unfortunate physician begged them to kill him at once, as he 'could not live under the same roof with such a monster'.

As stated in the early part of this article, an exhaustive inquiry before a commission in lunacy developed the fact that while in one mood the doctor was a most worthy man, in other he was a terrible monster. He was at once removed to a private insane asylum in Islington, and he is now the most intractable and dangerous madman confined in that establishment.

In order to account for the disappearance of the doctor from society a sham death and burial were gone through, and an empty coffin, which now reposes in the family vaults in Kensal Green, is supposed to contain the mortal remains of a great west end physician, whose untimely death all London mourned.

None of the keepers know that the desperate maniac who flings himself from side to side in his padded cell and makes the long watches of the night hideous with his piercing cries is the famous 'Jack the Ripper'. To them and the visiting inspectors he is simply known as Thomas Mason, alias No. 124.

To an uninformed reader this account could look like a startling but still plausible account of the Whitechapel murders. The details of the events are all set down in easily verifiable chronological order. There are the times pinpointed, people named, and locations clearly indicated. Where then is the catch?

The Print that Lies

Once the true facts of the murders are assembled it only takes a minute or two to recognize that the Chicago 'revelations' are blatantly false. It is deliberately worded as a self-revealing hoax. Every paragraph tells you that; for no single paragraph deals with *any* of the real Jack the Ripper murders.

The real murders were committed in a short period of just over ten weeks, and they were five in number. The Chicago piece stretches the crimes out over a period of years and clocks up *seventeen* deaths. And all the times in the article fail to match. As for the only named murder, the one staged in Crown Court, no such murder took place. The bloody postcard never existed, nor did any of the other events described ever happen. This story has as much validity as any other fairy tale. This is far from astonishing when you discover that the story was fabricated by an irreverent tall-story club founded by Chicago newsmen. It was an extra-special club from our viewpoint, since it was so taken with the Jack the Ripper murders that it actually named itself the Whitechapel Club. It thought nothing of creating news at slack periods, or any other time if the whim seized.

For those in the know there are many allusions built into the text to make them chuckle. The very opening tells them what to expect. By naming William Greer Harrison the leg-pull is openly signalled, for Harrison was the butt of many Bohemian jokes and hoaxes. He was a San Francisco broker who felt himself destined for literary greatness. This impelled him to join the Bohemian Club in San Francisco, so that he could rub shoulders with the artists, poets and writers who gathered there. But they despised him as a pretentious and pompous ass, and this made him ripe for duping and teasing. Ambrose Bierce went out of his way to pillory Harrison in verse; he found the stockbroker's poetry as 'rhythmic as the throb and gurgle of a roadside pump replenishing a horse-trough'. As for Lees, the Whitechapelers despised religion and cant, and Lees, to them, was steeped in both things. And the man had made claims that the spiritualists had secret information about the aid they gave the police. This made Lees a certain target for one of their hoaxes.

So was Lees just all humbug? Not a bit. He was a well-meaning man who suffered from delusions. It is doubtful if he ever realized when he had overstepped the bounds of truth. But one thing is certain: he did go to the police and offer to trace the Ripper but only after the double-event. And the result? He was ridiculed and shown the door. His own diary for 1888 even records the events:

> Tuesday 2nd October. Offered services to police to follow up East End murders – called a fool and a lunatic. Got trace of man from the spot in Berner Street.
> Wednesday 3rd October. Went to City police again – called a madman and a fool.
> Thursday 4th October. Went to Scotland Yard – same result but promised to write to me.

These entries are in Lees' own handwriting; they have not been tampered with in any way. The diary is there to be seen in the Britten Memorial Museum, at Stansted Hall, Stansted, Essex.

When the Chicago piece was first published the truth about Lees was not known, even so the story had very little impact anywhere. In Britain only one journalist was taken in by it, this was Joseph Hatton, who based a short piece on it in the 19 May 1895 issue of *People*. He was misled enough to imagine that the Dr Howard named in the hoax was an old acquaintance, Dr Benjamin Howard. Dr Benjamin Howard was out of the country at the time, but on his return in January 1896, he wrote an angry letter to the *People* :

> A number of persons have called my attention to 'A startling story' in your widely read *The People* – May 19 1895, directly charging me with 'the breach of a vow' etc.
>
> In this publication my name is dishonourably associated with Jack the Ripper – and in such a way – as if true – renders me liable to shew cause to the British Medical Council why my name with three degrees attached should not be expunged from the Official Register.
>
> Unfortunately for the Parties of the other part – there is not a single item of this startling statement concerning me which has the slightest foundation in fact.

Beyond what I may have read in newspapers, I have never known anything about Jack the Ripper. I have never made any public statement about Jack the Ripper – and at the time of the alleged public statement by me I was thousands of miles distant from San Francisco where it is alleged I made it.

In my absence from London this statement has passed uncontradicted so long that the damage has multiplied beyond private methods of correction.

In response to this letter of 26 January, the journalist behind the story replied, on 31 January, saying:

Dear Dr. Howard,
I took the 'Jack the Ripper' notes from a two-column report in the *Chicago Times*. It was published in such evident good faith that I never thought of doubting it. You will observe that I spoke of you not only with respect but with admiration.

I hope at all events that the incident may lead to a renewal of our friendship.

Tell me what you would like me to do and I shall only be too glad to comply with your wishes.

I always remember you as an appreciative acquaintance of the dear son whom I lost and of whom you predicted great things.

Won't you come to see me?

Joseph Hatton.

After that nothing more was heard of this Chicago nonsense in any known publication until 1931. Up until then the yarn had been treasured only by small bands of gullible spiritualists. Now, on 9 March 1931 the London *Daily Express* began to reprint the *Times-Herald* article, without telling its readers where it came from. The line taken by the *Express* was that this text was taken from a document left by Robert James Lees in the safe keeping of a close friend. This friend had instructions to release the document only after Lees' death. Robert Lees had died in January 1931, so the embargo on publication had been lifted. All this, of course, was pure chicanery.

There was no secret document; neither was there any close friend who acted as custodian of Lees' confessions. Behind this reappearance of the 1895 hoax was a frustrated crime reporter, Cyril Morton. He had heard that Lees knew the identity of the Ripper and as soon as Lees died he had rushed to Leicester and tried to buy the name from Lees' daughter Eva.

She refused to cooperate, the truth being that she knew nothing, but while in her home Morton caught sight of a copy of the original article of 1895. That was enough for him. If a story could not be bought it could at least be manufactured. Having secured a copy of the Chicago text, Morton chopped out all those bits that revealed its American origins. A few extra touches were added and this re-vamped version became 'the secret document'. But, tiny amendments apart, the text as printed in the *Daily Express* is word for word the exact text of the piece printed on 28 April 1895.

This reprinting of the hoax gave it a new vigour and it began to gain strength after strength. It was featured in the French press; it was repeated in Australia and it was given a resounding endorsement by ex-Detective Sergeant Edwin T. Woodhall. Woodhall was more interested in money than truth; he had no scruples about inventing things to fill the pages of the cheap books he was churning out. He was responsible for manufacturing a number of false stories involving the Ripper, so one more would hardly hurt. His version of the hoax appeared in at least five publications and by 1939, on the strength of this worthless tale, Lees was taken seriously by many.

On its own merits this tale was simply a boost for spiritualism; unfortunately, though, it contained elements that could be expanded to suggest a Royal involvement and a Royal cover-up. And this Royal entanglement was stressed even more strongly in the version of events that Lees himself came to evolve. This version was fully disclosed by Cynthia Legh in 1970. Miss Legh first met Lees in 1912 after her mother had become enthralled by Lees' book *Through the Mists*. From then on Lees became a frequent visitor to their home at Adlington Hall, in Cheshire. Miss Legh records:

Often when interested friends came over to see him, to ask about his Healing work and his many fascinating experiences, they might say 'What is the real story about Jack the Ripper?' I therefore heard the story myself at least half a dozen times and hope that I may omit nothing of real interest.

To keep strictly and briefly to the point, I must say first that Queen Victoria had upon several occasions sent for Mr. Lees and she had told him he could at any time ask for an audience with her; she recognized and valued his exceptional gifts. Perhaps I should explain here that Mr. Lees only – as he expressed it – 'recorded' his books or wrote them as 'dictated' by his spirit guides who were...able to 'materialize' quite simply in his much used and dedicated study; they would sit and dictate what he was to write, while Mr. Lees sat and wrote at his table.

When the first murder occurred the public was naturally shocked and horrified. Mr. Lees and his wife had previously done a good deal of rescue work in the East End of London, and he knew something of its underworld and could move amongst them unharmed. When the second murder was being planned one of his guides told Mr. Lees to go and see the head of Scotland Yard. Neither of them. of course, expected him to believe what he had to say, but this was the pattern he must follow. They had met before…all pleasant, but nothing to be done! However, said Mr. Lees, I had to come and tell you, and will you please make a note?

The second similar murder took place! The third time his guide spoke, Mr. Lees went back again: 'Were we right last time or not?' 'Yes, you were, but that was a coincidence, quite extraordinary, but I can't take action on this kind of "chance".'

The third murder took place! Here I regret that I cannot be sure whether a fourth followed or not, but it was at this point that his guide told Mr. Lees to go to the Queen.

He was given a long private audience, at the end of which Queen Victoria gave him a letter to hold until, and if, a further murder should be planned; this he was to take with him to the Chief.

The occasion unfortunately arose, and every possible facility was put at his disposal. He took with him a man of authority from Scotland Yard. They went together to a house in London and rang the bell; a manservant answered it. Yes, the 'Doctor' was at home…he was alone in his surgery. Mr. Lees walked in and greeted him; the doctor looked at him with some surprise and said, 'Well, James! I didn't think it would be you who would come for me.' These words stayed in my memory, for James Lees himself felt so infinitely sad, for the case of this man was the most complete example of Jekyll and Hyde he ever came across. I think he described him as a 'charming fellow ordinarily'. Late the same evening the doctor was taken (privately) to a place of detention and care, where he died a number of years later.

The Queen had asked Mr. Lees to leave London with his family for all events five years, and for this period he received from her a pension, as it entailed leaving his job.

People were so disturbed about the murders, and were asking so many questions, she felt they might find themselves in a very difficult situation; also it was a terrible position for the doctor's wife as she held a position at Court.

On this same memorable day a beggar died in the Seven Dials area, where people in those days often died unrecorded; his body was brought into the house during the night, he had a superficial resemblance to the doctor and was much the same height and weight and took his place in the coffin at the funeral! The following day the newspaper reported that Doctor…had had a sudden heart attack and had died during the night at his home.

And now you have the elements that insist on the involvement of the Crown. The Queen 'knows' the identity of the killer; the killer's wife held a position at the Court; the Royal medium was responsible for the capture of the Ripper; and the Queen herself asked the medium to leave town in order to make the cover-up foolproof.

Just six weeks after Cynthia Legh's story came out in *Light* Dr Thomas Eldon Stowell published his own version of the Royal cover-up. It appeared in the *Criminologist* and although it never once mentioned the name of the Ripper, all the details pointed the Duke of Clarence as the man he was indicting. The genesis of his incredible solution is fully worked out in my *Bloody Truth* but briefly it can be said that it is easily traced back to the Lees story and to the illusion that the Royal physician Sir William Gull was involved in that story.

Once the Stowell theory was out in the open, more than 3,000 newspapers took up the story and from that point on, reason gave way to the raptures of sensationalism. Joseph Sickert sold his own version of the Court cover-up to the BBC and then to Stephen Knight, who used it as the basis for his best-selling *Final Solution*. Michael Harrison rejected the idea of Clarence as the Ripper, but put Clarence's friend J. K. Stephen in the dock. Frank Spiering then combined Clarence and Stephen into a deadly alliance, and after that one would have thought that the fantasies had run themselves to earth. No shred of proof was ever offered for any of these outlandish nominations. And the real evidence showed that all of these ideas were of recent manufacture.

Unfortunately, old fallacies die hard. People choose the easy path all too often. And it is quite easy to simply repeat the old yarns, give them a new twist or two, and sell them as 'final solutions'. And so the Royal connection re-emerged in 1991 in the shape of *The Ripper and the Royals*. This again was a Sickert-inspired monstrosity. Originally Sickert had named three killers, headed by Gull; now he enlarged the group to include Sir Randolph Churchill (father of Winston) and an Italian-American pickpocket Frederico Albericci, also known as Fingers Freddie! Even the author now accepts that this solution is complete fiction. As for the fake Abberline diaries quoted in the above book, the least said about them the better.

Following on the heels of *The Ripper and the Royals* came an American offering called *Murder and Madness* by Dr David Abrahamsen. This book adopts a version of the fantasy created by Frank Spiering and makes the murders the joint work of J. K. Stephen and the Duke of Clarence. Its dottiness is only matched by the more recent *Jack the Ripper Revealed* by John Wilding.

Mr Wilding now insists on a deadly alliance between authentic suspect Montague Druitt and hoax candidate J. K. Stephen. Together they did it, and behold they left behind cipher messages in the famous writing on the wall and in two Jack the Ripper letters sent from Liverpool. Sad to say the so-called secret messages can be dragged out of other documents that Wilding would not accept. Even sadder for Mr Wilding is that the two letters from Liverpool which are crucial to his case, were never written, sent or received in 1888. They were among the many Ripper letters that were sent in 1889, when a new round of scares erupted.

Forbes Winslow, among others, received some of these letters, and they are all worthless except as curiosities. Without authentic hidden messages from 1888 Mr Wilding has nothing new to offer. But like Dr Abrahamsen he has neglected his research. If either had read my book, *The Bloody Truth*, they would have realized that each and every involvement of the Royal Family has been based on modern claptrap. And that goes for the Royal hangers-on as well. Perhaps we can now have a respite from this gothic Lewis Carroll world of pasteboard characters?

Fool's Gold

In 1992, at a time when the craze for hoaxes seemed to have petered out, along came the biggest Ripper hoax of the twentieth century. First reports spoke of a confessional diary penned by Jack the Ripper, unearthed in Liverpool and brought to London by its finder. Later reports were a little different. A one-time scrap-metal merchant named Mike Barrett had been *given* this diary by a drinking companion Tony Devereux.

Mr Devereux, alas, was now dead, so everything had to depend on Barrett's unsupported testimony. Despite this the rights were bought by the London publishing firm of Smith Gryphon and the trade began to learn of a promised 'scoop of scoops'. At that stage only the people called in by the publisher knew the 'true' name of the diary Ripper.

When I first heard of this document I made two forecasts. One, that it would be written in a journal or diary with a number of its front pages torn out. Secondly, that it would be written in a simple iron-gall ink. This type of ink is indistinguishable from those used in the 1880s, but is easily made and not difficult to buy. Indeed some thousands of packets of ink-powder, once used in schools, are still around, and often turn up in street markets and minor antique shops. When mixed, it is a Victorian-style ink.

I was able to make these forecasts since my experience had shown me that old journals, ledgers, diaries and scrapbooks are quite easy to find, but the majority of these have been used or part-used, so anyone needing some blank paper will have to make do with what is left.

At that point I warned Paul Begg, who was giving 'historical advice' on the diary, that there was no reliable way of dating such an ink once it had lain on the paper for eighteen months or so. This was the limit of any advice I could offer. I was not asked to look at the find, and the name of this new 'Ripper' was never mentioned.

Then the time came when someone put rumours and logic together and we learned that the diary was said to have been written by James Maybrick. Now, a great deal was known about James, mainly because his wife Florence was tried for his murder and convicted. Her neck was never stretched; a life sentence took the place of the original order to hang and for years people argued over the misconduct of the trial. This, of course, has nothing to do with Jack the Ripper, but the running debate prompted many newspaper articles and a number of books. And the man who faked the diary found it comparatively easy to know anything he wanted to about the Maybrick family in 1888 and 1889. After that year it didn't matter since James Maybrick died on 11 May 1889.

Investigating this diary was not easy. All the people who had been allowed to read the text were first obliged to sign a confidentiality agreement that effectively gagged them. If they had doubts or reservations they were not allowed to voice them. One-sidedly, though, statements seeming to endorse the diary as genuine were encouraged and published, helping to convince doubters who had never seen the original.

Before I saw the diary I pointed out publicly that although the publishers had released small snippets of the text, they had not displayed a single line of the handwriting found in the diary. This omission led to the conclusion that in all probability the journal was not in the known handwriting of James Maybrick. In the event, all my forecasts were proved accurate. The diary was written in a scrapbook with twenty of its front pages torn out, and the hoaxer had used a simple iron-gall ink which you or I can make up on a kitchen stove. The diary's handwriting in no way resembled that of James Maybrick.

In many ways the text is hilarious. It poses as a confession, meant for the outside world: a record of what really happened; but at intervals the diarist grows coy and writes about the clues he's left behind him. Yet he never says what they are. In my opinion the reason for this coyness is simple. Our penman is playing safe and relying on the intrigued believers to fill in the gaps for him. By being sparing with details the hoaxer avoids falling into traps. Yet he just wasn't clever enough. By claiming to have written the original Ripper missives, and by referring to the two farthings alleged to have been found in Annie Chapman's pocket, he blundered. Those Ripper missives are hoaxes; no serious historian challenges this; and all the document examiners agree that the writing in the diary is by a different hand. As for the two farthings, no coins of any sort were found near the body of Annie Chapman, or in her pockets. The two farthings were nothing but journalistic inventions. Richard Whittington-Egan has most amusingly commented on this myth, saying:

By 1929, when Leonard Matters published the first book on the subject, the 'trumpery' articles had metamorphosed into 'two or three coppers and odds and ends'. In 1959, Donald McCormick added two farthings – 'Two brass rings, a few pennies and two farthings were neatly laid out in a row at the woman's feet.' It only remained for Robin O'Dell in 1965, to supply the gloss of 'two new farthings', and the legend was complete.

There were many of these legends at the time, including the report that three rings had been found at Annie Chapman's feet.

Over the years, these myths were repeated by so many journalists and authors that our diary-hoaxer would feel confident that he was dealing with facts: he fell into the trap and gave himself away.

But forget the internal absurdities of this diary. Even if its text had been flawless, its handwriting would still have failed the crucial test. Here we are fortunate since we can examine an authentic, lengthy example of Maybrick's writing in the form of his will of 25 April 1889. Comparison shows the diary is a fake.

In the light of that information the publishers' claim that the diary had been 'authenticated' is questionable. In one statement Robert Smith told *Publishing News* that '…we did not begin any rights discussions until we were satisfied as to its authenticity'. And to the *Guardian* on 24 March 1993, Robert Smith said: 'None of the tests we have had done have thrown the slightest doubt on the diary's authenticity.'

This was the persistent public claim, but behind the scenes lay another story altogether. Evidence came to light showing that some of the gagged advisors held views that were in direct conflict with the publicity statements being used to boost the Smith Gryphon book based on the diary. Disquiet began to grow in those who were thinking of buying rights. In particular *The Sunday Times* launched its own private inquiries.

This paper had been about to buy the serialization rights when they were warned that they were being fooled. After its 'Hitler Diaries' fiasco the paper could not afford to be lumbered with yet another set of worthless scribblings. So, as can be imagined, their reappraisal of the diary and its publishers' claims was ruthless. And they were right to be so tough. Their searches brought the crucial Maybrick will to their eyes for the very first time. Smith Gryphon had not included this in their sales package, but once unearthed *The Sunday Times* recognized that this one document alone proved the diary to be a fake.

Meanwhile, in the United States, Warner Books who were due to publish an initial 200,000 copies of the book, began to have their own doubts.

These were aroused after David Streitfeld of the *Washington Post* prepared an article on the diary and gave advance notice of its contents to Warner's President Larry Kirshbaum. The article appeared on 30 July 1993 under the heading 'Jack the Ripoff?', and it disclosed that Warner Books were to conduct its own thorough and independent investigation into the diary's validity.

True to their word the US publishers commissioned a thorough investigation led by Kenneth Rendell, one of the leading experts in historical documents. It had to be a rushed job, since publication day was looming fast, and many questions had to remain unanswered. But despite its improvised feel, the Rendell report did ask and answer some essential questions. Its verdict was: FAKE, and Warner Books cancelled its contract.

In Britain *The Sunday Times* grew weary of being gagged and took action through the courts, as Maurice Chittenden explained in *The Sunday Times* on 19 September 1993:

> *The Sunday Times* first established that the 'diary' of Jack the Ripper was a fake three months ago, after it was offered exclusive serialization rights for £75,000.
>
> The newspaper told the publisher of the findings of its investigation and wanted to warn the public that there was a danger the Ripper's forged confessions could become the biggest international fraud in the book world since the 'discovery' of the Hitler diaries. The proposed print run of 250,000 copies and the worldwide sale of television and newspaper rights meant it was worth at least £4m.
>
> However, the newspaper had signed confidentiality agreements in which it agreed not to disclose the contents of the diary to a third party. Experts who had examined the diary were made to sign similar statements. Such agreements are common in the publishing world because they allow newspapers and magazines to read forthcoming books with a view to serialization. In this case the publisher tried to use the agreement to gag the newspaper, preventing it from printing the findings of its investigation into the authenticity of the diary and from quoting experts.
>
> This meant that while other papers began to speculate about the diary ('Is this man Jack the Ripper?' asked *The Independent on Sunday* on August 29), *The Sunday Times*, which knew the truth, had to stay silent. However, serious doubt was cast on the diary 11 days ago when Warner Books cancelled plans to publish it in the United States.
>
> Last week *The Sunday Times* won a High Court battle with Smith

Gryphon under which the publisher released this paper from any obligation of confidence and agreed to pay it £6,500.

Robert Smith approached *The Sunday Times* in early April this year and claimed he had a 'sensational document'. At subsequent meetings he revealed he had acquired the rights to the Ripper diary and knew exactly who he was: James Maybrick. *The Sunday Times* was required to pay a non-returnable £5,000 for an option to take up the serial rights, and to sign a series of confidentiality agreements.

The newspaper then launched its investigation. It uncovered Maybrick's will, in which handwriting did not match that of the diary, and a scientific report prepared for Smith 12 months earlier that had cast suspicion on the manuscript. A panel of experts assembled by *The Sunday Times* concluded that the diary was a forgery.

Told of the findings Smith threatened to sue for damages if *The Sunday Times* breached its confidentiality agreement. However, it was the newspaper that issued a writ in the High Court on July 20 seeking to be released from any obligations of confidence on the grounds of fraud, fraudulent misrepresentation or negligent misrepresentation. In addition, on July 29 *The Sunday Times* reported the matter to the police; the papers have been sent to Scotland Yard.

On July 23 Smith Gryphon published a four-page supplement to *The Bookseller* proclaiming that the world's greatest murder mystery would be solved with the publication of the diary on October 7. In August *The Sunday Times* applied for a speedy trial on the grounds that it was in the public interest that the book, *The Diary of Jack the Ripper: The Discovery, The Investigation, The Authentication*, be exposed before going on sale. Mr Justice Lindsay ruled that there was 'a real possibility that for a period in October, if nothing is done, the public or some of its members, may be deceived.' He ordered a speedy trial.

Last week Smith Gryphon agreed to repay the £5,000, make a small contribution to legal costs and release the newspaper and others from the confidentiality agreements.

The separate investigation carried out for Warner Books by Kenneth Rendell, an expert in historical documents, has confirmed most of *The Sunday Times'* findings. Rendell said last week: 'The victory in releasing the confidentiality agreements is the key to the whole thing.'

Fall of the Axe

Since the Rendell report had such a devastating effect on the publication plans of Smith Gryphon, it now counts as an historic document in the battle against this hoax. Unfortunately its full text is too long to reprint in full, but its essential conclusions can be found in the following extracts:

...A letter was sent on September 25, 1888 to 'The Boss, Central News Office, London.' This letter, genuinely written in 1888, was signed Jack the Ripper. It may or may not have been written by the murderer, but whether or not, the diary directly reflects the language found in it... The phrases that appear in the 1888 letter are clearly used repeatedly in the diary...(But) Sue Iremonger, a documents expert consulted by the English publisher in London, 'does not link the handwriting of the diary with that of the "Dear Boss" letter.' If she is correct, there can only be one conclusion: if the letter is written by Jack the Ripper, then the diary, which copies its language but does not match its handwriting, must be forged. If the 1888 letter is a hoax of the time, then the diary must still be a hoax since it copies its language but does not match its handwriting...

People who have not been involved in major literary forgeries are not aware of the resourcefulness of perpetrators of such hoaxes. In the present case many have stated that it is too elaborate to be a hoax; they are not aware that virtually everyone said no one could possibly forge nearly 60 Hitler diaries, nor could anyone create Howard Hughes' autobiography or Benito Mussolini's diaries, nor could a young man in Salt Lake City forge letters and manuscripts whose contents would shake the Mormon Church to its foundations. If an investigator assumes that something is too complex to be a fraud, then he or she is likely to be victimized. Forgers are not always motivated by money or fame – it can be the simple satisfaction of fooling experts. Knowing the psychology of forgers is almost as important as knowing how to analyse handwriting...

The original diary was brought to Chicago on August 20, 1993, by Robert Smith, the English publisher, for the examination of the handwriting, ink, and paper. I met him at the laboratory of Maureen Casey Owens, the former president of the American Society of Questioned Document Examiners, author of numerous papers on Forensic handwriting questions, and, for 25 years, the Chicago Police Department's expert in document examination. We were joined by Robert L. Kuranz, who had been a research ink chemist for more than 30 years, and Dr. Nickell.

My immediate reaction, and, I later learned, that of Mrs. Owens as well as Dr. Nickell, was that the diary was written much more recently than the later 1880s. I was also struck by the uniformity of the writing and ink – highly unusual in a diary – a uniformity that immediately reminded me of my first glimpse of the Hitler diaries.

I was also surprised that the diary was written in a scrapbook, not a normal diary book. Scrapbooks, much larger in format and containing very absorbent heavy paper, were used for mounting postcards, photographs, valentines, and other greetings cards, and I had not previously encountered one used as a diary. It was possible, but very unlikely.

We were all very suspicious of the fact that approximately 20 pages at the beginning of the book had been torn out. There are no logical explanations as to why the purported author, Maybrick, a man of means, would have done this. First of all, he would have bought a normal Victorian diary, but if for some reason he wanted a scrapbook, he would have bought a new one. He would be unlikely to take one he already had and tear out the contents. It was highly likely, on the other hand, that someone wanting to forge a diary, and not knowing the difference between a scrapbook and a diary, would have bought a scrapbook at a flea market, torn out the pages already used, and had the remainder of the pages for their creation...

The English publisher also had brought with him photocopies of Maybrick's marriage certificate bearing an unquestioned genuine signature, as well as photocopies of his will, which he indicated was generally considered to be a forgery, probably Maybrick's brother...

We had not expected to find any elements that would date the ink as recent but could not rule out the possibility. (It is relatively easy today to obtain or make ink with elements that were used in Victorian England.)

Some of the ink/paper samples extracted by Bob Kuranz had meanwhile been sent to Rod McNeil for an ion migration test to determine how long the ink had been on the paper. We had some concern that the nature of the book, a scrapbook with relatively more absorbent paper, might make this analysis difficult. Both Maureen Owens and myself continued to work on the handwriting, and it was becoming increasingly evident that the examination of the handwriting would be conclusive in itself...

Our further examination of the writing in the diary confirmed what Dr. Nickell, Mrs. Owens, and myself suspected the first time we saw the diary: the writing is not consistent with letter formations of the late 1880s; there is a uniformity of ink and slant of writing in going from one entry to the next (supposedly written at different times) that is unnatural and very indicative of a forger writing multiple entries at one time. A lack of variation in layout also leads to the same conclusion.

Most important and surprising of all, a careful examination of the Maybrick will conclusively indicates that the signature on the will is signed by the same person who signed the marriage certificate – James Maybrick – and that the text of the will was also written by Maybrick. This was an unexpected development as I had been told that the evidence that it was written by Maybrick's brother Michael was very strong. (I was never shown this evidence.)

An analysis and comparison of the Maybrick will with the Jack the Ripper diary conclusively shows that they were written by two different people. Both examples were supposedly written at the same time; both are lengthy examples. There is sufficient evidence to reach a definitive conclusion. There is no other possibility – the writer of the Jack the Ripper diary was not James Maybrick. Even without considering the evidence of the 'Dear Boss' letter and numerous inconsistencies in the overall story, the historical facts in the diary so clearly identify the author as James Maybrick, that proof that he did not write the diary leaves only the conclusion that this is a hoax!

In the end the examiners were convinced that the diary was a recent product, probably only a few years old. This seems to clash with the results of the independent ion migration test which dated the ink at 1921, plus or minus twenty years. But this particular test has been developed by one man only, as such its value is open to question. But this is of small importance since the evidence of fakery is there for all to see, without the aid of microscopes or complex laboratory equipment.

Other puzzles also cease to be baffling with a modicum of research. The link between the name of Maybrick and the Whitechapel murders struck many as novel and without any ancestry. But the fact is that the two cases have been joined together for many years. For example, in Michael Harrison's book, *Clarence* (1972) you find the argument that Mrs Maybrick's conviction was yet another crime chargeable to the Ripper! This, according to Harrison, resulted from her misfortune '…to be tried by a judge desperately grasping on to a disappearing sanity, his mind lost to him in the horror of contemplating what his own son was and had done'. That mad Judge was Sir James Stephen; his son was the poet J. K. Stephen, and the horror was generated by the Judge's discovery that his son was none other than the fiend of Whitechapel. All this is sheer nonsense, but such things act as a stimulus for our hoaxer. And there are a good number of suggestive passages in other books which were able to feed the fantasy of Maybrick as the Ripper. No genius was needed at any point.

Unseemly Bluff

We now know how this hoax could have been inspired; it only remains to add that the hoaxer could have drawn all his *factual* material from just a few books. In fact it's quite easy to demonstrate that the diary could have been concocted by drawing on *three* books at the most. So why were people impressed by its contents?

In the first place there was no exchange of accurate information among those consulted. Some of them believed that the writing had been proven to be as old as the 1880s. And there were claims that the handwriting matched that of the original 'Dear Boss' letter. Because these entries were so old (so the argument ran) some details recorded showed the writer to be the killer, since he knew things that were not publicly known until 1987. All these claims turned out to be sheer moonshine.

The Rendell report was certainly the greatest setback for the hoax, but even so the publishers still went ahead with their plans. Then, on Monday 4 October came the London book launch of *The Diary of Jack the Ripper.* The invitations read: 'the author and the experts will be on hand to answer detailed questions.'

As expected, I was not sent an invitation; my awkward, but perfectly legitimate questions, were unwelcome. But this had been anticipated; an invitation soon came my way, and the day dawned. I waited until the press had asked its questions, and waited again, until it became clear that no one was about to put the essential questions, then I uncoiled myself from my back seat and made two very basic requests. 'Where,' I asked, 'is the expert who will put his reputation on the line and state that this diary is an authentic document written by James Maybrick in 1888 and 1889? And where is there another expert also prepared to put his reputation on the line and state that James Maybrick's will is a forgery?' The silence was uncanny. Mr Smith was left alone at the bridge of the *Titanic.* His experts had either deserted him or they had never existed.

The publisher mumbled something about the Maybrick will having been disputed by the lawyer Alexander MacDougall in 1891. At this point, I had to remind Mr Smith of the one and only time he had spoken to me on the phone.He had then tried this line of denigrating the will by quoting MacDougall. His answers to me indicated that he had not read the book he was quoting from. But I had. I then drew his attention to the passages in that book which proved that MacDougall was not only inaccurate about this will, but also gave contradictory accounts of it. I reminded Mr Smith that his reliance on the texts of Alexander Mac-Dougall was absurd since there is on file at Somerset House a certified copy of the Maybrick will. This certified copy was made on 29 July 1889 by the firm of Layton, Steel and Springman, the Liverpool solicitors who handled the estate. The text of this solicitor's copy agrees in all essentials with the wording of the will in Maybrick's own hand dated and witnessed on 25 April 1889.

Here is proof beyond doubt that the so-called transcript of this will in MacDougall's book is flawed and worthless as evidence. This is not to say that MacDougall deliberately altered the text – his errors most likely arose at some stage of his copying or dictating for the book. But nothing can excuse the continual use by diary apologists of his discredited text, especially since I brought MacDougall's errors to Mr Smith's notice in August 1993.

The book launch was memorable for two other oddities. There was no mention of the Rendell report in the book, so readers were to be kept in ignorance of those major objections. And over the subtitle to the book was stuck a white label which carried this message: 'Is It GENUINE? Read the evidence, then judge for yourself.' Since the subtitle read: 'The discovery, the investigation, the authentication', this represented something of a climb-down. Yet since the book excluded the essential objections to the diary, how could the average reader even begin to judge? It was bluff once more, but there was worse to come. Close examination of the book's narrative discloses a sorry state of affairs.

In my view – a view shared by many others – the book itself distorts history in an unacceptable fashion. The conclusions reached in order to get round the uncomfortable fact of the Maybrick will are not supported by historical evidence. On page 125, for example, the narrative states:

> The will that has survived...poses more questions than it answers. Most important of all, we know from Florie's letter to her mother that in December 1888 Maybrick had torn up his will and written a new

one. Maybrick knew that there was a will already in existence. So why does this blue will (of 25 April) begin: 'In case I die before having made a regular and proper will in legal form I wish this to be taken as my last will and testament...'?

Here we have a false claim that is then used to justify false reasoning. The letter mentioned was written on 31 December 1888. At no point in this letter does Florrie state that her husband James *had written a new will*. Let us emphasize this, since justice demands it. The letter says nothing to justify the interpretation being drawn by Mrs Harrison, so as a matter of course all the arguments based on her initial premise are invalid. This is elementary.

Now this is not simply an opinion of mine, it is a bald statement of fact. I have submitted the texts to experienced editors and lawyers. Every person asked to examine the wording of the crucial letter agrees that the interpretation put on it by Mrs Harrison is baseless. Florrie's letter actually reads:

> In his fury he tore up his will this morning as he had made me the sole legatee and trustee for the children in it. Now he proposes to settle everything he can on the children alone, allowing me only the one third by law. I am sure it matters little to me as long as the children are provided for...

And there you have the text that proves my point. Nowhere in this letter is the statement that on 31 December 1888, James Maybrick tore up his will and then wrote a new will, as Mrs Harrison alleges. The words of Florrie's letter are direct and not open to misunderstanding. She writes that he tore up an existing will and made it known that he proposed to write a new one; one that would be decidedly different. This is so simple that I am surprised that anyone could mistake its meaning.

What then prompts Shirley Harrison, author of the narrative, to tell us that the letter says '...Maybrick had torn up his will and written a new one'? To be charitable, it looks like a case of wishful thinking. Unfortunately this leaves her readers with the illusion that there 'was a will already in existence' on 25 April 1889.

But how on earth do we account for the following claim by Mrs Harrison? She writes:

> It is puzzling, too, that there are discrepancies between the wording of the will in Somerset House and the one seen and copied by Mac-Dougall. For instance the words 'bequeath' and 'made out' are missing

in MacDougall's version, as is the phrase 'in his presence', all important phrases.

The truth is that there is no puzzle at all. She is relying on a book whose
faults make it worthless. To prove this I include the faulty texts here. The
certified copy of this will confirms at once that MacDougall is hopelessly
wrong (*see* Appendix Ten). So Robert Smith's claim that '...the author
gives you the facts and the evidence as objectively as possible...' is in my
view not borne out by the contents of the book.

As for Mr Smith himself, in his contribution to the diary he tries to
dismiss the idea of a hoaxer by stating that such a hoaxer would have to have
a comprehensive '...understanding of the motivations and unexpected
behaviour of serial killers'; '...be qualified in ink and paper chemistry';
'...be a crime historian who had acquired intimate knowledge, well beyond
the accessible published sources of two famous Victorian cases...'; and
have '...a rare and precise knowledge of the physical and psychological
effects of arsenic addictions'.

I find this almost beyond belief. He really seems to be quite out of touch
with the mass of popular literature – the crime magazines, cheap pulp
paperbacks, trashy novels – which were easily able to supply all the garish
colour and sordid bits and pieces that we find in this diary. In these times you
don't have to be an expert on serial killers to know about them. Pick up
some of the many 'True Crime' types of magazines and soon enough there
are all the insights one could need. Finding out about arsenic and strychnine
addictions is almost as easy. As for expertise in inks and paper, this is never
called for. Stick with an authentic Victorian paper, use a simple ink (plenty of recipes around) and the game's afoot. Just three source books are all you
need to provide the crime facts and their backgrounds.

Perhaps the most incredible part of Mr Smith's sales-pitch is his claim that
two special items in the diary '...argue its authenticity'. One of these items
is the mention of an empty tin matchbox, found at the scene of Catherine
Eddowes' murder. This, he says, was not known until 1987. So what? We
are dealing with a recent hoax, just a few years old, not an ancient piece of
penmanship. His second point is even more amazing:

> Until 1987, when the inquest report on Mary Jane Kelly first came to
> light, no one knew that her heart had been removed by the Ripper;
> nor was it reported at the time of the murders. Yet, after the only
> reference to her name in the diary are the words: 'no heart, no heart'.

We groan in disbelief! What on earth have his advisors been up to? Can they all have been asleep in their sentry-boxes? That the heart had been removed from the body was reported in the *Star* on 10 November 1888, in *The Times* and *Pall Mall Gazette* of the same day, and in the *Pall Mall Budget* for 15 November 1888. And I don't doubt that other papers ran the same basic report, which in *The Times* version read: 'The kidneys and heart had also been removed from the body and placed on the table...' Since then, these reports have been drawn on by many writers; so much for the Smith-myth.

And let us now dispose of any nonsensical bending of the words to make them apply to removing the heart *from the room*. The hoaxing diarist states, without qualification: 'Regret I did not take any of it away with me...'

After Warner Books cancelled its contract, another American publisher, Hyperion, agreed to publish, but wisely they included the Rendell report in their edition. Quite fairly Robert Smith was allowed to comment on it, but his attempted rebuttal simply shows the emptiness of his case. He seized on the R. J. McNeil ion migration test as the weak point of the report. But if he had considered the significance of the placing of these test results right at the end of the report, then he might have realized that they were never considered of great importance. That the test was done at all was simply in the interests of completeness. The overwhelming verdict of all who have considered this diary is that it is a modern fake, created after 1987. Incredibly, though, Mr Smith still plugs away with his myth about the heart, saying:

> Nor does Rendell comment on the clear reference in the diary to the Ripper removing the heart of Mary Jane Kelly. That knowledge was contained only in the 'closed' coroner's inquest records. They were never available to the press or public, and they disappeared in 1888 and were anonymously returned to Scotland Yard in 1987.

And once again we meet a repetition of the claims based on the Mac-Dougall transcript of the will:

> There are also many differences between the words in the 'will' as it appears in a transcript taken down by a lawyer, Alexander MacDougall, soon after Maybrick's death, and published in his book of 1891 on the Maybrick case, and the 'will' that exists in Somerset House today. For instance the 'will' today has the legally important words 'bequeath' and 'in his presence' mysteriously added. One hand, maybe two, have been at work here, but not, we suggest, James Maybrick's.

One wonders at Mr Smith's capacity to deceive himself.

He now goes on record to state that MacDougall took this transcript *soon after Maybrick's death*, but the very transcript he is talking about proves this claim to be inaccurate. MacDougall actually gives the date of the document he was looking at: its date was 29 July 1889. In other words he saw the will only *after* it had been executed and *after* the certified copy had been made by the Liverpool solicitors. As I've already shown, that copy matches up with the copy written by Maybrick, so the continual use by Mr Smith of this worthless transcript is to be deplored.

But Mr Smith is lost once he accepts the Maybrick will as authentic, so he tries to wave aside the findings of disputed document examiners. He was warned by examiner Sue Iremonger that there was no possible chance of the diary and the will being written by the same person. Maureen Casey Owens and Dr Joe Nickell say exactly the same thing, as does every other examiner who has been asked to look at the two documents. For solace Smith Gryphon turned to the dubious field of graphology.

Graphology is a now fashionable pseudo-science that has taken in a good many people. But so has palmistry, phrenology and astrology. Because it uses handwriting as the basis for its conclusions it is too often confused with the handwriting examination techniques used in criminal investigations. But it should be stressed that the two processes have nothing in common. Graphologists attempt to forecast character and ability from handwriting. And there lies the danger in taking their reports seriously.

A further danger lies in the fact that the graphologist can often be influenced by a client's needs. This is made clear from a report furnished by Mr Reed Hayes of Hawaii. In the book he is described as 'an eminent document examiner'. What is not stated is that he is a member of one of the warring factions within graphology, a section known as the International Graphoanalysis Society.

The objectional technique of trying to match evidence so that it suits a character interpretation, is well illustrated by the following quote (not in the book) from his report of 21 September 1993 on the Maybrick will:

Have you noticed that both times Michael Maybrick's name appears on the will...that the word Michael is nearly disintegrated? This suggests to me that whoever wrote the will felt very anxious about Michael...I see several similarities that lead me to think *maybe* Michael wrote James' will. (I'm basing this not only on some similarities in

the writing, but also on my analysis that Michael had such a guilt
problem as we discussed, and the fact that the word Michael is so
disjointed.)

In these few sentences Mr Hayes reveals that he has discussed 'a guilt
problem' with his client. This is not an objective approach by any
standards. Here, it is an interchange of illusions. This, in my opinion, has
nothing to do with reality.

But Reed Hayes was small fry compared with the Smith Gryphon
star, Anna Koren from Israel. A member of the American Association
of Graphologists, among other things, she specializes in 'character analysis'. Over a page of her analysis of the writing of the diary appears in
the book. We learn many amazing things about the writer. 'His percep-
tion of sexuality and mating is distorted to the point of a tendency to
sadism.' 'His feelings of inferiority, emotional repression, and lack of
inner confidence may cause him to lose control every now and then and
he may explode very violently.' 'The diary shows an unstable personality.' 'Tendencies to despotism, irascibility and brutality are clearly
discerned.' 'He suffers from extreme changes of mood...' 'A tendency
to hypochondria and a use of drugs or alcohol is evident.' 'A psychotic disease impedes his ability to distinguish between good or evil, forbidden or
permissible and may lead to criminal activity.' 'He suffers from psychological disorders which produce illogical, obsessive, destructive, and
aggressive behaviour.'

And there is much more along these lines. I am not alone in finding it
incredible that anyone could take this seriously. It's all so obvious, but it
has been dressed up to look like a wondrous revelation. This lady has
just been reading a document which talks about gouging eyes out, throw-
ing acid in faces, and knifing women; a vile document, resplendent with
hate. Are we to believe that she is not influenced by the text? The truth
is that anyone knowing the jargon could turn out a report on very similar lines. And they could do it without seeing a single line of the
handwriting. The typescript on its own would provide them with everything they could need.

Reed Hayes and Anna Koren, then, seem to be the only 'experts' who
bring any kind of succour to the Smith Gryphon camp. Yet what the
book does not reveal is the fact that Anna Koren's reports reach no serious conclusions. Unrevealed to the book's readers is the truth that Anna
Koren has in fact nothing positive to contribute. Here are some vital
sentences from her report of 11 September 1993 as proof:

Unfortunately I have not managed to reach unequivocal conclusions with regard to the comparison of the letter 'Dear Boss', the letter of the 6th of October, the will of James Maybrick and the diaries signed by 'Jack the Ripper'. I have invested many many hours into examining these writings during the 9 months that have elapsed since I first saw the Diary in December 1992...I have found both similarities and contradictions in the documents and it is impossible for me to reach a verdict.

Contrast those words of abdication with the considered opinions of disputed document examiners. Sue Iremonger's careful examination of the Maybrick will and Maybrick's marriage register signature led her to conclude that the will was signed by the same person who signed the marriage document. Further to that she found that the text of the will was written by Maybrick as well. These were firm conclusions without waffle or evasion. And Sue Iremonger's conclusions were independently confirmed by the later examination conducted by Maureen Casey Owens. The will was an authentic document penned by James Maybrick. In this particular case no amount of special pleading based on the reliability or otherwise of hand-writing analysis makes any difference.

Fortunately for the truth, James Maybrick's handwriting has some quite distinctive features which can be readily seen even by a layman. The 'bric' section in his signature shows an odd way of forming the alliance between the letters. This results in the letter 'r' being shaped with a small loop or hole at its base. This loop is present on the marriage document, on both signatures on the will and on the name Maybrick when it appears in the body of the will. A highly skilled forger could, of course, turn out something along these lines. But what would be the point? The will does no more than provide for the children using the brothers as the legatees in trust. This is quite along the lines made known to Florence back on 31 December 1888, and communicated by her to her mother.

The ridiculous idea of a conspiracy to forge the will is simply the result of an attempt to demolish the basic evidence which proves the diary to be a fake. Why then, asks the Smith Gryphon camp, did the faker fail to imitate Maybrick's handwriting in the diary? The answer to that is short and simple. Even if he had seen Maybrick's writing the diary-faker did not have the skill to imitate it. The chances are, though, that he never even knew of the existence of the will. Like most people he would know only about the availability of marriage, death and birth certificates. That section of the public which knows about the availability of wills is quite small indeed.

That this diary is a fake is now accepted by Martin Fido, Don Rumbelow, Martin Howells, Stewart Evans and many others with a strong interest in the Whitechapel murders. The detectives at Scotland Yard, who looked at the possible fraudulent aspects of the diary's promotion, also agree that the diary is a hoax and a recent one at that. Indeed it is becoming increasingly difficult to find anyone who actually believes in its ramblings. And that seems promising. But unfortunately every hoax contaminates the fields of honest research, even if it is exposed. Like the Clarence hoax this one will not die overnight. Its time-wasting stupidities will linger on to dog historians for years to come.

James Maybrick's Will

Transcript of the Certified Copy of Maybrick's Will

Liverpool 25th April 1889

In case I die before having made a regular & proper will in legal form, I wish this to be taken as my last will & testament.

I leave & bequeath all my worldly possessions, of whatever kind or description, including furniture pictures wines linen & plate Life Insurances, cash, shares, property, in fact everything I possess In trust with my brothers Michael Maybrick & Thomas Maybrick, for my two Children James Chandler Maybrick and Gladys Eveleyn Maybrick. The furniture I desire to remain intact & to be used in furnishing a home which can be shared by my widow and Children but the furniture is to be the Childrens.

I further desire that all moneys be invested in the names of the above Trustees (Michael & Thomas Maybrick) & the income of same used for the Childrens benefit & Education such education to be left to the discretion of said Trustees.

My widow will have for her portion of my Estate the Policies on my life, say £500 with the Scottish Widows Fund and £2000 with the Mutual Reserve Fund Life Association of New York, both Policies being made out in her name – The Interest on this £2,500 together with the £125 a year which she receives from her New York property will make a provision of about £125 a year, a sum although small will yet be the means of keeping her respectably. –

It is also my desire that my widow shall live under the same roof with the Children so long as she remains my widow. -

If it is legally possible I wish the £2,500 of Life Insurance on my life in my wifes name to be invested in the names of the said Trustees, but that she should have the sole use of the interest thereof during her lifetime but at her

James Maybrick's will in his own handwriting

Association of New York, both Policies
being made out in her name. The interest
on this £2500, together with the £125 a year
which she receives from her New York property
will make a provision of about £425 a
year, a sum although small will yet be
the means of keeping her respectably.—

It is also my desire that my widow shall
live under the same roof with the Children
so long as she remains my widow.

If it is legally possible I wish the £2000
of Life Insurance on my life in my wife's
name to be invested in the names of
the said Trustees, but that she should
have the sole use of the interest thereof
during her lifetime, but at her death the
principal to revert to my said Children
James Chandler & Gladys Evelyn Maybrick.

      Witness my hand & Seal this
      twenty fifth day of April 1889.

Signed by the Testator in the
presence of us who at his
request in his presence
and in the presence of each
other have hereunto affixed
our names as Witnesses

  James Maybrick

George R Davidson.
Geo. Smith

death the principal to revert to my said Children. James Chandler & Gladys
Eveleyn Maybrick.

    Witness my hand & seal this twenty fifth day
of April 1889
Signed by the Testator in the presence
of us who at his request in his presence
and in the presence of each other have hereunto   }   James Maybrick
affixed our names as witnesses

Geo. R Davidson

Geo. Smith

    At Liverpool on the 29th July 1889 Administration (with the will annexed)
of the personal Estate of James Maybrick late of the City of Liverpool and of
Riversdale Road Aigburth in the County of Lancaster, deceased who died
on the 11th May 1889 at Riversdale Road aforesaid was granted to Michael
Maybrick and Thomas Maybrick the brothers the Universal Legatees in trust
named in the said will they having been first sworn. No Executor being
named in the said will. –

Personal Estate Gross £5,016..1..0   Net £3,770..16..6¾

Layton, Steel and Springman, Solicitors, Liverpool

Certified to be a correct copy

MacDougall's Faulty Transcription of 1891

Liverpool, 25th April, 1889.

In case I die before having made a regular and proper will in legal form, I wish this to be taken as my last will and testament. I leave all my worldly possessions, of what kind or description, including furniture, pictures, wines, linen, and plate, life insurances, cash, shares, property – in fact, everything I possess, in trust with my brothers Michael Maybrick and Thomas Maybrick for my two children, James Chandler Maybrick and Gladys Evelyn Maybrick. The furniture I desire to remain intact, and to be used in furnishing a home which can be shared by my widow and children, but the furniture is to be the children's. I further desire that all moneys be invested in the names of the above trustees (Michael and Thomas Maybrick), and the income of same used for the children's benefit and education, such education to be left to the discretion of said trustees. My widow will have for her portion of my estate the policies on my life, say, £500 with the Scottish Widows' Fund and £2,000 with the Mutual Reserve Fund Life Association of New York, both policies being in her name. The interest on this £2,500, together with the £125 a year which she receives from her New York property, will make a provision of about £125 a year, a sum which, although small, will yet be the means of keeping her respectable. It is also my desire that my widow shall live under the same roof with the children so long as she remains my widow. If it is legally possible, I wish the £2,500 of life insurance on my life, in my wife's name, to be invested in the names of the said trustees, but that she should have the sole use of the interest thereof during her lifetime, but at her death the principal to revert to my said children James Chandler Maybrick and Gladys Evelyn Maybrick.

Witness my hand and seal this
    twenty-fifth day of April, 1889,   JAMES MAYBRICK

Signed by the testator in the presence of us, who, at his request and in the presence of each other, have hereunto affixed our names as witnesses, Geo. R. Davidson, Geo. Smith.

The affidavit of due execution filed T. E. Paget, District Registrar at Liverpool on the 29th July, 1889.

Administration (with the will annexed) of the personal estate of James Maybrick, late of the city of Liverpool, and of Riversdale Road, Aigburth, in the county of Lancaster deceased, was granted to Michael Maybrick and Thomas Maybrick the brothers, the universal legatees in trust named in the said will; they have been first sworn, no executor being named in the said will.

Personal Estate, gross...£5,016   1   0

    "   "   nett 3,770   16   6¾

LAYTON, STEEL, AND SPRINGMAN,
Solicitors, Liverpool

Select Bibliography

ADAM, HARGRAVE LEE, *Trial of George Chapman*, Hodge (London) 1930

ANDERSON, SIR ROBERT, *Criminals and Crime*, Nisbet (London) 1907

ANDERSON, SIR ROBERT, *The Lighter Side of My Official Life*, Hodder and Stoughton (London) 1910

ARLEN, MICHAEL, *Hell! said the Duchess*, William Heinemann (London) 1934

BANKS, HAROLD, *The Strangler. The Story of Terror in Boston*, Mayflower-Dell (London) 1967

BARNARD, ALLAN (Ed.), *The Harlot Killer*, Dodd Mead (New York) 1953

BARNETT, HENRIETTA OCTAVIA WESTON, *Canon Barnett*, 2 vols, John Murray (London) 1918

BEAUMONT, F. A., *The Fiend of East London, The Fifty Most Amazing Crimes of the Last 100 Years*, Odhams (London) 1936

BEGG, PAUL, FIDO, MARTIN and SKINNER, KEITH, *The Jack the Ripper A to Z*, Headline (London) 1991

BEGG, PAUL, *Jack the Ripper, the Uncensored Facts*, Robson (London) 1988

BRUSSEL, JAMES, *Casebook of a Crime Psychiatrist*, Mayflower (London) 1970

CAMPS, PROFESSOR FRANCIS E. AND BARBER, RICHARD, *The Investigation of Murder*, Michael Joseph (London) 1966

CROWLEY, ALEISTER, *The Confessions of Aleister Crowley*, Jonathan Cape (London) 1969

CULLEN, TOM A., *Autumn of Terror: Jack the Ripper, his Crimes and Times*, Bodley Head (London) 1965, Fontana (London) 1973

DEACON, RICHARD, *A History of the British Secret Service*, Muller (London) 1969

DEACON, RICHARD, *A History of the Russian Secret Service*, Muller (London) 1972

DEW, WALTER, *I Caught Crippen*, Blackie (London) 1938

DOUGLAS, ARTHUR, *Will the Real Jack the Ripper*, Countryside Publications (Chorley, Lancs.) 1979

EMMONS, ROBERT, *The Life and Opinions of Walter Richard Sickert*, Faber & Faber (London) 1941

FARSON, DANIEL, *Jack the Ripper*, Michael Joseph (London) 1972

FIDO, MARTIN, *The Crimes, Detection & Death of Jack the Ripper*, Weidenfeld & Nicolson (London) 1987. Rev. ed. 1989

FRANK, GEROLD, *The Boston Strangler*, Jonathan Cape & Co. (London)1967

GRIFFITHS, ARTHUR GEORGE FREDERICK, *Mysteries of Police and Crime*, Cassell (London) 1898

HALSTED, DENNIS GRATWICK, *Doctor in the Nineties*, Johnson (London) 1959

HARRISON, MICHAEL, *Clarence: the Life of the Duke of Clarence and Avondale*, W. H. Allen (London) 1972

HARRISON, SHIRLEY, *The Diary of Jack the Ripper*, Smith Gryphon (London) 1993

HOWELLS, MARTIN & SKINNER, KEITH, *The Ripper Legacy*, Sidgwick and Jackson (London) 1987

KEYES, EDWARD, *The Michigan Murders*, New English Library, 1977

KNIGHT, STEPHEN, *Jack the Ripper: The Final Solution*, Harrap (London) 1976, Treasure Press (London) 1984

LARSEN, RICHARD, *Bundy, The Deliberate Stranger*, Prentice Hall (USA) 1980

LEESON, BENJAMIN, *Lost London: The Memoirs of An East End Detective*, Stanley Paul (London) 1934

LEYTON, ELLIOT, *Compulsive Killers*, New York University Press (New York) 1986

LE QUEUX, WILLIAM, *Things I Know About Kings, Celebrities and Crooks*, Nash & Grayson (London) 1923

LILLY, MARJORIE, *Sickert: The Painter and His Circle*, Elek (London) 1971

MacLEOD, C. M., 'A Ripper Handwriting Analysis,' *Criminologist* (London) August 1968

MACNAGHTEN, SIR MELVILLE L., *Days of My Years*, Arnold (London) 1914

MARJORIBANKS, EDWARD, *The Life of Sir Edward Marshall Hall*, Gollancz (London) 1929

MATTERS, LEONARD W., *The Mystery of Jack the Ripper*, W. H. Allen (London) 1948

McCORMICK, DONALD, *The Identity of Jack the Ripper*, Jarrolds (London) 1959; John Long (rev. edn)(London)1970

MOORE-ANDERSON, ARTHUR P., *Sir Robert Anderson and Lady Agnes Anderson*, Marshall, Morgan & Scott (London) 1947

PEARSALL, RONALD, *The Worm in the Bud*, Weidenfeld & Nicolson (London) 1969

RESSLER, ROBERT, *Whoever Fights Monsters*, Simon & Schuster (USA) 1992

RULE, ANN, *The 1-5 Killer*, Signet Books (North American Library) 1984

RULE, ANN, *The Stranger Beside Me*, W. W. Norton & Co. (New York) 1980

RUMBELOW, DONALD, *The Complete Jack the Ripper*, W. H. Allen (London) 1975, Star Books (London) 1979

SCHWARZ, TED, *The Hillside Strangler*, Doubleday & Co., Inc (USA) 1981

SIMPSON, COLIN; CHESTER, LEWIS; LEITCH, DAVID, *The Cleveland Street Affair*, Little, Brown & Co., (Boston, USA) 1976

SMITH, SIR HENRY, *From Constable to Commissioner*, Chatto & Windus (London) 1910

SPIERING, FRANK, *Prince Jack*, Doubleday & Co. (New York) 1978

STEWART, WILLIAM, *Jack the Ripper: A New Theory*, Quality Press (London) 1939

STOWELL, THOMAS E. A., 'Jack the Ripper – A Solution?' *Criminologist* (London) November 1970

SYMONDS, JOHN, *The Great Beast: The Life and Magick of Aleister Crowley*, Macdonald (London) 1971

WAGNER, GILLIAN, *Barnado*, Eyre & Spottiswoode (London) 1980

WHITTINGTON-EGAN, RICHARD, *A Casebook on Jack the Ripper*, Wildy & Sons (London) 1975

WINSLOW, FORBES, *Recollections of Forty Years*, Ouseley (London) 1910

The all-important Lees story is to be found in the following:

Chicago *Sunday Times-Herald*, 28 April 1895

Daily Express, London, 7, 9 & 10 March 1931

Fifty Strangest Stories Ever Told, Odhams (London) 1937

Light, (London) Autumn, 1970

Prediction, (London) January 1937

Two Worlds, (London) 21 February 1959

ARCHER, FRED, *Ghost Detectives*, W. H. Allen (London) 1970

HILL, WILLIAM BOYLE, *A New Earth and A New Heaven*, Watts (London) 1936

NEIL, CHARLES (Ed.), *The World's Greatest Mysteries*, Neil (Australia) 1936

SAXON, PETER, *The Man Who Dreamed of Murder*, Sexton Blake Library (London) November 1958

WOODHALL, EDWIN T., *Crime and the Supernatural*, John Long (London) 1935

WOODHALL, EDWIN T., *Jack the Ripper, Or When London Walked In Terror*, Melifont (London) 1937

The known writings of Roslyn D'Onston:

'Who Is The Whitechapel Demon? (By One Who Thinks He Knows)', *Pall Mall Gazette*, 1 December 1888, Unsigned

'The Real Origin of "She", By One Who Knew Her', *Pall Mall Gazette*, 3 January 1889, Signed R. D.

'What I Know Of Obeeyahism, By the Author of the Original of "She"', *Pall Mall Gazette*, 15 February 1889, Signed Roslyn D'Onston

'African Magic', *Lucifer*, November 1890, Signed 'Tautriadelta'

'Dead or Alive' in *More Ghost Stories*, W. T. Stead's special New Year's Extra Number (1892) of his *Review of Reviews*. This later appeared in book form under the title *Real Ghost Stories*, 1897.

'A Modern Magician', *Borderland*, April 1896, Signed 'Tautriadelta'

'Elementals' (Essay on Vampires, Demons etc), *Borderland*, London, July 1896

The Patristic Gospels, Under the name Roslyn D'Onston, Grant Richards (London) 1904

LETTERS

Paul Harrison has written that D'Onston '…wrote letters to the press of the day regularly. They would print them enthusiastically, using one of Stephenson's assorted pseudonyms – Doctor Death, Sudden Death and his most popular one, Tautriadelta…' In fact no paper anywhere printed D'Onston's letters 'enthusiastically' or otherwise, for the very good reason that he never wrote any! His one and only published writing on the Whitechapel murders is the 1 December 1888 *Pall Mall* piece included in this book. The only pseudonym he ever used, Tautriadelta, did not appear in print until November 1890, two years after the end of the murders, when it appeared on the article commissioned by *Lucifer*.

Index